*For Mark—a true friend, and fellow creator.*

# Table of Contents

# Preface

Even though this is my second book on technologies in the JavaScript ecosystem, I still find myself somewhat surprised at my role as a JavaScript expert and evangelist. Like so many programmers, I held a strong prejudice against JavaScript up until about 2012. To do such an about-face still feels a little disorienting.

My prejudice was for the usual reasons: I considered JavaScript a "toy" language (without really learning it properly, and therefore not knowing of what I spoke) that was practiced by dangerous, sloppy, untrained amateur programmers. There is a little truth in both of these reasons. ES6 was developed quickly, and even its inventor Brendan Eich admits there are things that he didn't get right the first time around—and by the time he realized it, too many people were relying on the problematic behavior for him to effectively change it (show me the language that doesn't suffer from this problem, however). As for the second reason, JavaScript *did* make programming suddenly accessible. Not only did everyone have a browser, but with only a little effort, they could see the JavaScript that enabled the websites that were rapidly proliferating on the Web. People learned by trial and error, by reading each other's code and—in so many cases—emulating poorly written code with insufficient understanding.

I'm glad I have learned enough about JavaScript to recognize that—far from being a toy language—it is based on extremely solid foundations, and is powerful, flexible, and expressive. I'm also glad I have come to embrace the accessibility that JavaScript brings. I certainly hold no animosity toward amateurs: everyone has to start somewhere, programming is a profitable skill, and a career in programming has many advantages.

To the new programmer, the amateur, I say this: there is no shame in being an amateur. There is some shame in *staying* an amateur (if you make programming your profession, certainly). If you want to practice programming, *practice it*. Learn everything you can, from every source you can. Keep an open mind and—perhaps most importantly—question everything. Question every expert. Question every experienced programmer. Constantly ask "Why?"

For the most part, I have tried to keep this book to the "facts" of JavaScript, but it is impossible to completely avoid opinion. Where I offer opinions, take them for what they are. You are welcome to disagree, and you are encouraged to seek out the opinions of other experienced developers.

You are learning JavaScript at a very exciting time. The Web is leaving its infancy (technically speaking), and web development isn't the confusing, complicated Wild West that it was 5 and 10 years ago. Standards like HTML5 and ES6 are making it easier to learn web development, and easier to develop high-quality applications. Node.js is extending the reach of JavaScript beyond the browser, and now it is a viable choice for system scripting, desktop application development, backend web development, and even embedded applications. Certainly I haven't had this much fun programming since I started in the mid-1980s.

## A Brief History of JavaScript

JavaScript was developed by Brendan Eich, a developer at Netscape Communications Corporation, in 1995. Its initial development was very rapid, and much of the criticism leveled at JavaScript has cited the lack of planning foresight during its development. However, Brendan Eich was not a dabbler: he had a solid foundation in computer science, and incorporated remarkably sophisticated and prescient ideas into JavaScript. In many ways, it was ahead of its time, and it took 15 years for mainstream developers to catch on to the sophistication the language offered.

JavaScript started life with the name Mocha, and was briefly named LiveScript before being officially renamed to JavaScript in a Netscape Navigator release in 1995. The word "Java" in "JavaScript" was not coincidental, but it is confusing: aside from a common syntactic ancestry, JavaScript has more in common with Self (a prototype-based language developed at Xerox PARC in the mid-'80s) and Scheme (a language developed in the 1970s by Guy Steele and Gerald Sussman, which was in turn heavily influenced by Lisp and ALGOL) than with Java. Eich was familiar with both Self and Scheme, and used some of their forward-thinking paradigms in developing JavaScript. The name JavaScript was partially a marketing attempt to tie into the success Java was enjoying at the time.[1]

In November 1996, Netscape announced that they had submitted JavaScript to Ecma, a private, international nonprofit standards organization that carries significant influence in the technology and communications industries. Ecma International published the first edition of the ECMA-26 specification, which was, in essence, JavaScript.

1 Eich confessed in a 2014 interview to enjoying thumbing his nose at Sun Microsystems, who "hated JavaScript."

The relationship between Ecma's specifications—which specify a language called ECMAScript—and JavaScript is mostly academic. Technically, JavaScript is an *implementation* of ECMAScript, but for practical purposes, JavaScript and ECMAScript can be thought of interchangeably.

The last major ECMAScript version was 5.1 (generically referred to as ES5), published in June 2011. Browsers "in the wild" that are old enough not to support ECMAScript 5.1 have fallen well below the single digits, and it's safe to say that ECMAScript 5.1 is the current lingua franca of the Web.

ECMAScript 6 (ES6)—which is the focus of this book—was published by Ecma International in June 2015. The working name for the specification prior to publication was "Harmony," and you will hear ES6 referred to as "Harmony," "ES6 Harmony," "ES6," "ES2015," and "ECMAScript 2015." In this book, we will refer to it simply as ES6.

# ES6

If ES5 is the current lingua franca of the Web, the attentive reader might be wondering why this book focuses on ES6.

ES6 represents a significant advancement in the JavaScript language, and some of ES5's major shortcomings are addressed in ES6. I think you will find that ES6 is generally a much more pleasant and powerful language to work with (and ES5 was quite enjoyable to start with). Also—thanks to transcompilers—you can write ES6 today and transcompile it to "web-compatible" ES5.

With ES6 finally published, browser support for it will grow steadily, and at some point, transcompilation will no longer be necessary to reach a broad audience (I am not foolish enough to make a prediction—even a rough one—about when that will happen).

What's clear is that ES6 represents the future of JavaScript development, and by investing your time in learning it now, you will be prepared for the future, with transcompilers preventing us from sacrificing portability now.

However, not every developer will have the luxury of writing ES6 today. It's possible that you're working on a very large existing ES5 code base that would be prohibitively expensive to convert to ES6. And some developers simply won't wish to go through the extra effort involved in transcompilation.

With the exception of Chapter 1, this book will cover ES6, not ES5. Where appropriate, I will point out where ES6 differs from ES5, but there will not be side-by-side code examples, or extensive discussion of doing things "the ES5 way" when there is a better way in ES6. If you fall into that category of programmers who, for whatever reason, need to stick to ES5, this may not be the book for you (though I hope you will return to it at some point in the future!).

The editorial choice to focus on ES6 was made carefully. The improvements in ES6 are significant enough that it would have been difficult to maintain a clear pedagogical framework. In short, a book that attempts to cover ES5 *and* ES6 would do both topics a disservice.

# Who This Book Is For

This book is primarily for readers who already have some experience with programming (even an introductory programming class, or an online course). If you're new to programming, this book will be helpful, but you might want to supplement it with an introductory text or class.

Those who already have some JavaScript experience (especially if it's only in ES5) will find a practical and thorough coverage of important language concepts.

Programmers who are coming from another language should feel right at home with the content in this book.

This book does attempt to comprehensively cover the language features, related tools, techniques, and paradigms that drive modern JavaScript development. Therefore, the material in this book necessarily ranges from the simple and straightforward (variables, control flow, functions) to the complicated and esoteric (asynchronous programming, regular expressions). Depending on your level of experience, you may find some chapters more challenging than others: the beginning programmer will no doubt need to revisit some of the material more than once.

# What This Book Is Not

This book is not a comprehensive reference to JavaScript or its related libraries. The Mozilla Developer Network (MDN) maintains an excellent, thorough, up-to-date, and free online JavaScript reference (*https://developer.mozilla.org/en-US/docs/Web/JavaScript*), which will be referenced liberally throughout this book. If you prefer a physical book, David Flanagan's *JavaScript: The Definitive Guide* is quite comprehensive (though it does not cover ES6 at the time of this writing).

# Conventions Used in This Book

The following typographical conventions are used in this book:

*Italic*
: Indicates new terms, URLs, email addresses, filenames, and file extensions.

`Constant width`
: Used for program listings, as well as within paragraphs to refer to program elements such as variable or function names, databases, data types, environment variables, statements, and keywords.

**`Constant width bold`**
: Shows commands or other text that should be typed literally by the user.

*`Constant width italic`*
: Shows text that should be replaced with user-supplied values or by values determined by context.

This element signifies a tip or suggestion.

This element signifies a general note.

This element indicates a warning or caution.

## Safari® Books Online

*Safari Books Online* is an on-demand digital library that delivers expert content in both book and video form from the world's leading authors in technology and business.

Technology professionals, software developers, web designers, and business and creative professionals use Safari Books Online as their primary resource for research, problem solving, learning, and certification training.

Safari Books Online offers a range of plans and pricing for enterprise, government, education, and individuals.

Members have access to thousands of books, training videos, and prepublication manuscripts in one fully searchable database from publishers like O'Reilly Media,

Prentice Hall Professional, Addison-Wesley Professional, Microsoft Press, Sams, Que, Peachpit Press, Focal Press, Cisco Press, John Wiley & Sons, Syngress, Morgan Kaufmann, IBM Redbooks, Packt, Adobe Press, FT Press, Apress, Manning, New Riders, McGraw-Hill, Jones & Bartlett, Course Technology, and hundreds more. For more information about Safari Books Online, please visit us online.

## How to Contact Us

Please address comments and questions concerning this book to the publisher:


O'Reilly Media, Inc.
1005 Gravenstein Highway North
Sebastopol, CA 95472
800-998-9938 (in the United States or Canada)
707-829-0515 (international or local)
707-829-0104 (fax)


We have a web page for this book, where we list errata, examples, and any additional information. You can access this page at *http://bit.ly/learningJS_3E.*

To comment or ask technical questions about this book, send email to *bookquestions@oreilly.com.*

For more information about our books, courses, conferences, and news, see our website at *http://www.oreilly.com.*

Find us on Facebook: *http://facebook.com/oreilly*

Follow us on Twitter: *http://twitter.com/oreillymedia*

Watch us on YouTube: *http://www.youtube.com/oreillymedia*

## Acknowledgments


The opportunity to write books for O'Reilly is a tremendous honor, and I owe a debt of gratitude to Simon St. Laurent for seeing the potential in me, and bringing me on board. Meg Foley, my editor, has been supportive, encouraging, and ever-helpful (there's a certain green T-shirt in the mail for you, Meg!). An O'Reilly book is a team effort, and my copyeditor Rachel Monaghan, production editor Kristen Brown, and proofreader Jasmine Kwityn were fast, thorough, and insightful: thank you all for your effort!

To my technical reviewers—Matt Inman, Shelley Powers, Nick Pinkham, and Cody Lindley—thanks for your astute feedback, for your brilliant ideas, and for helping make this book great. To say I couldn't have done it without you is an understatement. While everyone's feedback was incredibly helpful, I want to give special recognition to Matt: his experience as an educator provided valuable insight on all matters of pedagogy, and the liberal use of Stephen Colbert images in his feedback helped me maintain my sanity!

Shelley Powers—author of previous editions of this book—deserves special thanks not just for passing this title on to me, but for providing her experienced feedback and for making this a better book (and for sparking some spirited discussions!).

I would like to thank all the readers of of my previous book (*Web Development with Node and Express*). If you hadn't bought that book—and reviewed it so positively!—I would probably not have had the opportunity to write this book. Special thanks to the readers who took the time to send in feedback and corrections: I have learned a lot from your responses!

To everyone at Pop Art, where I am honored to work: you are my rock. Your support humbles me, your enthusiasm motivates me, and your professionalism and dedication are what get me out of bed in the morning. Tom Paul in particular deserves my gratitude: his unwavering principles, innovative business ideas, and exceptional leadership inspire me not only to do my best today, but to do even better tomorrow. Thanks to Steve Rosenbaum for founding Pop Art, weathering stormy seas, and successfully passing the torch on to Tom. As I have taken time to finish this book, Colwyn Fritze-Moor and Eric Buchmann worked extra hard to cover duties that I normally would have handled: thank you both. Thanks to Dylan Hallstrom for being the very model of reliability. Thanks to Liz Tom and Sam Wilskey for joining Team Pop Art! Thanks to Carole Hardy, Nikki Brovold, Jennifer Erts, Randy Keener, Patrick Wu, and Lisa Melogue for all of your support. Lastly, thanks always to my predecessors, from whom I learned so much: Tony Alferez, Paul Inman, and Del Olds.

My enthusiasm for this book—and the subject of programming languages in particular—was sparked by Dr. Dan Resler, Associate Professor at Virginia Commonwealth University. I registered for his class on compiler theory with a singular lack of interest, and left that class with a passion for formal language theory. Thank you for passing your enthusiasm—and some small part of your depth of understanding—on to me.

Thanks to all of my friends in the PSU part-time MBA cohort—it's been such a pleasure getting to know you all! Special thanks to Cathy, Amanda, Miska, Sahar, Paul S., Cathy, John R., Laurie, Joel, Tyler P., Tyler S., and Jess: you've all enriched my life so much!

If my coworkers at Pop Art motivate me to greatness and inspire my days, my friends motivate me to deepness and light up my nights. Mark Booth: no friend knows me better, and there is no one I would sooner trust my deepest secrets to. Your creativity and talent put me to shame: don't let me show you up with this stupid book. Katy Roberts is as reliable as the incoming tide, and as beautiful. Katy, thank you for your deep and abiding kindness and friendship. Sarah Lewis: I love your face. Byron and Amber Clayton are true and loyal friends who always bring a smile to my face. Lorraine, it's been years, but you still bring out the best in me. To Kate Nahas: I'm so glad we have reconnected after so many years; I look forward to sharing a toast to Duke's memory. To Desember: thank you for your trust, warmth, and companionship. Lastly, thanks to my new friends Chris Onstad and Jessica Rowe: you two have brought so much joy and laughter into my life in the last two years, I don't know what I would have done without you.

To my mother, Ann: thank you for your unwavering support, love, and patience. My father, Tom, remains my prototype for curiosity, innovation, and dedication, and without him I would be a poor engineer (or perhaps not an engineer at all). My sister, Meris, will always be a fixed point in my life, representing loyalty and conviction.

# CHAPTER 1
# Your First Application

Often, the best way to learn is to *do*: so we're going to start off by creating a simple application. The point of this chapter is not to explain everything that's going on: there's a lot that's going to be unfamiliar and confusing, and my advice to you is to relax and not get caught up in trying to understand everything right now. The point of this chapter is to get you excited. Just enjoy the ride; by the time you finish this book, everything in this chapter will make perfect sense to you.

If you don't have much programming experience, one of the things that is going to cause you a lot of frustration at first is how *literal* computers are. Our human minds can deal with confusing input very easily, but computers are terrible at this. If I make a grammatical error, it may change your opinion about my writing ability, but you will probably still understand me. JavaScript—like all programming languages—has no such facility to deal with confusing input. Capitalization, spelling, and the order of words and punctuation are crucial. If you're experiencing problems, make sure you've copied everything correctly: you haven't substituted semicolons for colons or commas for periods, you haven't mixed single quotation and double quotation marks, and you've capitalized all of your code correctly. Once you've had some experience, you'll learn where you can "do things your way," and where you have to be perfectly literal, but for now, you will experience less frustration by entering the examples exactly as they're written.

Historically, programming books have started out with an example called "Hello, World" that simply prints the phrase "hello world" to your terminal. It may interest you to know that this tradition was started in 1972 by Brian Kernighan, a computer scientist working at Bell Labs. It was first seen in print in 1978 in *The C Programming*

*Language*, by Brian Kernighan and Dennis Ritchie. To this day, *The C Programming Language* is widely considered to be one of the best and most influential programming language books ever written, and I have taken much inspiration from that work in writing this book.

While "Hello, World" may seem dated to an increasingly sophisticated generation of programming students, the implicit meaning behind that simple phrase is as potent today as it was in 1978: they are the first words uttered by something that *you* have breathed life into. It is proof that you are Prometheus, stealing fire from the gods; a rabbi scratching the true name of God into a clay golem; Doctor Frankenstein breathing life into his creation.[1] It is this sense of creation, of genesis, that first drew me to programming. Perhaps one day, some programmer—maybe you—will give life to the first artificially sentient being. And perhaps its first words will be "hello world."

In this chapter, we will balance the tradition that Brian Kernighan started 44 years ago with the sophistication available to programmers today. We will see "hello world" on our screen, but it will be a far cry from the blocky words etched in glowing phosphor you would have enjoyed in 1972.

## Where to Start

In this book, we will cover the use of JavaScript in all its current incarnations (server-side, scripting, desktop, browser-based, and more), but for historical and practical reasons, we're going to start with a browser-based program.

One of the reasons we're starting with a browser-based example is that it gives us easy access to graphics libraries. Humans are inherently visual creatures, and being able to relate programming concepts to visual elements is a powerful learning tool. We will spend a lot of time in this book staring at lines of text, but let's start out with something a little more visually interesting. I've also chosen this example because it organically introduces some very important concepts, such as event-driven programming, which will give you a leg up on later chapters.

## The Tools

Just as a carpenter would have trouble building a desk without a saw, we can't write software without some tools. Fortunately, the tools we need in this chapter are minimal: a browser and a text editor.

I am happy to report that, as I write this, there is not one browser on the market that is not suited to the task at hand. Even Internet Explorer—which has long been a

1 I hope you have more compassion for your creations than Dr. Frankenstein—and fare better.

thorn in the side of programmers—has cleaned up its act, and is now on par with Chrome, Firefox, Safari, and Opera. That said, my browser of choice is Firefox, and in this text, I will discuss Firefox features that will help you in your programming journey. Other browsers also have these features, but I will describe them as they are implemented in Firefox, so the path of least resistance while you go through this book will be to use Firefox.

You will need a text editor to actually write your code. The choice of text editors can be a very contentious—almost religious—debate. Broadly speaking, text editors can be categorized as text-mode editors or windowed editors. The two most popular text-mode editors are vi/vim and Emacs. One big advantage to text-mode editors is that, in addition to using them on your computer, you can use them over SSH—meaning you can remotely connect to a computer and edit your files in a familiar editor. Windowed editors can feel more modern, and add some helpful (and more familiar) user interface elements. At the end of the day, however, you are editing text only, so a windowed editor doesn't offer an inherent advantage over a text-mode editor. Popular windowed editors are Atom, Sublime Text, Coda, Visual Studio, Notepad++, TextPad, and Xcode. If you are already familiar with one of these editors, there is probably no reason to switch. If you are using Notepad on Windows, however, I highly recommend upgrading to a more sophisticated editor (Notepad++ is an easy and free choice for Windows users).

Describing all the features of your editor is beyond the scope of this book, but there are a few features that you will want to learn how to use:

*Syntax highlighting*
: Syntax highlighting uses color to distinguish syntactic elements in your program. For example, literals might be one color and variables another (you will learn what these terms mean soon!). This feature can make it easier to spot problems in your code. Most modern text editors will have syntax highlighting enabled by default; if your code isn't multicolored, consult your editor documentation to learn how to enable it.

*Bracket matching*
: Most programming languages make heavy use of parentheses, curly braces, and square brackets (collectively referred to as "brackets"). Sometimes, the contents of these brackets span many lines, or even more than one screen, and you'll have brackets within brackets, often of different types. It's critical that brackets match up, or "balance"; if they don't, your program won't work correctly. Bracket matching provides visual cues about where brackets begin and end, and can help you spot problems with mismatched brackets. Bracket matching is handled differently in different editors, ranging from a very subtle cue to a very obvious one. Unmatched brackets are a common source of frustration for beginners, so I

strongly recommend that you learn how to use your editor's bracket-matching feature.

*Code folding*
Somewhat related to bracket matching is *code folding*. Code folding refers to the ability to temporarily hide code that's not relevant to what you're doing at the moment, allowing you to focus. The term comes from the idea of folding a piece of paper over on itself to hide unimportant details. Like bracket matching, code folding is handled differently by different editors.

*Autocompletion*
Autocompletion (also called *word completion* or *IntelliSense*[2]) is a convenience feature that attempts to guess what you are typing before you finish typing it. It has two purposes. The first is to save typing time. Instead of typing, for example, **`encodeURIComponent`**, you can simply type **`enc`**, and then select `encodeURIComponent` from a list. The second purpose is called *discoverability*. For example, if you type **`enc`** because you want to use `encodeURIComponent`, you'll find (or "discover") that there's also a function called `encodeURI`. Depending on the editor, you may even see some documentation to distinguish the two choices. Autocompletion is more difficult to implement in JavaScript than it is in many other languages because it's a loosely typed language, and because of its scoping rules (which you will learn about later). If autocompletion is an important feature to you, you may have to shop around to find an editor that meets your needs: this is an area in which some editors definitely stand out from the pack. Other editors (vim, for example) offer very powerful autocompletion, but not without some extra configuration.

## A Comment on Comments

JavaScript—like most programming languages—has a syntax for making *comments* in code. Comments are completely ignored by JavaScript; they are meant for you or your fellow programmers. They allow you to add natural language explanations of what's going on when it's not clear. In this book, we'll be liberally using comments in code samples to explain what's happening.

In JavaScript, there are two kinds of comments: inline comments and block comments. An inline comment starts with two forward slashes (`//`) and extends to the end of the line. A block comment starts with a forward slash and an asterisk (`/*`) and ends with an asterisk and a forward slash (`*/`), and can span multiple lines. Here's an example that illustrates both types of comments:

2 Microsoft's terminology.

```
console.log("echo");     // prints "echo" to the console
/*
   In the previous line, everything up to the double forward slashes
   is JavaScript code, and must be valid syntax.  The double
   forward slashes start a comment, and will be ignored by JavaScript.

   This text is in a block comment, and will also be ignored
   by JavaScript.  We've chosen to indent the comments of this block
   for readability, but that's not necessary.
*/
/*Look, Ma, no indentation!*/
```

Cascading Style Sheets (CSS), which we'll see shortly, also use JavaScript syntax for block comments (inline comments are not supported in CSS). HTML (like CSS) doesn't have inline comments, and its block comments are different than JavaScript. They are surrounded by the unwieldy `<!--` and `-->`:

```
<head>
   <title>HTML and CSS Example</title>
   <!-- this is an HTML comment...
            which can span multiple lines. -->
   <style>
      body: { color: red; }
      /* this is a CSS comment...
            which can span multiple lines. */
   </style>
   <script>
      console.log("echo"); // back in JavaScript...
      /* ...so both inline and block comments
            are supported. */
   </script>
</head>
```

## Getting Started

We're going to start by creating three files: an HTML file, a CSS file, and a JavaScript source file. We could do everything in the HTML file (JavaScript and CSS can be embedded in HTML), but there are certain advantages to keeping them separate. If you're new to programming, I strongly recommend that you follow along with these instructions step by step: we're going to take a very exploratory, incremental approach in this chapter, which will facilitate your learning process.

It may seem like we're doing a lot of work to accomplish something fairly simple, and there's some truth in that. I certainly could have crafted an example that does the same thing with many fewer steps, but by doing so, I would be *teaching you bad habits*. The extra steps you'll see here are ones you'll see over and over again, and while it may seem overcomplicated now, you can at least reassure yourself that you're learning to do things *the right way*.

One last important note about this chapter. This is the lone chapter in the book in which the code samples will be written in ES5 syntax, not ES6 (Harmony). This is to ensure that the code samples will run, even if you aren't using a browser that has implemented ES6. In the following chapters, we will talk about how to write code in ES6 and "transcompile" it so that it will run on legacy browsers. After we cover that ground, the rest of the book will use ES6 syntax. The code samples in this chapter are simple enough that using ES5 doesn't represent a significant handicap.

For this exercise, you'll want to make sure the files you create are in the same directory or folder. I recommend that you create a new directory or folder for this example so it doesn't get lost among your other files.

Let's start with the JavaScript file. Using a text editor, create a file called *main.js*. For now, let's just put a single line in this file:

```
console.log('main.js loaded');
```

Then create the CSS file, *main.css*. We don't actually have anything to put in here yet, so we'll just include a comment so we don't have an empty file:

```
/* Styles go here. */
```

Then create a file called *index.html*:

```
<!doctype html>
<html>
  <head>
    <link rel="stylesheet" href="main.css">
  </head>
  <body>
    <h1>My first application!</h1>
    <p>Welcome to <i>Learning JavaScript, 3rd Edition</i>.</p>

    <script src="main.js"></script>
  </body>
</html>
```

While this book isn't about HTML or web application development, many of you are learning JavaScript for that purpose, so we will point out some aspects of HTML as they relate to JavaScript development. An HTML document consists of two main parts: the *head* and the *body*. The head contains information that is *not directly displayed in your browser* (though it can affect what's displayed in your browser). The body contains the contents of your page that will be rendered in your browser. It's important to understand that elements in the head will never be shown in the browser, whereas elements in the body usually are (certain types of elements, like `<script>`, won't be visible, and CSS styles can also hide body elements).

In the head, we have the line `<link rel="stylesheet" href="main.css">`; this is what links the currently empty CSS file into your document. Then, at the end of the body, we have the line `<script src="main.js"></script>`, which is what links the JavaScript file into your document. It may seem odd to you that one goes in the head and the other goes at the end of the body. While we could have put the `<script>` tag in the head, there are performance and complexity reasons for putting it at the end of the body.

In the body, we have `<h1>My first application!</h1>`, which is first-level header text (which indicates the largest, most important text on the page), followed by a `<p>` (paragraph) tag, which contains some text, some of which is italic (denoted by the `<i>` tag).

Go ahead and load *index.html* in your browser. The easiest way to do this on most systems is to simply double-click on the file from a file browser (you can also usually drag the file onto a browser window). You'll see the body contents of your HTML file.

There are many code samples in this book. Because HTML and JavaScript files can get very large, I won't present the whole files every time: instead, I will explain in the text where the code sample fits into the file. This may cause some trouble for beginning programmers, but understanding the way code fits together is important, and can't be avoided.

## The JavaScript Console

We've already written some JavaScript: `console.log('main.js loaded')`. What did that do? The *console* is a text-only tool for programmers to help them diagnose their work. You will use the console extensively as you go through this book.

Different browsers have different ways of accessing the console. Because you will be doing this quite often, I recommend learning the keyboard shortcut. In Firefox, it's Ctrl-Shift-K (Windows and Linux) or Command-Option-K (Mac).

In the page in which you loaded *index.html*, open the JavaScript console; you should see the text "main.js loaded" (if you don't see it, try reloading the page). `console.log` is a method[3] that will print whatever you want to the console, which is very helpful for debugging and learning alike.

One of the many helpful features of the console is that, in addition to seeing output from your program, you can *enter JavaScript directly in the console*, thereby testing

3 You will learn more about the difference between a *function* and a *method* in Chapter 9.

things out, learning about JavaScript features, and even modifying your program temporarily.

## jQuery

We're going to add an extremely popular client-side scripting library called *jQuery* to our page. While it is not necessary, or even germane to the task at hand, it is such a ubiquitous library that it is often the first one you will include in your web code. Even though we could easily get by without it in this example, the sooner you start getting accustomed to seeing jQuery code, the better off you will be.

At the end of the body, *before* we include our own *main.js*, we'll link in jQuery:

```
<script src="https://code.jquery.com/jquery-2.1.1.min.js"></script>

<script src="main.js"></script>
```

You'll notice that we're using an Internet URL, which means your page won't work correctly without Internet access. We're linking in jQuery from a publicly hosted *content delivery network* (CDN), which has certain performance advantages. If you will be working on your project offline, you'll have to download the file and link it from your computer instead. Now we'll modify our *main.js* file to take advantage of one of jQuery's features:

```
$(document).ready(function() {
    'use strict';
    console.log('main.js loaded');
});
```

Unless you've already had some experience with jQuery, this probably looks like gibberish. There's actually a lot going on here that won't become clear until much later. What jQuery is doing for us here is making sure that the browser has loaded all of the HTML before executing our JavaScript (which is currently just a single `console.log`). Whenever we're working with browser-based JavaScript, we'll be doing this just to establish the practice: any JavaScript you write will go between the `$(document).ready(function() {` and `});` lines. Also note the line `'use strict';` this is something we'll learn more about later, but basically this tells the JavaScript interpreter to treat your code more rigorously. While that may not sound like a good thing at first, it actually helps you write better JavaScript, and prevents common and difficult-to-diagnose problems. We'll certainly be learning to write very rigorous JavaScript in this book!

## Drawing Graphics Primitive

Among many of the benefits HTML5 brought was a standardized graphics interface. The HTML5 *canvas* allows you to draw graphics primitives like squares, circles, and polygons. Using the canvas directly can be painful, so we'll use a graphics library called Paper.js (*http://paperjs.org*) to take advantage of the HTML5 canvas.

Paper.js is not the only canvas graphics library available: KineticJS (*http://kineticjs.com*), Fabric.js (*http://fabricjs.com*), and EaselJS (*http://www.createjs.com/#!/EaselJS*) are very popular and robust alternatives. I've used all of these libraries, and they're all very high quality.

Before we start using Paper.js to draw things, we'll need an HTML canvas element to draw on. Add the following to the body (you can put it anywhere; after the intro paragraph, for example):

```
<canvas id="mainCanvas"></canvas>
```

Note that we've given the canvas an `id` attribute: that's how we will be able to easily refer to it from within JavaScript and CSS. If we load our page right now, we won't see anything different; not only haven't we drawn anything on the canvas, but it's a white canvas on a white page and has no width and height, making it very hard to see indeed.

Every HTML element can have an ID, and for the HTML to be valid (correctly formed), each ID must be unique. So now that we've created a canvas with the `id` "mainCanvas", we can't reuse that ID. Because of this, it's recommended that you use IDs sparingly. We're using one here because it's often easier for beginners to deal with one thing at a time, and by definition, an ID can only refer to one thing on a page.

Let's modify *main.css* so our canvas stands out on the page. If you're not familiar with CSS, that's OK—this CSS is simply setting a width and height for our HTML element, and giving it a black border:[4]

```
#mainCanvas {
   width: 400px;
   height: 400px;
```

4 If you want to learn more about CSS and HTML, I recommend the Codecademy's free HTML & CSS track (*https://www.codecademy.com/tracks/web*).

```
    border: solid 1px black;
}
```

If you reload your page, you should see the canvas now.

Now that we have something to draw on, we'll link in Paper.js to help us with the drawing. Right after we link in jQuery, but before we link in our own *main.js*, add the following line:

```
<script src="https://cdnjs.cloudflare.com/ajax/libs/paper.js/0.9.24/ ↩
paper-full.min.js"></script>
```

Note that, as with jQuery, we're using a CDN to include Paper.js in our project.

You might be starting to realize that the order in which we link things in is very important. We're going to use both jQuery and Paper.js in our own *main.js*, so we have to link in both of those first. Neither of them depends on the other, so it doesn't matter which one comes first, but I always include jQuery first as a matter of habit, as so many things in web development depend on it.

Now that we have Paper.js linked in, we have to do a little work to configure Paper.js. Whenever you encounter code like this—repetitive code that is required before you do something—it's often called *boilerplate*. Add the following to *main.js*, right after `'use strict'` (you can remove the `console.log` if you wish):

```
paper.install(window);
paper.setup(document.getElementById('mainCanvas'));

// TODO

paper.view.draw();
```

The first line installs Paper.js in the global scope (which will make more sense in Chapter 7). The second line attaches Paper.js to the canvas, and prepares Paper.js for drawing. In the middle, where we put `TODO` is where we'll actually be doing the interesting stuff. The last line tells Paper.js to actually draw something to the screen.

Now that all of the boilerplate is out of the way, let's draw something! We'll start with a green circle in the middle of the canvas. Replace the "TODO" comment with the following lines:

```
var c = Shape.Circle(200, 200, 50);
c.fillColor = 'green';
```

Refresh your browser, and behold, a green circle. You've written your first real JavaScript. There's actually a lot going on in those two lines, but for now, it's only important to know a few things. The first line creates a circle *object*, and it does so with three *arguments*: the *x* and *y* coordinates of the center of the circle, and the radius of the circle. Recall we made our canvas 400 pixels wide and 400 pixels tall, so the center of the canvas lies at (200, 200). And a radius of 50 makes a circle that's an eighth of the width and height of the canvas. The second line sets the *fill* color, which is distinct from the outline color (called the *stroke* in Paper.js parlance). Feel free to experiment with changing those arguments.

## Automating Repetitive Tasks

Consider what you'd have to do if you wanted not just to add one circle, but to fill the canvas with them, laid out in a grid. If you space the circles 50 pixels apart and make them slightly smaller, you could fit 64 of them on the canvas. Certainly you could copy the code you've already written 63 times, and by hand, modify all of the coordinates so that they're spaced out in a grid. Sounds like a lot of work, doesn't it? Fortunately, this kind of repetitive task is what computers excel at. Let's see how we can draw out 64 circles, evenly spaced. We'll replace our code that draws a single circle with the following:

```
var c;
for(var x=25; x<400; x+=50) {
   for(var y=25; y<400; y+=50) {
      c = Shape.Circle(x, y, 20);
      c.fillColor = 'green';
   }
}
```

If you refresh your browser, you'll see we have 64 green circles! If you're new to programming, what you've just written may seem confusing, but you can see it's better than writing the 128 lines it would take to do this by hand.

What we've used is called a `for` loop, which is part of the control flow syntax that we'll learn about in detail in Chapter 4. A `for` loop allows you to specify an initial condition (25), an ending condition (less than 400), and an increment value (50). We use one loop inside the other to accomplish this for both the x-axis and y-axis.

There are many ways we could have written this example. The way we've written it, we've made the *x* and *y* coordinates the important pieces of information: we explicitly specify where the circles will start and how far apart they'll be spaced. We could have approached this problem from another direction: we could have said what's important is the number of circles we want (64), and let the program figure out how to space them so that they fit on the canvas. The reason we went with this solution is that it better matches what we would have done if we had cut and pasted our circle code 64 times and figured out the spacing ourselves.

## Handling User Input

So far, what we've been doing hasn't had any input from the user. The user can click on the circles, but it doesn't do anything. Likewise, trying to drag a circle would have no effect. Let's make this a little more interactive, by allowing the *user* to choose where the circles get drawn.

It's important to become comfortable with the *asynchronous* nature of user input. An *asynchronous event* is an event whose timing you don't have any control over. A user's mouse click is an example of an asynchronous event: you can't be inside your users' minds, knowing when they're going to click. Certainly you can prompt their click response, but it is up to them when—and if—they actually click. Asynchronous events arising from user input make intuitive sense, but we will cover much less intuitive asynchronous events in later chapters.

Paper.js uses an object called a *tool* to handle user input. If that choice of names seems unintuitive to you, you are in good company: I agree, and don't know why the Paper.js developers used that terminology.[5] It might help you to translate "tool" to "user input tool" in your mind. Let's replace our code that drew a grid of circles with the following code:

```
var tool = new Tool();

tool.onMouseDown = function(event) {
   var c = Shape.Circle(event.point.x, event.point.y, 20);
   c.fillColor = 'green';
};
```

The first step in this code is to create our tool object. Once we've done that, we can attach an *event handler* to it. In this case, the event handler is called `onMouseDown`. Whenever the user clicks the mouse, *the function we've attached to this handler is invoked.* This is a very important point to understand. In our previous code, the code ran right away: we refreshed the browser, and the green circles appeared automatically. That is not happening here: if it were, it would draw a single green circle somewhere on the screen. Instead, the code contained between the curly braces after `function` is executed *only when the user clicks the mouse on the canvas.*

The event handler is doing two things for you: it is executing your code *when* the mouse is clicked, and it is telling you *where* the mouse was clicked. That location is stored in a property of the argument, `event.point`, which has two properties, `x` and `y`, indicating where the mouse was clicked.

5 Technical reviewer Matt Inman suggested that the Paper.js developers might have been Photoshop users familiar with "hand tool," "direct selection tool," and so on.

Note that we could save ourselves a little typing by passing the point directly to the circle (instead of passing the *x* and *y* coordinates separately):

```
var c = Shape.Circle(event.point, 20);
```

This highlights a very important aspect of JavaScript: it's able to ascertain information about the variables that are passed in. In the previous case, if it sees three numbers in a row, it knows that they represent the *x* and *y* coordinates and the radius. If it sees two arguments, it knows that the first one is a point object, and the second one is the radius. We'll learn more about this in Chapters 6 and 9.

# Hello, World

Let's conclude this chapter with a manifestation of Brian Kernighan's 1972 example. We've already done all the heavy lifting: all that remains is to add the text. Before your `onMouseDown` handler, add the following:

```
var c = Shape.Circle(200, 200, 80);
c.fillColor = 'black';
var text = new PointText(200, 200);
text.justification = 'center';
text.fillColor = 'white';
text.fontSize = 20;
text.content = 'hello world';
```

This addition is fairly straightforward: we create another circle, which will be a backdrop for our text, and then we actually create the text object (`PointText`). We specify where to draw it (the center of the screen) and some additional properties (justification, color, and size). Lastly, we specify the actual text contents ("hello world").

Note that this is not the first time we emitted text with JavaScript: we did that first with `console.log` earlier in this chapter. We certainly could have changed that text to "hello world." In many ways, that would be more analogous to the experience you would have had in 1972, but the point of the example is not the text or how it's rendered: the point is that you're creating something autonomous, which has observable effects.

By refreshing your browser with this code, you are participating in a venerable tradition of "Hello, World" examples. If this is your first "Hello, World," let me welcome you to the club. If it is not, I hope that this example has given you some insight into JavaScript.

CHAPTER 2

# JavaScript Development Tools

While you can write JavaScript with nothing more than an editor and a browser (as we saw in the previous chapter), JavaScript developers rely on some useful development tools. Furthermore, because we are focusing on ES6 for the rest of this book, we'll need a way to convert our ES6 code to portable ES5 code. The tools discussed in this chapter are very common, and you are likely to encounter them in any open source project or software development team. They are:

- Git, a version control tool that helps you manage your project as it grows, and collaborate with other developers.
- Node, which allows you to run JavaScript outside of the browser (and comes with npm, which gives you access to the rest of the tools on this list).
- Gulp, a *build tool* that automates common development tasks (Grunt is a popular alternative).
- Babel, a *transcompiler* that converts ES6 code to portable ES5 code.
- ESLint, a *linter* that helps you avoid common mistakes and makes you a better programmer!

Don't think of this chapter as a distraction from the topic at hand (JavaScript). Think of it as a practical introduction to some important tools and techniques that are commonly used in JavaScript development.

## Writing ES6 Today

I have good news and bad news. The good news is that ES6 (aka Harmony, aka JavaScript 2015) is an exciting, delightful evolution in the history of JavaScript. The bad news is that the world isn't quite ready for it. That doesn't mean you can't use it now, but it is going to put an extra burden on the programmer, as ES6 code has to be transcompiled into "safe" ES5 to ensure that it can run anywhere.

Programmers who have been around a while might be thinking "big deal; back in my day, there was no such thing as a language that didn't have to be compiled and linked!" I've been writing software long enough to remember that time, but I do not miss it: I enjoy the lack of fuss in interpreted languages like JavaScript.[1]

One of the advantages of JavaScript has always been its ubiquity: it became the standard browser scripting language almost overnight, and with the advent of Node, its use broadened beyond the browser. So it is a bit painful to recognize that it will probably be a few years before you can ship ES6 code without worrying about browsers that don't support it. If you're a Node developer, the situation is a little bit brighter: because you only have one JavaScript engine to worry about, you can track the progress of ES6 support in Node.

The ES6 examples in this book can be run in Firefox, or on a website such as ES6 Fiddle (*http://www.es6fiddle.net/*). For "real-world code," however, you will want to know the tools and techniques in this chapter.

One interesting aspect about JavaScript's transition from ES5 to ES6 is that, unlike language releases of the past, the *adoption is gradual*. That is, the browser you're using right now probably has some—but not all—features available in ES6. This gradual transition is made possible in part by the dynamic nature of JavaScript, and in part by the changing nature of browser updates. You may have heard the term *evergreen* used to describe browsers: browser manufacturers are moving away from the concept of having discrete browser versions that have to be updated. Browsers, they reason, should be able to keep themselves up to date because they are always connected to the Internet (at least if they are going to be useful). Browsers still have versions, but it is now more reasonable to assume that your users have the *latest* version—because evergreen browsers don't give users the option *not* to upgrade.

Even with evergreen browsers, however, it will be a while before you can rely on all of the great features of ES6 being available on the client side. So for the time being, transcompilation (also called *transpilation*) is a fact of life.

## ES6 Features

There are a lot of new features in ES6—so many that even the transcompilers we'll be talking about don't currently support all of them. To help control the chaos, New

1 Some JavaScript engines (Node, for example) do compile your JavaScript, but it happens transparently.

York–based developer kangax (*https://twitter.com/kangax*) maintains an excellent compatibility table (*https://kangax.github.io/compat-table/es6/*) of ES6 (and ES7) features. As of August 2015, the most complete implementation (Babel) is only at 72%. While that may sound discouraging, it's the most important features that have been implemented first, and all of the features discussed in this book are available in Babel.

We have a little bit of prep work to do before we can start transcompiling. We'll need to make sure we have the necessary tools, and learn how to set up a new project to use them—a process that will become automatic after you do it a few times. In the meantime, you will probably want to refer back to this chapter as you start new projects.

## Installing Git

If you don't have Git installed on your system, you can find downloads and instructions for your operating system on the Git home page (*https://git-scm.com/*).

## The Terminal

Throughout this chapter, we'll be working in the *terminal* (also known as the *command line* or *command prompt*). The terminal is a text-based way of interacting with your computer, and is commonly used by programmers. Though it is certainly possible to be an effective programmer without ever using the terminal, I believe it is an important skill to have: many tutorials and books assume you're using a terminal, and many tools are designed to be used on the terminal.

The most ubiquitous terminal experience is a shell (terminal interface) called *bash*, and it is available by default on Linux and OS X machines. While Windows has its own command-line experience, Git (which we will install next) provides a bash command line, which I recommend you use. In this book, we will be using bash.

On Linux and OS X, look in your programs for the *Terminal* program. On Windows, after you install Git, look for "Git Bash" in your programs.

When you start the terminal, you see a *prompt*, which is where you will type commands. The default prompt may include the name of your computer or the directory you're in, and it will normally end with a dollar sign ($). Thus, in the code samples in this chapter, I will use a dollar sign to indicate the prompt. What follows the prompt is what you should type. For example, to get a listing of the files in the current directory, type **`ls`** at the prompt:

```
$ ls
```

In Unix, and therefore bash, directory names are separated with a forward slash (/). Even in Windows, where directories are normally separated by backslashes (\), Git

Bash translates backslashes to forward slashes. Bash also uses the tilde (~) as a shortcut for your home directory (where you should normally be storing your files).

The basics you'll need are the ability to change the current directory (`cd`), and make new directories (`mkdir`). For example, to go to your home directory, type:

```
$ cd ~
```

The command `pwd` (print working directory) tells you what directory you're currently in:

```
$ pwd
```

To create a subdirectory called *test*, type:

```
$ mkdir test
```

To change to this newly created directory, type:

```
$ cd test
```

Two periods (`..`) are a shortcut for "parent directory." So to go "up" a directory (if you've been following along, this will take you back to your home directory), type:

```
$ cd ..
```

There's a lot more to learn about the terminal, but these basic commands are all you need to get through the material in this chapter. If you want to learn more, I recommend the Console Foundations course on Treehouse (*http://teamtreehouse.com/library/console-foundations*).

## Your Project Root

You'll want to create a directory for each project. We'll call this directory the *project root*. For example, if you're following along with the examples in this book, you could create an *lj* directory, which would be your project root. In all the command-line examples in this book, we'll assume that you're in the project root. If you try an example and it doesn't work, the first thing to verify is that you're in the project root. Any files we create will be relative to the project root. For example, if your project root is */home/joe/work/lj*, and we ask you to create a file *public/js/test.js*, the full path to that file should be */home/joe/work/lj/public/js/test.js*.

## Version Control: Git

We won't discuss version control in detail in this book, but if you're not using it, you should be. If you're not familiar with Git, I encourage you to use this book as an opportunity to practice.

First, from your project root, initialize a repository:

```
$ git init
```

This will create a project repository for you (there's now a hidden directory called *.git* in your project root).

Inevitably, there will be some files you never want tracked in version control: build artifacts, temporary files, and the like. These files can be explicitly excluded in a file called *.gitignore*. Go ahead and create a *.gitignore* file now with the following contents:

```
# npm debugging logs
npm-debug.log*

# project dependencies
node_modules

# OSX folder attributes
.DS_Store

# temporary files
*.tmp
*~
```

If there are any other "junk" files that you know of, you're welcome to add them here (for example, if you know your editor creates *.bak* files, you would add **.bak* to this list).

A command you'll be running a lot is `git status`, which tells you the current status of your repository. Go ahead and run it now. You should see:

```
$ git status
On branch master

Initial commit

Untracked files:
  (use "git add <file>..." to include in what will be committed)

        .gitignore

nothing added to commit but untracked files present (use "git add" to track)
```

The important thing that Git is telling you is that there's a new file in the directory (*.gitignore*), but it's *untracked*, meaning Git doesn't recognize it.

The basic unit of work in a Git repository is the *commit*. Currently, your repository doesn't have any commits (you've just initialized it and created a file, but you haven't registered any of that work with Git). Git doesn't make any assumptions about what files you want to track, so you have to explicitly add *.gitignore* to the repository:

```
$ git add .gitignore
```

We still haven't created a commit; we've simply *staged* the file *.gitignore* to go in the next commit. If we run `git status` again, we will see:

```
$ git status
On branch master

Initial commit

Changes to be committed:
  (use "git rm --cached <file>..." to unstage)

        new file:   .gitignore
```

Now *.gitignore* is *to be committed*. We still haven't created a commit yet, but when we do, our changes to *.gitignore* will be in it. We could add more files, but let's go ahead and create a commit now:

```
$ git commit -m "Initial commit: added .gitignore."
```

The string that follows `-m` is the commit *message*: a brief description of the work you've done in this commit. This allows you to look back at your commits and see the history of your project unfold.

You can think of a commit as a snapshot of your project at a moment in time. We've now taken a snapshot of the project (with only the *.gitignore* file in it), and you could go back to that at any time. If you run `git status` now, Git will tell you:

```
On branch master
nothing to commit, working directory clean
```

Let's make some additional changes to our project. In our *.gitignore* file, we're ignoring any files named *npm-debug.log*, but let's say we want to ignore any files with the *.log* extension (which is standard practice). Edit the *.gitignore* file and change that line to `*.log`. Let's also add a file called *README.md*, which is a standard file that explains the project in the popular *Markdown* format:

```
= Learning JavaScript, 3rd Edition
== Chapter 2: JavaScript Development Tools

In this chapter we're learning about Git and other
development tools.
```

Now type **`git status`**:

```
$ git status
On branch master
Changes not staged for commit:
  (use "git add <file>..." to update what will be committed)
  (use "git checkout -- <file>..." to discard changes in working directory)

        modified:   .gitignore
```

```
Untracked files:
  (use "git add <file>..." to include in what will be committed)

        README.md
```

We now have two changes: one to a tracked file (*.gitignore*) and one to a new file (*README.md*). We could add the changes as we did before:

```
$ git add .gitignore
$ git add README.md
```

But this time we'll use a shortcut to add *all* changes, then create a commit with all of those changes:

```
$ git add -A
$ git commit -m "Ignored all .log files and added README.md."
```

This is a common pattern you'll be repeating frequently (adding changes and then committing them). Try to make your commits small and logically consistent: think of them as telling a story to someone else, explaining your thought process. Whenever you make changes to your repository, you'll be following the same pattern: add one or more changes, then create a commit:

```
$ git add -A
$ git commit -m "<brief description of the changes you just made>"
```

Beginners are often confused by `git add`; the name makes it seem like you're adding files to the repository. Those changes *can* be new files, but just as likely they're changes to files already in the repository. In other words, you're adding *changes*, not files (and a new file is just a special type of change).

This represents the simplest possible Git workflow; if you want to learn more about Git, I recommend GitHub's Git Tutorial (*https://try.github.io/levels/1/challenges/1*) and Jon Loeliger and Matthew McCullough's book, *Version Control with Git*, Second Edition (*http://bit.ly/versionControlGit_2e*).

## Package Management: npm

Understanding npm is not strictly necessary to JavaScript development, but it's increasingly becoming the package management tool of choice. For Node development, it's practically essential. Whether you're actually writing Node apps or just doing browser development, you'll find that life is a lot easier with npm. In particular, we'll be using npm to install our build tools and transcompilers.

npm comes bundled with Node, so if you haven't installed Node already, go to the Node.js home page (*https://nodejs.org/*) and click on the big green "INSTALL" button.

Once you've installed Node, verify that npm and Node are functioning on your system. From the command line, do the following:

```
$ node -v
v4.2.2
$ npm -v
2.14.7
```

Your version numbers may vary as Node and npm are updated. Broadly speaking, npm manages installed packages. A package can be anything from a full application, to sample code, to a module or library that you'll use in your project.

npm supports installing packages at two levels: globally and locally. Global packages are usually command-line tools that you'll use in the development process. Local packages are project-specific. Installing a package is done with the `npm install` command. Let's install the popular *Underscore* package to see how it works. In your project root, run the following:

```
$ npm install underscore
underscore@1.8.3 node_modules\underscore
```

npm is telling you that it installed the latest version of Underscore (1.8.3 as I write this; yours will probably be different). Underscore is a module with no dependencies, so the output from npm is very brief; for some complex modules, you may see pages of text go by! If we wanted to install a specific version of Underscore, we can specify the version number explicitly:

```
$ npm install underscore@1.8.0
underscore@1.8.0 node_modules\underscore
```

So where did this module actually get installed? If you look in your directory, you'll see a new subdirectory called *node_modules*; any local modules you install will go in this directory. Go ahead and delete the *node_modules* directory; we'll be re-creating it in a moment.

As you install modules, you'll want to keep track of them somehow; the modules you install (and use) are called *dependencies* of your project. As your project matures, you'll want a concise way to know what packages your project depends on, and npm does this with a file called *package.json*. You don't have to create this file yourself: you can run `npm init`, and interactively answer some questions (you can simply press Enter for each question and accept the defaults; you can always edit the file and change your answers later). Go ahead and do this now, and take a look at the generated *package.json* file.

Dependencies are split into regular dependencies and *dev dependencies*. Dev dependencies are packages that your app can run without, but are helpful or necessary in building your project (we'll see examples of these soon). From here on out, when you install local packages, you should add either the `--save` or `--saveDev` flag; if you don't, the package will be installed, but not listed in the *package.json* file. Let's go ahead and reinstall Underscore with the `--save` flag:

```
$ npm install --save underscore
npm WARN package.json lj@1.0.0 No description
npm WARN package.json lj@1.0.0 No repository field.
underscore@1.8.3 node_modules\underscore
```

You might be wondering what all of these warnings are. npm is telling you that there are some components missing from your package. For the purposes of this book, you can ignore these warnings: you only need to worry about them if you're using npm to publish your own packages, which is beyond the scope of this book.

Now if you look at your *package.json* file, you'll see that Underscore is listed as a dependency. The idea of dependency management is that the dependency versions referenced in *package.json* are all that's necessary to re-create (download and install) the dependencies themselves. Let's try this out. Delete the *node_modules* directory again, and then run `npm install` (note we don't specify any particular package name). npm will install any packages listed in the *package.json* file. You can look at the newly created *node_modules* directory to verify this.

## Build Tools: Gulp and Grunt

For most development, you'll probably want a *build tool*, which automates the repetitive tasks you perform as part of the development process. Currently, the two most popular build tools for JavaScript are Grunt (*http://gruntjs.com/*) and Gulp (*http://gulpjs.com/*). These are both capable build systems. Grunt has been around a couple of years longer than Gulp, so the community is larger, but Gulp is catching up fast. Because Gulp seems to be the increasingly popular choice for new JavaScript programmers, we'll use it in this book, though I am not prepared to say Gulp is superior to Grunt (or vice versa).

First, you'll install Gulp globally with:

```
$ npm install -g gulp
```

If you're on Linux or OS X, you'll need elevated privileges to use the `-g` (global) switch when running npm: `sudo install -g gulp`. You'll be prompted for your password and given superuser privileges (for that command only). If you are on a system that someone else manages, you might have to ask them to put you in the *sudoers* file.

You'll only need to install Gulp globally once for each system you develop on. Then, for each project, you'll need a local Gulp, so from your project root, run `npm install --save-dev gulp` (Gulp is an example of a dev dependency: your app won't need it to run, but you'll use it to help with your development process). Now that Gulp has been installed, we create a *Gulpfile* (*gulpfile.js*):

```
const gulp = require('gulp');
// Gulp dependencies go here

gulp.task('default', function() {
    // Gulp tasks go here
});
```

We haven't actually configured Gulp to *do* anything yet, but we can verify that Gulp can run successfully now:

```
$ gulp
[16:16:28] Using gulpfile /home/joe/work/lj/gulpfile.js
[16:16:28] Starting 'default'...
[16:16:28] Finished 'default' after 68 μs
```

If you're a Windows user, you may get the error "The build tools for Visual Studio 2010 (Platform Toolset = *v100*) cannot be found." Many npm packages have a dependency on Visual Studio build tools. You can get a free version of Visual Studio from the product download page (*https://www.visualstudio.com/en-us/visual-studio-homepage-vs.aspx*). Once you've installed Visual Studio, look for "Developer Command Prompt" in your program files. In that command prompt, navigate to your project root and try to install Gulp again, and you should have better luck. You don't need to continue using the Visual Studio Developer Command Prompt, but it's the easiest way to install npm modules that have dependencies on Visual Studio.

## Project Structure

Before we use Gulp and Babel to convert our ES6 code to ES5, we need to think about where we're going to put our code within our project. There's no one universal standard for project layout in JavaScript development: the ecosystem is just too diverse for that. Very commonly, you'll see source code in *src* or *js* directories. We're going to put our source in *es6* directories, to make it perfectly clear that we're writing ES6 code.

Because many projects include both server-side (Node) code and client-side (browser) code, we're going to separate these two categories as well. Server-side code will simply go in the *es6* directory in our project root, and code destined for the browser will go in *public/es6* (by definition, any JavaScript sent to the browser is public, and this is a very common convention).

In the next section, we'll take our ES6 code and convert it to ES5, so we'll need a place to put that ES5 code (we don't want to mix it in with ES6 code). A common convention is to put that code in a directory called *dist* (for "distribution").

Putting it all together, your project root will look something like this:

```
.git                    # Git
.gitignore

package.json            # npm
node_modules

es6                     # Node source
dist

public/                 # browser source
    es6/
    dist/
```

# The Transcompilers

As I write this, the two most popular transcompilers are Babel (*https://babeljs.io/*) and Traceur (*https://github.com/google/traceur-compiler*). I have used both, and they are both quite capable and easy to use. I am currently leaning slightly toward Babel, and we'll be using it as the transcompiler in this book. So let's get started!

Babel started as a ES5 to ES6 transcompiler, and has grown to be a general-purpose transcompiler that's capable of many different transformations, including ES6, React, and even ES7. Starting with version 6 of Babel, transformations are no longer included with Babel. To perform our ES5 to ES6 transformation, we need to install the ES6 transformations and configure Babel to use them. We make these settings local to our project, as it is conceivable that we'll want to use ES6 on one project, React on another, and ES7 (or some other variant) on another. First, we install the ES6 (aka ES2015) preset:

```
$ npm install --save-dev babel-preset-es2015
```

Then we create a file in our project root called *.babelrc* (the leading period indicates the file should be normally hidden). The contents of this file are:

```
{ "presets": ["es2015"] }
```

With this file in place, any use of Babel in this project recognizes that you're using ES6.

## Running Babel with Gulp

Now we can use Gulp to do something actually useful: convert the ES6 code we'll be writing to portable ES5 code. We'll convert any code in *es6* and *public/es6* to ES5 code in *dist* and *public/dist*. We'll be using a package called `gulp-babel`, so we start by installing it with `npm install --save-dev gulp-babel`. Then we edit *gulpfile.js*:

```
const gulp = require('gulp');
const babel = require('gulp-babel');

gulp.task('default', function() {
  // Node source
  gulp.src("es6/**/*.js")
    .pipe(babel())
    .pipe(gulp.dest("dist"));
  // browser source
  gulp.src("public/es6/**/*.js")
    .pipe(babel())
    .pipe(gulp.dest("public/dist"));
});
```

Gulp uses the concept of a *pipeline* to do its work. We start off by telling Gulp what files we're interested in: `src("es6/**/*.js")`. You might be wondering about the `**`; that's a wildcard for "any directory, including subdirectories." So this source filter will pick up all *.js* files in *es6*, and any subdirectories thereof, no matter how deep. Then we *pipe* those source files to Babel, which is what transforms them from ES6 to ES5. The final step is to pipe the compiled ES5 to its destination, the *dist* directory. Gulp will preserve the names and directory structure of your source files. For example, the file *es6/a.js* will be compiled to *dist/a.js*, and *es6/a/b/c.js* will be compiled to *dist/a/b/c.js*. We repeat the same process for the files in our *public/es6* directory.

We haven't learned any ES6 yet, but let's create an ES6 sample file, and verify that our Gulp configuration is working. Create the file *es6/test.js* that shows off some of the new features of ES6 (don't worry if you don't understand this file; when you're done with this book, you will!):

```
'use strict';
// es6 feature: block-scoped "let" declaration
const sentences = [
    { subject: 'JavaScript', verb: 'is', object: 'great' },
    { subject: 'Elephants', verb: 'are', object: 'large' },
];
// es6 feature: object destructuring
function say({ subject, verb, object }) {
    // es6 feature: template strings
    console.log(`${subject} ${verb} ${object}`);
}
// es6 feature: for..of
for(let s of sentences) {
    say(s);
}
```

Now create a copy of this file in *public/es6* (you can change the contents of the *sentences* array if you want to verify that your files are different). Now type **`gulp`**. When it's done, look in the *dist* and *public/dist* directories. You'll see a *test.js* file in both places. Go ahead and look at that file, and note that it differs from its ES6 equivalent.

Now let's try running the ES6 code directly:

```
$ node es6/test.js
/home/ethan/lje3/es6/test.js:8
function say({ subject, verb, object }) {
             ^

SyntaxError: Unexpected token {
    at exports.runInThisContext (vm.js:53:16)
    at Module._compile (module.js:374:25)
    at Object.Module._extensions..js (module.js:417:10)
    at Module.load (module.js:344:32)
    at Function.Module._load (module.js:301:12)
    at Function.Module.runMain (module.js:442:10)
    at startup (node.js:136:18)
    at node.js:966:3
```

The error you get from Node may be different, as Node is in the process of implementing ES6 features (if you're reading this book far enough in the future, it may work completely!). Now let's run the ES5 equivalent:

```
$ node dist\test.js
JavaScript is great
Elephants are large
```

We've successfully converted ES6 code to portable ES5 code, which should run anywhere! As a last step, add *dist* and *public/dist* to your *.gitignore* file: we want to keep track of the ES6 source, not the ES5 files that are generated from it.

## Linting

Do you run a lint roller over your dress or suit before you go to a fancy party or an interview? Of course you do: you want to look your best. Likewise, you can *lint* your code to make it (and by extension, you) look its best. A linter takes a critical eye to your code and lets you know when you're making common mistakes. I've been writing software for 25 years, and a good linter will still find mistakes in my code before I do. For the beginner, it's an invaluable tool that can save you a *lot* of frustration.

There are several JavaScript linters out there, but my preference is Nicholas Zakas's *ESLint*. Install ESLint:

```
npm install -g eslint
```

Before we start using ESLint, we need to create an *.eslintrc* configuration file for our project. Each project you work on may have different technologies or standards, and the *.eslintrc* allows ESLint to lint your code accordingly.

The easiest way to create an *.eslintrc* file is to run `eslint --init`, which will interactively ask you some questions and create a default file for you.

In your project root, run `eslint --init`. The answers you will need to have are:

- Do you use tabs or space to indent? A recent StackOverflow poll (*http://stackoverflow.com/research/developer-survey-2015#tech-tabsspaces*) showed that the majority of programmers prefer tabs, but that more experienced programmers prefer spaces. I will let you choose your own path here....
- Do you prefer single or double quotes for strings? It doesn't matter what you answer here...we want to be able to use either equally.
- What line endings do you use (Unix or Windows)? If you're on Linux or OS X, choose Unix. If you're on Windows, choose Windows.
- Do you require semicolons? Yes.
- Are you using ECMAScript 6 (ES6) features? Yes.
- Where will your code run (Node or in the browser)? Ideally, you would use a different configuration for browser and Node code, but that's a more advanced configuration. Go ahead and choose Node.
- Do you want to use JSX? No. (JSX is a XML-based extension to JavaScript that is used in Facebook's *React* UI library. We won't be using it in this book.)
- What format do you want your config file to be in (JSON or YAML)? Choose JSON (YAML is a popular data serialization format like JSON, but JSON is more appropriate for JavaScript development).

After you've answered all the questions, you will have a *.eslintrc* file, and we can start using ESLint.

There are several ways to run ESLint. You can run it directly (for example, `eslint es6/test.js`), integrate into your editor, or add it to your Gulpfile. Editor integration is great, but the instructions differ for every editor and operating system: if you want editor integration, I recommend Googling the name of your editor with "eslint."

Whether or not you use editor integration, I recommend adding ESLint to your Gulpfile. After all, we have to run Gulp when we want to build, so that's also a great time to check the quality of our code. First, run:

```
npm install --save-dev gulp-eslint
```

Then modify *gulpfile.js*:

```
const gulp = require('gulp');
const babel = require('gulp-babel');
const eslint = require('gulp-eslint');

gulp.task('default', function() {
```

```
    // Run ESLint
    gulp.src(["es6/**/*.js", "public/es6/**/*.js"])
      .pipe(eslint())
      .pipe(eslint.format());
    // Node source
    gulp.src("es6/**/*.js")
      .pipe(babel())
      .pipe(gulp.dest("dist"));
    // browser source
    gulp.src("public/es6/**/*.js")
      .pipe(babel())
      .pipe(gulp.dest("public/dist"));
});
```

Now let's see what ESLint doesn't like about our code. Because we included ESLint in our `default` task in the Gulpfile, we can simply run Gulp:

```
$ gulp
[15:04:16] Using gulpfile ~/git/gulpfile.js
[15:04:16] Starting 'default'...
[15:04:16] Finished 'default' after 84 ms
[15:04:16]
/home/ethan/lj/es6/test.js
  4:59  error  Unexpected trailing comma     comma-dangle
  9:5   error  Unexpected console statement  no-console

✖ 2 problems (2 errors, 0 warnings)
```

Clearly, Nicholas Zakas and I disagree about trailing commas. Fortunately, ESLint lets you make your own choices about what's an error and what's not. The `comma-dangle` rule defaults to `"never"`, and we have the option of turning it off altogether, or changing it to `"always-multiline"` (my preference). Let's edit the *.eslintrc* file to change this setting (if you agree with Nicholas about trailing commas, you can use the default of `"never"`). Each rule in the *.eslintrc* is an array. The first element is a number, where 0 turns the rule off, 1 considers it a warning, and 2 considers it an error:

```
{
   "rules": {
      /* changed comma-dangle default...ironically,
         we can't use a dangling comma here because
         this is a JSON file. */
      "comma-dangle": [
         2,
         "always-multiline"
      ],
      "indent": [
         2,
         4
      ],
      /* ... */
```

Now if you run `gulp` again, you'll see that our dangling comma no longer causes an error. As a matter of fact, if we remove it, it will cause an error!

The second error refers to using `console.log`, which is generally considered "sloppy" (even dangerous if you're targeting legacy browsers) when used in production browser code. For learning purposes, however, you can disable this, as we'll be using `console.log` throughout this book. Also, you will probably want to turn off the `"quotes"` rule. I'll leave it as a reader's exercise to disable these rules.

ESLint has a lot of configuration options; they're all thoroughly documented on the ESLint website (*http://eslint.org/*).

Now that we can write ES6, transcompile it to portable ES5, and lint our code to improve it, we're ready to dive into ES6!

# Conclusion

In this chapter, we learned that ES6 support is not widespread yet, but it shouldn't stop you from enjoying the benefits of ES6 today, as you can transcompile your ES6 to portable ES5.

When you're setting up a new development machine, you'll want:

- A good editor (see Chapter 1)
- Git (visit *https://git-scm.com/* for installation instructions)
- Gulp (`npm install -g gulp`)
- ESLint (`npm install -g eslint`)

When you start a new project (whether it be a scratch project to run the examples in this book, or a real project), you'll want the following components:

- A dedicated directory for your project; we call this the *project root*
- A Git repository (`git init`)
- A *package.json* file (`npm init`)
- A Gulpfile (*gulpfile.js*; use the one from this chapter)
- Gulp and Babel local packages (`npm install --save-dev gulp gulp-babel babel-preset-es2015`)
- A *.babelrc* file (contents: `{ "presets": ["es2015"] }`)
- An *.eslintrc* file (use `eslint --init` to create it, and edit to your preferences)
- A subdirectory for Node source (*es6*)

- A subdirectory for browser source (*public/es6*)

Once you have everything set up, your basic workflow will look like this:

1. Make logically consistent, related changes.
2. Run Gulp to test and lint your code.
3. Repeat until your changes work and are lint-free.
4. Check to make sure you're not about to commit anything you don't want to (`git status`). If there are files you don't want in Git, add them to your *.gitignore* file.
5. Add all of your changes to Git (`git add -A`; if you don't want to add all the changes, use `git add` for each file instead).
6. Commit your changes (`git commit -m "<description of your changes>"`).

Depending on the project, there may be other steps, such as running tests (usually as a Gulp task), and pushing your code to a shared repository such as GitHub or Bitbucket (`git push`). However, the steps listed here are a great framework to build on.

Throughout the rest of the book, we'll present source code without repeating the steps necessary to build and run it. Unless the example is explicitly browser code, all of the code samples should run with Node. So, for example, if you're given an example *example.js*, you would put that file in *es6*, and run it with:

```
$ gulp
$ node dist/example.js
```

You can also skip the Gulp step and run it directly with `babel-node` (though you will not be saving any time, as `babel-node` also has to transcompile):

```
$ babel-node es6/example.js
```

Now it's time to learn some JavaScript!

# CHAPTER 3
# Literals, Variables, Constants, and Data Types

This chapter is about *data*, and how we translate data into a format that JavaScript can understand.

You're probably aware that all data is ultimately represented inside a computer as long sequences of ones and zeros—but for most day-to-day tasks, we want to think about data in a way that's more natural to us: numbers, text, dates, and so on. We will call these abstractions *data types*.

Before we dive into the data types available in JavaScript, we will discuss *variables*, *constants*, and *literals*, which are the mechanisms available to us in JavaScript for *holding* data.

The importance of vocabulary is often overlooked when you're learning to program. While it may not seem important to understand how a literal differs from a value, or a statement from an expression, not knowing these terms will hamper your ability to learn. Most of these terms are not specific to JavaScript, but are commonly understood in computer science. Having a good grasp of the concepts is important, of course, but paying attention to vocabulary makes it easy for you to transfer your knowledge to other languages, and learn from more sources.

## Variables and Constants

A *variable* is essentially a named value, and as the name implies, the value can change at any time. For example, if we're working on a climate control system, we might have a variable called `currentTempC`:

```
let currentTempC = 22;  // degrees Celsius
```

The `let` keyword is new in ES6; prior to ES6, the only option was the `var` keyword, which we will discuss in Chapter 7.

This statement does two things: it declares (creates) the variable `currentTempC` and assigns it an initial value. We can change the value of `currentTempC` at any time:

```
currentTempC = 22.5;
```

Note that we don't use `let` again; `let` specifically declares a variable, and you can only do it once.

With numbers, there's no way to associate units with the value. That is, there's no language feature that allows us to say that `currentTempC` is in degrees Celsius, thereby producing an error if we assign a value in degrees Fahrenheit. For this reason, I chose to add "C" to the variable name to make it clear that the units are degrees Celsius. The language can't enforce this, but it's a form of documentation that prevents casual mistakes.

When you declare a variable, you don't have to provide it with an initial value. If you don't, it implicitly gets a special value, `undefined`:

```
let targetTempC;  // equivalent to "let targetTempC = undefined";
```

You can also declare multiple variables with the same `let` statement:

```
let targetTempC, room1 = "conference_room_a", room2 = "lobby";
```

In this example, we've declared three variables: `targetTempC` isn't initialized with a variable, so it implicitly has the value `undefined`; `room1` is declared with an initial value of `"conference_room_a"`; and `room2` is declared with an initial value of `"lobby"`. `room1` and `room2` are examples of *string* (text) variables.

A *constant* (new in ES6) also holds a value, but unlike a variable, can't be changed after initialization. Let's use a constant to express a comfortable room temperature and a maximum temp (`const` can also declare multiple constants):

```
const ROOM_TEMP_C = 21.5, MAX_TEMP_C = 30;
```

It is conventional (but not required) for constants that refer to a specific number or string to be named with all uppercase letters and underscores. This makes them easy to spot in your code, and is a visual cue that you shouldn't try to change their value.

## Variables or Constants: Which to Use?

In general, you should prefer constants over variables. You'll find that more often than not you want a handy name for some piece of data, but you don't need its value to change. The advantage of using constants is that it makes it harder to accidentally change the value of something that shouldn't be changed. For example, if you're working on a part of your program that performs some kind of action on a user, you might have a variable called `user`. If you're dealing with only one user, it would probably indicate an error in your code if the value of `user` changed. If you were working with two users, you might call them `user1` and `user2`, instead of simply reusing a single variable `user`.

So your rule of thumb should be to use a constant; if you find you have a legitimate need to change the value of the constant, you can always change it to a variable.

There is one situation in which you will always want to use variables instead of constants: variables used in loop control (which we'll learn about in Chapter 4). Other situations where you might want to use variables are when the value of something is naturally changing over time (such as `targetTempC` or `currentTemp` in this chapter). If you get in the habit of preferring constants, however, you might be surprised by how seldom you really need a variable.

In the examples in this book, I have tried to use constants instead of variables whenever possible.

## Identifier Names

Variable and constant names (as well as function names, which we'll cover in Chapter 6) are called *identifiers*, and they have naming rules:

- Identifiers must start with a letter, dollar sign ($), or underscore (_).
- Identifiers consist of letters, numbers, the dollar sign ($), and underscore (_).
- Unicode characters are allowed (for example, π or ö).
- Identifiers cannot be a reserved word (see Appendix A).

Note that the dollar sign is not a special character the way it is in some other languages: it's simply another character you can use in identifier names (many libraries, such as jQuery, have taken advantage of this, and used the dollar sign by itself as an identifier).

Reserved words are words that JavaScript might confuse with part of the language. For example, you can't have a variable called `let`.

There's no single convention for JavaScript identifiers, but the two most common are:

*Camel case*

`currentTempC`, `anIdentifierName` (so named because the capital letters look like the humps in a camel's back).

*Snake case*

`current_temp_c`, `an_identifier_name` (slightly less popular).

You can use whichever convention you prefer, but consistency is a good idea: select one and stick with it. If you are working on a team or making your project available to a community, try choosing whatever the preferred convention is.

It is also advisable to adhere to the following conventions:

- Identifiers shouldn't start with a capital letter *except* for classes (which we'll cover in Chapter 9).
- Very often, identifiers that start with one or two underscores are used to represent special or "internal" variables. Unless you need to create your own special category of variables, avoid starting variable names with an underscore.
- When using jQuery, identifiers that start with a dollar sign conventionally refer to jQuery-wrapped objects (see Chapter 19).

## Literals

We've already seen some *literals*: when we gave `currentTempC` a value, we provided a *numeric literal* (`22` at initialization, and `22.5` in the next example). Likewise, when we initialized `room1`, we provided a *string literal* (`"conference_room_a"`). The word *literal* means that you're providing the value directly in the program. Essentially, a literal is a way to *create a value*; JavaScript takes the literal value you provide and creates a data value from it.

It's important to understand the difference between a *literal* and an *identifier*. For example, think back to our earlier example where we created a variable called `room1`, which had the value `"conference_room_a"`. `room1` is an identifier (referring to a constant), and `"conference_room_a"` is a string literal (and also the value of `room1`). JavaScript is able to distinguish the identifier from the literal by the use of quotation marks (numbers don't need any sort of quotation because identifiers can't start with a number). Consider the following example:

```
let room1 = "conference_room_a";        // "conference_room_a" (in quotes) is
                                        // a literal

let currentRoom = room1;                // currentRoom now has the same value
                                        // as room1 ("conference_room_a")
```

```
let currentRoom = conference_room_a;    // produces an error; no identifier
                                        // called conference_room_a exists
```

You can use a literal anywhere you can use an identifier (where a value is expected). For example, in our program, we could just use the numeric literal `21.5` everywhere instead of using `ROOM_TEMP_C`. If you use the numeric literal in a couple places, this may be OK. But if you use it in 10 or 100 places, you should be using a constant or variable instead: it makes your code easier to read, and you can change the value in one place instead of many.

It is up to you, the programmer, to decide what to make a variable and what to make a constant. Some things are quite obviously constants—such as the approximate value of π (the ratio of a circle's circumference to its diameter), or `DAYS_IN_MARCH`. Other things, such as `ROOM_TEMP_C`, are not quite as obvious: 21.5°C might be a perfectly comfortable room temperature for me, but not for you, so if this value is configurable in your application, you would make it a variable instead.

# Primitive Types and Objects

In JavaScript, values are either *primitives* or *objects*. Primitive types (such as string and number) are *immutable*. The number 5 will always be the number 5; the string `"alpha"` will always be the string `"alpha"`. This seems obvious for numbers, but it often trips people up with strings: when people concatenate strings together (`"alpha" + "omega"`), they sometimes think it's the same string, just modified. It is not: it is a new string, in the same way that 6 is a different number than 5. There are six primitive types that we will cover:

- Number
- String
- Boolean
- Null
- Undefined
- Symbol

Note that immutability doesn't mean the *contents of a variable* can't change:

```
let str = "hello";
str = "world";
```

First `str` is initialized with the (immutable) value `"hello"`, and then it is assigned a new (immutable) value, `"world"`. What's important here is that `"hello"` and `"world"` are different strings; only the value that `str` holds has changed. Most of the time, this distinction is academic, but the knowledge will come in handy later when we discuss functions in Chapter 6.

In addition to these six primitive types, there are *objects*. Unlike primitives, objects can take on different forms and values, and are more chameleon-like.

Because of their flexibility, objects can be used to construct custom data types. As a matter of fact, JavaScript provides some built-in object types. The built-in object types we'll cover are as follows:

- `Array`
- `Date`
- `RegExp`
- `Map` and `WeakMap`
- `Set` and `WeakSet`

Lastly, the primitive types number, string, and boolean have corresponding object types, `Number`, `String`, and `Boolean`. These corresponding objects don't actually store a value (that's what the primitive does), but rather provide functionality that's related to the corresponding primitive. We will discuss these object types along with their primitives.

# Numbers

While some numbers (like 3, 5.5, and 1,000,000) can be represented accurately by a computer, many numbers are necessarily approximations. For example, π cannot be represented by a computer at all, because its digits are infinite and do not repeat. Other numbers, such as 1/3, can be represented by special techniques, but because of their forever repeating decimals (3.33333…), they are normally approximated as well.

JavaScript—along with most other programming languages—approximates real numbers through a format called *IEEE-764 double-precision floating-point* (which I will refer to simply as a "double" from here on out). The details of this format are beyond the scope of this book, but unless you are doing sophisticated numerical analysis, you probably don't need to understand them. However, the consequences of the approximations required by this format often catch people off guard. For example, if you ask JavaScript to calculate 0.1 + 0.2, it will return 0.30000000000000004. This does not mean that JavaScript is "broken" or bad at math: it's simply an unavoidable consequence of approximating infinite values in finite memory.

JavaScript is an unusual programming language in that it only has this one numeric data type.[1] Most languages have multiple integer types and two or more floating-point types. On one hand, this choice simplifies JavaScript, especially for beginners. On the other hand, it reduces JavaScript's suitability for certain applications that require the performance of integer arithmetic, or the precision of fixed-precision numbers.

JavaScript recognizes four types of numeric literal: decimal, binary, octal, and hexadecimal. With decimal literals, you can express integers (no decimal), decimal numbers, and numbers in base-10 exponential notation (an abbreviation of scientific notation). In addition, there are special values for infinity, negative infinity, and "not a number" (these are not technically numeric literals, but they do result in numeric values, so I am including them here):

```
let count = 10;             // integer literal; count is still a double
const blue = 0x0000ff;      // hexadecimal (hex ff = decimal 255)
const umask = 0o0022;       // octal (octal 22 = decimal 18)
const roomTemp = 21.5;      // decimal
const c = 3.0e6;            // exponential (3.0 × 10^6 = 3,000,000)
const e = -1.6e-19;         // exponential (-1.6 × 10^-19 = 0.00000000000000000016)
const inf = Infinity;
const ninf = -Infinity;
const nan = NaN;            // "not a number"
```

No matter what literal format you use (decimal, hexadecimal, exponential, etc.), the number that gets created is stored in the same format: a double. The various literal formats simply allow you to specify a number in whatever format is convenient. JavaScript has limited support for displaying numbers in different formats, which we'll discuss in Chapter 16.

The mathematicians in the crowd might be calling foul: infinity is not a number! Indeed, it isn't; but of course, neither is `NaN`. These are not numbers you do computation with; rather, they are available as placeholders.

In addition, there are some useful properties of the corresponding `Number` object that represent important numeric values:

```
const small = Number.EPSILON;               // the smallest value that can be
                                            // added to 1 to get a distinct number
                                            // larger than 1, approx. 2.2e-16
const bigInt = Number.MAX_SAFE_INTEGER;     // the largest representable integer
const max = Number.MAX_VALUE;               // the largest representable number
const minInt = Number.MIN_SAFE_INTEGER;     // the smallest representable integer
const min = Number.MIN_VALUE;               // the smallest representable number
const nInf = Number.NEGATIVE_INFINITY;      // the same as -Infinity
```

1 This may change in the future: dedicated integer types are an oft-discussed language feature.

```
const nan = Number.NaN;                    // the same as NaN
const inf = Number.POSITIVE_INFINITY;      // the same as Infinity
```

We'll discuss the importance of these values in Chapter 16.

# Strings

A *string* is simply text data (the word *string* comes from "string of characters"—a word originally used in the late 1800s by typesetters, and then later by mathematicians, to represent a sequence of symbols in a definite order).

Strings in JavaScript represent *Unicode* text. Unicode is a computing industry standard for representing text data, and includes *code points* for every character or symbol in most known human languages (including "languages" that might surprise you, such as Emoji). While Unicode itself is capable of representing text in any language, that does not mean that the software rendering the Unicode will be capable of rendering every code point correctly. In this book, we'll stick to fairly common Unicode characters that are most likely available in your browser and console. If you are working with exotic characters or languages, you'll want to do additional research on Unicode to understand how code points are rendered.

In JavaScript, string literals are represented with single quotes, double quotes, or backticks.[2] The backtick was introduced in ES6 to enable *template strings*, which we will cover shortly.

## Escaping

When you're trying to represent text data in a program that's made up of text data, the problem is always distinguishing text data from the program itself. Setting off strings within quotes is a start, but what if you want to use quotes *in* a string? To solve this problem, there needs to be a method of *escaping* characters so they are not taken as string termination. Consider the following examples (which do not require escaping):

```
const dialog = 'Sam looked up, and said "hello, old friend!", as Max walked in.';
const imperative = "Don't do that!";
```

In `dialog`, we can use double quotes without fear because our string is set off with single quotes. Likewise, in `imperative`, we can use an apostrophe because the string is set off with double quotes. But what if we needed to use both? Consider:

```
// this will produce an error
const dialog = "Sam looked up and said "don't do that!" to Max.";
```

2 Also called a *grave accent* mark.

This dialog string will fail no matter which quotation mark we choose. Fortunately, we can *escape* quotation marks with a backslash (\), which is a signal to JavaScript that the string is *not* ending. Here's the preceding example rewritten to use both types of quotation marks:

```
const dialog1 = "He looked up and said \"don't do that!\" to Max.";
const dialog2 = 'He looked up and said "don\'t do that!" to Max.';
```

Then, of course, we get into the chicken-and-egg problem that arises when we want to use a backslash in our string. To solve this problem, a backslash can escape itself:

```
const s = "In JavaScript, use \\ as an escape character in strings.";
```

Whether you use single or double quotes is up to you. I generally prefer double quotation marks when I'm writing text that might be presented to the user, because I use contractions (like *don't*) more often than I use double quotation marks. When I'm expressing HTML inside a JavaScript string, I tend to prefer single quotation marks so that I can use double quotation marks for attribute values.

# Special Characters

The backslash is used for more than simply escaping quotation marks: it is also used to represent certain nonprintable characters, such as newlines and arbitrary Unicode characters. Table 3-1 lists the commonly used special characters.

*Table 3-1. Commonly used special characters*

| Code | Description | Example |
|---|---|---|
| \n | Newline (technically a line feed character: ASCII/Unicode 10) | "Line1\nLine2" |
| \r | Carriage return (ASCII/Unicode 13) | "Windows line 1\r\nWindows line 2" |
| \t | Tab (ASCII/Unicode 9) | "Speed:\t60kph" |
| \' | Single quote (note that you can use this even when not necessary) | "Don\'t" |
| \" | Double quote (note that you can use this even when not necessary) | 'Sam said \"hello\".' |
| \` | Backtick (or "accent grave"; new in ES6) | `New in ES6: \` strings.` |
| \$ | Dollar sign (new in ES6) | `New in ES6: ${interpolation}` |
| \\ | Backslash | "Use \\\\ to represent \\!" |

| Code | Description | Example |
|---|---|---|
| `\uXXXX` | Arbitrary Unicode code point (where +XXXX+ is a hexadecimal code point) | `"De Morgan's law: \u2310(P \u22c0 Q) \u21D4 (\u2310P) \u22c1 (\u2310Q)"` |
| `\xXX` | Latin-1 character (where +XX+ is a hexadecimal Latin-1 code point) | `"\xc9p\xe9e is fun, but foil is more fun."` |

Note that the Latin-1 character set is a subset of Unicode, and any Latin-1 character `\xXX` can be represented by the equivalent Unicode code point `\u00XX`. For hexadecimal numbers, you may use lowercase or uppercase letters as you please; I personally favor lowercase, as I find them easier to read.

You don't need to use escape codes for Unicode characters; you can also enter them directly into your editor. The way to access Unicode characters varies among editors and operating systems (and there is usually more than one way); please consult your editor or operating system documentation if you wish to enter Unicode characters directly.

Additionally, there are some rarely used special characters, shown in Table 3-2. To my recollection, I have never used any of these in a JavaScript program, but I include them here for the sake of completeness.

*Table 3-2. Rarely used special characters*

| Code | Description | Example |
|---|---|---|
| `\0` | The NUL character (ASCII/Unicode 0) | `"ASCII NUL: \0"` |
| `\v` | Vertical tab (ASCII/Unicode 11) | `"Vertical tab: \v"` |
| `\b` | Backspace (ASCII/Unicode 8) | `"Backspace: \b"` |
| `\f` | Form feed (ASCII/Unicode 12) | `"Form feed: \f"` |

## Template Strings

A very common need is to express values in a string. This can be accomplished through a mechanism called *string concatenation*:

```
let currentTemp = 19.5;
// 00b0 is the Unicode code point for the "degree" symbol
const message = "The current temperature is " + currentTemp + "\u00b0C";
```

Up until ES6, string concatenation was the only way to accomplish this (short of using a third-party library). ES6 introduces *string templates* (also known as *string interpolation*). String templates provide a shorthand way of injecting values into a string. String templates use backticks instead of single or double quotes. Here is the previous example rewritten using string templates:

```
let currentTemp = 19.5;
const message = `The current temperature is ${currentTemp}\u00b0C`;
```

Inside a string template, the dollar sign becomes a special character (you can escape it with a backslash): if it's followed by a value[3] wrapped in curly braces, that value is inserted into the string.

Template strings are one of my favorite features of ES6, and you'll see them used throughout this book.

## Multiline Strings

Before ES6, multiline string support was spotty at best. The language specification allows for escaping the newline at the end of a line of source code, but it's a feature I've never used due to unreliable browser support. With ES6, the feature is more likely to be available, but there are some quirks that you should be aware of. Note that these techniques probably won't work in a JavaScript console (like the one in your browser) so you'll have to actually write a JavaScript file to try these out. For single- and double-quoted strings, you can escape the newline thusly:

```
const multiline = "line1\
line2";
```

If you expect `multiline` to be a string with a newline in it, you'll be surprised: the slash at the end of the line escapes the newline, but does not insert a newline into the string. So the result will be `"line1line2"`. If you want an actual newline, you'll have to do this:

```
const multiline = "line1\n\
line2";
```

Backtick strings behave a little more like you might expect:

```
const multiline = `line1
line2`;
```

This will result in a string with a newline. With both techniques, however, any indentation at the beginning of the line will be included in the resulting string. For example, the following will result in a string with newlines *and* whitespace before `line2` and `line3`, which may not be desirable:

3 You can actually use any *expression* inside the curly braces. We will cover expressions in Chapter 5.

```
const multiline = `line1
    line2
    line3`;
```

For this reason, I avoid multiline string syntax: it forces me to either abandon indentation that makes code easier to read, or include whitespace in my multiline strings that I may not want. If I do want to break strings up over multiple lines of source code, I usually use string concatenation:

```
const multiline = "line1\n" +
    "line2\n" +
    "line3";
```

This allows me to indent my code in an easy-to-read fashion, and get the string I want. Note that you can mix and match types of strings in string concatenation:

```
const multiline = 'Current temperature:\n' +
    `\t${currentTemp}\u00b0C\n` +
    "Don't worry...the heat is on!";
```

## Numbers as Strings

If you put a number in quotation marks, it's not a number—it's a string. That said, JavaScript will automatically convert strings that contain numbers to numbers as necessary. When and how this happens can be very confusing, as we will discuss in Chapter 5. Here's an example that illustrates when this conversion happens, and when it doesn't:

```
const result1 = 3 + '30';  // 3 is converted to a string; result is string '330'
const result2 = 3 * '30';  // '30' is converted to a number; result is numeric 90
```

As a rule of thumb, when you want to use numbers, use numbers (that is, leave off the quotes), and when you want to use strings, use strings. The gray area is when you're accepting user input, which almost always comes as a string, leaving it up to you to convert to a number where appropriate. Later in this chapter, we will discuss techniques for converting among data types.

# Booleans

Booleans are value types that have only two possible values: `true` and `false`. Some languages (like C) use numbers instead of booleans: 0 is `false` and every other number is `true`. JavaScript has a similar mechanism, allowing *any* value (not just numbers) to be considered "truthy" or "falsy," which we'll discuss further in Chapter 5.

Be careful not to use quotation marks when you intend to use a boolean. In particular, a lot of people get tripped up by the fact that the string `"false"` is actually truthy! Here's the proper way to express boolean literals:

```
let heating = true;
let cooling = false;
```

## Symbols

New in ES6 are *symbols*: a new data type representing unique tokens. Once you create a symbol, it is unique: it will match no other symbol. In this way, symbols are like objects (every object is unique). However, in all other ways, symbols are primitives, lending themselves to useful language features that allow extensibility, which we'll learn more about in Chapter 9.

Symbols are created with the `Symbol()` constructor.[4] You can optionally provide a description, which is just for convenience:

```
const RED = Symbol();
const ORANGE = Symbol("The color of a sunset!");
RED === ORANGE  // false: every symbol is unique
```

I recommend using symbols whenever you want to have a unique identifier that you don't want inadvertently confused with some other identifier.

## null and undefined

JavaScript has two special types, `null` and `undefined`. `null` has only one possible value (`null`), and `undefined` has only one possible value (`undefined`). Both `null` and `undefined` represent something that doesn't exist, and the fact that there are two separate data types has caused no end of confusion, especially among beginners.

The general rule of thumb is that `null` is a data type that is available to you, the programmer, and `undefined` should be reserved for JavaScript itself, to indicate that something hasn't been given a value yet. This is not an enforced rule: the `undefined` value is available to the programmer to use at any time, but common sense dictates that you should be extremely cautious in using it. The only time I explicitly set a variable to `undefined` is when I want to deliberately mimic the behavior of a variable that hasn't been given a value yet. More commonly, you want to express that the value of a variable isn't known or isn't applicable, in which case `null` is a better choice. This may seem like splitting hairs, and sometimes it is—the beginning programmer is advised to use `null` when unsure. Note that if you declare a variable without explicitly giving it a value, it will have a value of `undefined` by default. Here are examples of using `null` and `undefined` literals:

4 If you're already familiar with object-oriented programming in JavaScript, note that creating a symbol with the `new` keyword is not allowed, and is an exception to the convention that identifiers that start with capital letters should be used with `new`.

```
let currentTemp;              // implicit value of undefined
const targetTemp = null;      // target temp null -- "not yet known"
currentTemp = 19.5;           // currentTemp now has value
currentTemp = undefined;      // currentTemp appears as if it had never
                              // been initialized; not recommended
```

## Objects

Unlike the immutable primitive types, which only ever represent one value, objects can represent multiple or complex values, and can change over their lifetime. In essence, an object is a *container*, and the contents of that container can change over time (it's the same object with different contents). Like the primitive types, objects have a literal syntax: curly braces ({ and }). Because curly braces come in pairs, it allows us to express an object's contents. Let's start with an empty object:

```
const obj = {};
```

We can name our object anything we want, and normally you would use a descriptive name, such as `user` or `shoppingCart`. We're just learning the mechanics of objects, and our example doesn't represent anything specific so we just generically call it `obj`.

The contents of an object are called *properties* (or *members*), and properties consist of a *name* (or *key*) and *value*. Property names must be strings or symbols, and values can be any type (including other objects). Let's add a property `color` to `obj`:

```
obj.size;              // undefined
obj.color;             // "yellow"
```

To use the member access operator, the property name must be a valid identifier. If you want property names that are not valid identifiers, you have to use the *computed member access* operator (you can also use this for valid identifiers):

```
obj["not an identifier"] = 3;
obj["not an identifier"];          // 3
obj["color"];                      // "yellow"
```

You also use the computed member access operator for symbol properties:

```
const SIZE = Symbol();
obj[SIZE] = 8;
obj[SIZE];                         // 8
```

At this point, `obj` contains three properties with keys `"color"` (a string that is a valid identifier), `"not an identifier"` (a string that is not a valid identifier), and `SIZE` (a symbol).

If you're following along in a JavaScript console, you may notice that the console doesn't list the `SIZE` symbol as a property of `obj`. It is (you can verify this by typing `obj[SIZE]`), but symbol properties are handled differently and are not displayed by default. Also note that the key for this property is the symbol `SIZE`, *not* the string `"SIZE"`. You can verify this by typing `obj.SIZE = 0` (the member access property *always* operates on string properties) and then `obj[SIZE]` and `obj.SIZE` (or `obj["SIZE"]`).

At this juncture, let's pause and remind ourselves of the differences between primitives and objects. Throughout this section, we have been manipulating and modifying the object contained by the variable `obj`, but `obj` *has been pointing to the same object all along*. If `obj` had instead contained a string or a number or any other primitive, it would be a *different* primitive value every time we change it. In other words, `obj` has pointed to the same object all along, but the object itself has changed.

In the instance of `obj`, we created an empty object, but the object literal syntax also allows us to create an object that has properties right out of the gate. Inside the curly braces, properties are separated by commas, and the name and value are separated by a colon:

```
const sam1 = {
    name: 'Sam',
    age: 4,
};

const sam2 = { name: 'Sam', age: 4 };    // declaration on one line

const sam3 = {
    name: 'Sam',
    classification: {                    // property values can
        kingdom: 'Anamalia',             // be objects themselves
        phylum: 'Chordata',
        class: 'Mamalia',
        order: 'Carnivoria',
        family: 'Felidae',
        subfaimily: 'Felinae',
        genus: 'Felis',
        species: 'catus',
    },
};
```

In this example, we've created three new objects that demonstrate the object literal syntax. Note that the properties contained by `sam1` and `sam2` are the same; however, they are *two distinct objects* (again, contrast to primitives: two variables that both contain the number 3 refer to the same primitive). In `sam3`, property `classification` is itself an object. Consider the different ways we can access Sam the cat's family (it also doesn't matter if we use single or double quotes or even backticks):

```
sam3.classification.family;         // "Felinae"
sam3["classification"].family;      // "Felinae"
sam3.classification["family"];      // "Felinae"
sam3["classification"]["family"];   // "Felinae"
```

Objects can also contain *functions*. We'll learn about functions in depth in Chapter 6, but for now, what you need to know is that a function contains code (essentially a subprogram). Here's how we add a function to `sam3`:

```
sam3.speak = function() { return "Meow!"; };
```

We can now *call* that function by adding parentheses to it:

```
sam3.speak();            // "Meow!"
```

Lastly, we can delete a property from an object with the `delete` operator:

```
delete sam3.classification;         // the whole classification tree is removed
delete sam3.speak;                  // the speak function is removed
```

If you're familiar with object-oriented programming (OOP), you may be wondering how JavaScript objects relate to OOP. For now, you should think of an object as a generic container; we will discuss OOP in Chapter 9.

## Number, String, and Boolean Objects

We mentioned earlier in this chapter that numbers, strings, and booleans have corresponding object types (`Number`, `String`, and `Boolean`). These objects serve two purposes: to store special values (such as `Number.INFINITY`), and to provide functionality in the form of function. Consider the following:

```
const s = "hello";
s.toUpperCase();         // "HELLO"
```

This example makes it look like `s` is an object (we accessed a function property as if it were). But we know better: `s` is a primitive string type. So how is this happening? What JavaScript is doing is creating a *temporary* `String` object (which has a function `toUpperCase`, among others). As soon as the function has been called, JavaScript discards the object. To prove the point, let's try to assign a property to a string:

```
const s = "hello";
s.rating = 3;            // no error...success?
s.rating;                // undefined
```

JavaScript allows us to do this, making it seem like we're assigning a property to the string `s`. What's really happening, though, is that we're assigning a property to the temporary `String` object that's created. That temporary object is immediately discarded, which is why `s.rating` is `undefined`.

This behavior will be transparent to you, and rarely (if ever) do you have to think about it, but it can be useful to know what JavaScript is doing behind the scenes.

## Arrays

In JavaScript, arrays are a special type of object. Unlike regular objects, array contents have a natural order (element 0 will always come before element 1), and keys are numeric and sequential. Arrays support a number of useful methods that make this data type an extremely powerful way to express information, which we will cover in Chapter 8.

If you're coming from other languages, you'll find that arrays in JavaScript are something of a hybrid of the efficient, indexed arrays of C and more powerful dynamic arrays and linked lists. Arrays in JavaScript have the following properties:

- Array size is not fixed; you can add or remove elements at any time.
- Arrays are not homogeneous; each individual element can be of any type.
- Arrays are zero-based. That is, the first element in the array is element 0.

Because arrays are special types of objects with some extra functionality, you can assign non-numeric (or fractional or negative) keys to an array. While this is possible, it contradicts the intended purpose of arrays, can lead to confusing behavior and difficult-to-diagnose bugs, and is best avoided.

To create an array literal in JavaScript, use square brackets, with the elements of the array separated by commas:

```
const a1 = [1, 2, 3, 4];                          // array containing numbers
const a2 = [1, 'two', 3, null];                   // array containing mixed types
const a3 = [                                      // array on multiple lines
    "What the hammer?  What the chain?",
    "In what furnace was thy brain?",
    "What the anvil?  What dread grasp",
    "Dare its deadly terrors clasp?",
];
const a4 = [                                      // array containing objects
    { name: "Ruby", hardness: 9 },
    { name: "Diamond", hardness: 10 },
    { name: "Topaz", hardness: 8 },
];
const a5 = [                                      // array containing arrays
    [1, 3, 5],
    [2, 4, 6],
];
```

Arrays have a property `length`, which returns the number of elements in the array:

```
const arr = ['a', 'b', 'c'];
arr.length;                             // 3
```

To access individual elements of an array, we simply use the numeric index of the element inside square brackets (similar to how we access properties on an object):

```
const arr = ['a', 'b', 'c'];

// get the first element:
arr[0];                                  // 'a'

// the index of the last element in arr is arr.length-1:
arr[arr.length - 1];                     // 'c'
```

To overwrite the value at a specific array index, you can simply assign to it:[5]

```
const arr = [1, 2, 'c', 4, 5];
arr[2] = 3;      // arr is now [1, 2, 3, 4, 5]
```

In Chapter 8, we'll learn many more techniques for modifying arrays and their contents.

## Trailing Commas in Objects and Arrays

The alert reader may have already noticed that in these code samples, when the content of objects and arrays spans multiple lines, there is a *trailing* (or *dangling* or *terminal*) comma:

```
const arr = [
   "One",
   "Two",
   "Three",
];
const o = {
   one: 1,
   two: 2,
   three: 3,
};
```

Many programmers avoid adding this because in early versions of Internet Explorer, trailing commas produced an error (even though it has always been allowed in the JavaScript syntax). I prefer trailing commas because I am frequently cutting and pasting within arrays and objects, and adding things to the end of the object, so having the trailing comma means I never need to remember to add a comma on the line before; it's simply always there. This is a hotly contested convention, and my preference is just that: a preference. If you find the trailing comma troubling (or your team's style guide prohibits its use), by all means, omit it.

5 If you assign an index that is equal to or larger than the length of the array, the size of the array will increase to accommodate the new element.

JavaScript Object Notation (JSON), a JavaScript-like data syntax used quite frequently, does *not* allow trailing commas.

## Dates

Dates and times in JavaScript are represented by the built-in `Date` object. `Date` is one of the more problematic aspects of the language. Originally a direct port from Java (one of the few areas in which JavaScript actually has any direct relationship to Java), the `Date` object can be difficult to work with, especially if you are dealing with dates in different time zones.

To create a date that's initialized to the current date and time, use `new Date()`:

```
const now = new Date();
now;    // example: Thu Aug 20 2015 18:31:26 GMT-0700 (Pacific Daylight Time)
```

To create a date that's initialized to a specific date (at 12:00 a.m.):

```
const halloween = new Date(2016, 9, 31);  // note that months are
                                          // zero-based: 9=October
```

To create a date that's initialized to a specific date and time:

```
const halloweenParty = new Date(2016, 9, 31, 19, 0);   // 19:00 = 7:00 pm
```

Once you have a date object, you can retrieve its components:

```
halloweenParty.getFullYear();       // 2016
halloweenParty.getMonth();          // 9
halloweenParty.getDate();           // 31
halloweenParty.getDay();            // 1 (Mon; 0=Sun, 1=Mon,...)
halloweenParty.getHours();          // 19
halloweenParty.getMinutes();        // 0
halloweenParty.getSeconds();        // 0
halloweenParty.getMilliseconds();   // 0
```

We will cover dates in detail in Chapter 15.

## Regular Expressions

A *regular expression* (or *regex* or *regexp*) is something of a sublanguage of JavaScript. It is a common language extension offered by many different programming languages, and it represents a compact way to perform complex search and replace operations on strings. Regular expressions will be covered in Chapter 17. Regular expressions in JavaScript are represented by the `RegExp` object, and they have a literal syntax consisting of symbols between a pair of forward slashes. Here are some examples (which will look like gibberish if you've never seen a regex before):

```
// extremely simple email recognizer
const email = /\b[a-z0-9._-]+@[a-z_-]+(?:\.[a-z]+)+\b/;

// US phone number recognizer
const phone = /(:?\+1)?(:?\(\d{3}\)\s?|\d{3}[\s-]?)\d{3}[\s-]?\d{4}/;
```

# Maps and Sets

ES6 introduces the data types `Map` and `Set`, and their "weak" counterparts, `WeakMap` and `WeakSet`. Maps, like objects, map keys to values, but offer some advantages over objects in certain situations. Sets are similar to arrays, except they can't contain duplicates. The weak counterparts function similarly, but they make functionality tradeoffs in exchange for more performance in certain situations.

We will cover maps and sets in Chapter 10.

# Data Type Conversion

Converting between one data type and another is a very common task. Data that comes from user input or other systems often has to be converted. This section covers some of the more common data conversion techniques.

## Converting to Numbers

It's very common to want to convert strings to numbers. When you collect input from a user, it's usually as a string, even if you're collecting a numeric value from them. JavaScript offers a couple of methods to convert strings to numbers. The first is to use the `Number` object constructor:[6]

```
const numStr = "33.3";
const num = Number(numStr);    // this creates a number value, *not*
                               // an instance of the Number object
```

If the string can't be converted to a number, `NaN` will be returned.

The second approach is to use the built-in `parseInt` or `parseFloat` functions. These behave much the same as the `Number` constructor, with a couple of exceptions. With `parseInt`, you can specify a *radix*, which is the base with which you want to parse the number. For example, this allows you to specify base 16 to parse hexadecimal numbers. It is always recommended you specify a radix, even if it is 10 (the default). Both `parseInt` and `parseFloat` will discard everything they find past the number, allowing you to pass in messier input. Here are examples:

6 Normally, you wouldn't use a constructor without the `new` keyword, which we'll learn about in Chapter 9; this is a special case.

```
const a = parseInt("16 volts", 10); // the " volts" is ignored, 16 is
                                    // parsed in base 10
const b = parseInt("3a", 16);       // parse hexadecimal 3a; result is 58
const c = parseFloat("15.5 kph");   // the " kph" is ignored; parseFloat
                                    // always assumes base 10
```

A `Date` object can be converted to a number that represents the number of milliseconds since midnight, January 1, 1970, UTC, using its `valueOf()` method:

```
const d = new Date();          // current date
const ts = d.valueOf();        // numeric value: milliseconds since
                               // midnight, January 1, 1970 UTC
```

Sometimes, it is useful to convert boolean values to 1 (true) or 0 (false). The conversion uses the conditional operator (which we will learn about in Chapter 5):

```
const b = true;
const n = b ? 1 : 0;
```

## Converting to String

All objects in JavaScript have a method `toString()`, which returns a string representation. In practice, the default implementation isn't particularly useful. It works well for numbers, though it isn't often necessary to convert a number to a string: that conversion usually happens automatically during string concatenation or interpolation. But if you ever do need to convert a number to a string value, the `toString()` method is what you want:

```
const n = 33.5;
n;                         // 33.5 - a number
const s = n.toString();
s;                         // "33.5" - a string
```

`Date` objects implement a useful (if lengthy) `toString()` implementation, but most objects will simply return the string `"[object Object]"`. Objects can be modified to return a more useful string representation, but that's a topic for Chapter 9. Arrays, quite usefully, take each of their elements, convert them to strings, and then join those strings with commas:

```
const arr = [1, true, "hello"];
arr.toString();                  // "1,true,hello"
```

## Converting to Boolean

In Chapter 5, we'll learn about JavaScript's idea of "truthy" and "falsy," which is a way of coercing all values to true or false, so we won't go into all those details here. But we will see that we can convert any value to a boolean by using the "not" operator (`!`) twice. Using it once converts the value to a boolean, but the opposite of what you want; using it again converts it to what you expect. As with numeric conversion, you can also use the `Boolean` constructor (again, without the `new` keyword) to achieve the same result:

```
const n = 0;                // "falsy" value
const b1 = !!n;             // false
const b2 = Boolean(n);      // false
```

# Conclusion

The data types available to you in a programming language are your basic building blocks for the kind of things you can express in the language. For most of your day-to-day programming, the key points you want to take away from this chapter are as follows:

- JavaScript has six primitive types (string, number, boolean, null, undefined, and symbol) and an object type.
- All numbers in JavaScript are double-precision floating-point numbers.
- Arrays are special types of objects, and along with objects, represent very powerful and flexible data types.
- Other data types you will be using often (dates, maps, sets, and regular expressions) are special types of objects.

Most likely, you will be using strings quite a lot, and I highly recommend that you make sure you understand the escaping rules for strings, and how string templates work, before proceeding.

CHAPTER 4

# Control Flow

A common metaphor given to beginning programmers is *following a recipe*. That metaphor can be useful, but it has an unfortunate weakness: to achieve repeatable results in the kitchen, one has to *minimize* choices. Once a recipe is refined, the idea is that it is followed, step by step, with little to no variation. Occasionally, of course, there will be choices: "substitute butter for lard," or "season to taste," but a recipe is primarily a list of steps to be followed in order.

This chapter is all about *change* and *choice*: giving your program the ability to respond to changing conditions and intelligently automate repetitive tasks.

If you already have programming experience, especially in a language with a syntax inherited from C (C++, Java, C#), and are comfortable with control flow statements, you can safely skim or skip the first part of this chapter. If you do, however, you won't learn anything about the gambling habits of 19th-century sailors.

## A Control Flow Primer

Chances are, you've been exposed to the concept of a *flowchart*, which is a visual way of representing control flow. As our running example in this chapter, we're going to write a *simulation*. Specifically, we are going to simulate a Midshipman in the Royal Navy in the mid-19th century playing *Crown and Anchor*, a betting game popular at the time.

The game is simple: there's a mat with six squares with symbols for "Crown," "Anchor," "Heart," "Club," "Spade," and "Diamond." The sailor places any number of coins on any combination of the squares: these become the bets. Then he[1] rolls three six-sided dice with faces that match the squares on the mat. For each die that matches a square that has a bet on it, the sailor wins that amount of money. Here are some examples of how the sailor might play, and what the payout is:

| Bet | Roll | Payout |
|---|---|---|
| 5 pence on Crown | Crown, Crown, Crown | 15 pence |
| 5 pence on Crown | Crown, Crown, Anchor | 10 pence |
| 5 pence on Crown | Crown, Heart, Spade | 5 pence |
| 5 pence on Crown | Heart, Anchor, Spade | 0 |
| 3 pence on Crown, 2 on Spade | Crown, Crown, Crown | 9 pence |
| 3 pence on Crown, 2 on Spade | Crown, Spade, Anchor | 5 pence |
| 1 pence on all squares | Any roll | 3 pence (not a good strategy!) |

I chose this example because it is not too complex, and with a little imagination, demonstrates the main control flow statements. While it's unlikely that you will ever need to simulate the gambling behaviors of 19th-century sailors, this type of simulation is quite common in many applications. In the case of *Crown and Anchor*, perhaps we have constructed a mathematical model to determine if we should open a *Crown and Anchor* booth to raise money for charity at our next company event. The simulation we construct in this chapter can be used to support the correctness of our model.

The game itself is simple, but there are many thousands of ways it could be played. Our sailor—let's call him Thomas (a good, solid British name)—will start off very generic, and his behavior will become more detailed as we proceed.

Let's begin with the basics: starting and stopping conditions. Every time Thomas gets shore leave, he takes 50 pence with him to spend on *Crown and Anchor*. Thomas has a limit: if he's lucky enough to double his money, he quits, walking away with at least 100 pence in his pocket (about half his monthly wages). If he doesn't double his money, he gambles until he's broke.

We'll break the playing of the game into three parts: placing the bets, rolling the dice, and collecting the winnings (if any). Now that we have a very simple, high-level pic-

1 As loath as I am to use a gender-specific example, women didn't serve in the Royal Navy until 1917.

ture of Thomas's behavior, we can draw a flowchart to describe it, shown in Figure 4-1.

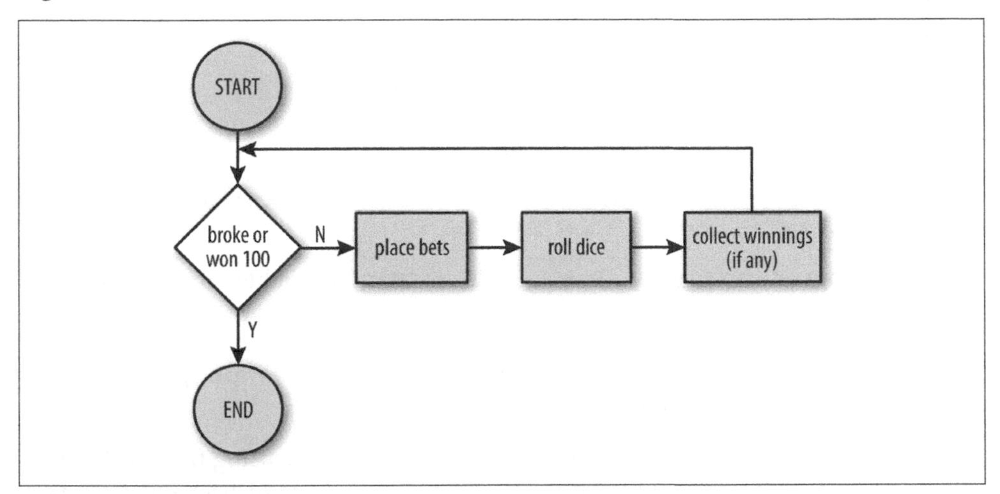


*Figure 4-1. Crown and Anchor simulation flowchart*

In a flowchart, the diamond shapes represent "yes or no" *decisions*, and the rectangles represent *actions*. We use circles to describe where to start and end.

The flowchart—as we've drawn it—isn't quite ready to be turned directly into a program. The steps here are easy for a human to understand, but too sophisticated for computers. For example, "roll dice" would not be obvious to a computer. What are dice? How do you roll them? To solve this problem, the steps "place bets," "roll dice," and "collect winnings" will have their *own* flowcharts (we have indicated this in the flowchart by shading those actions). If you had a big enough piece of paper, you could put them all together, but for the purposes of this book, we'll present them separately.

Also, our decision node is too vague for a computer: "broke or won 100 pence?" isn't something a computer can understand. So what *can* a computer understand? For the purposes of this chapter, we'll restrict our flowchart actions to the following:

- Variable assignment: `funds = 50`, `bets = {}`, `hand = []`
- Random integer between *m* and *n*, inclusive: `rand(1, 6)` (this is a "helper function" we will be providing later)
- Random face string ("heart," "crown," etc.): `randFace()` (another helper function)
- Object property assignment: `bets["heart"] = 5`, `bets[randFace()] = 5`
- Adding elements to an array: `hand.push(randFace())`

- Basic arithmetic: `funds - totalBet`, `funds + winnings`
- Increment: `roll++` (this is a common shorthand that just means "add one to the variable `roll`")

And we'll limit our flowchart decisions to the following:

- Numeric comparisons (`funds > 0`, `funds < 100`)
- Equality comparisons (`totalBet === 7`; we'll learn why we use three equals signs in Chapter 5)
- Logical operators (`funds > 0 && funds < 100`; the double ampersand means "and," which we'll learn about in Chapter 5)

All of these "allowed actions" are actions that we can write in JavaScript with little or no interpretation or translation.

One final vocabulary note: throughout this chapter, we will be using the words *truthy* and *falsy*. These are not simply diminutive or "cute" versions of *true* and *false*: they have meaning in JavaScript. What these terms mean will be explained in Chapter 5, but for now you can just translate them to "true" and "false" in your head.

Now that we know the limited language we can use, we'll have to rewrite our flowchart as shown in Figure 4-2.

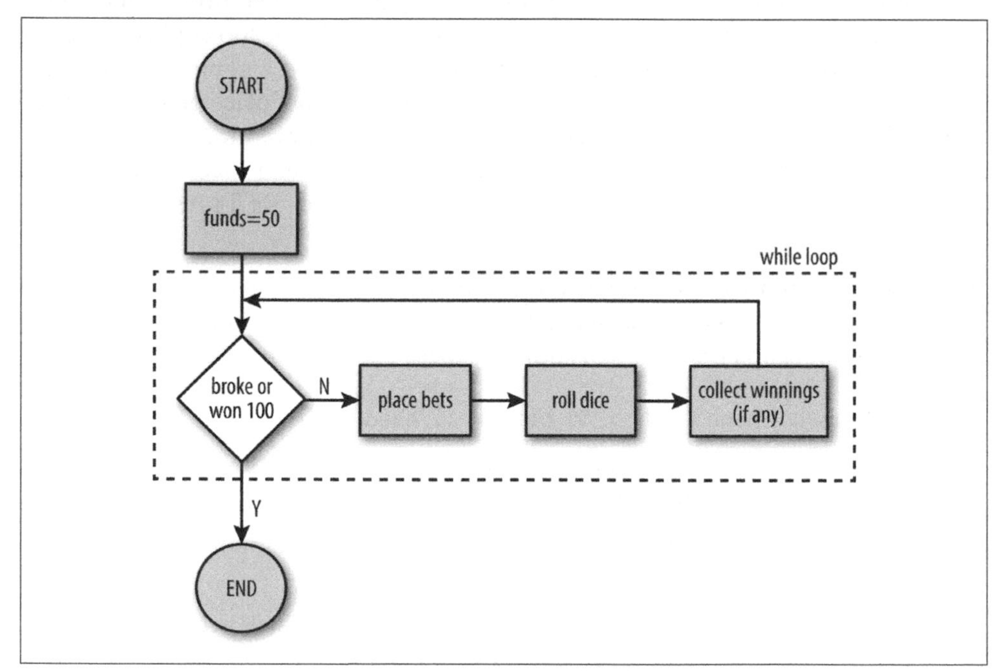


*Figure 4-2. Crown and Anchor simulation flowchart (refined)*

## while Loops

We finally have something that we can translate directly into code. Our flowchart already has the first control flow statement we'll be discussing, a `while` loop. A `while` loop repeats code as long as its *condition* is met. In our flowchart, the condition is `funds > 1 && funds < 100`. Let's see how that looks in code:

```
let funds = 50;     // starting conditions

while(funds > 1 && funds < 100) {
    // place bets

    // roll dice

    // collect winnings
}
```

If we run this program as is, it will run forever, because funds start at 50 pence, and they never increase or decrease, so the condition is always true. Before we start filling out details, though, we need to talk about *block statements*.

## Block Statements

Block statements (sometimes called *compound statements*) are not control flow statements, but they go hand in hand with them. A block statement is just a series of statements enclosed in curly braces that is treated by JavaScript as a single unit. While it is possible to have a block statement by itself, it has little utility. For example:

```
{   // start block statement
    console.log("statement 1");
    console.log("statement 2");
}   // end block statement

console.log("statement 3");
```

The first two calls to `console.log` are inside a block; this is a meaningless but valid example.

Where block statements become useful is with control flow statements. For example, the loop we're executing with our `while` statement will execute the *entire block statement* before testing the condition again. For example, if we wanted to take "two steps forward and one step back," we could write:

```
let funds = 50;     // starting conditions

while(funds > 1 && funds < 100) {

    funds = funds + 2;  // two steps forward
```

```
    funds = funds - 1;  // one step back
}
```

This `while` loop will eventually terminate: every time through the loop, `funds` increases by two and decreases by one for a net of 1. Eventually, `funds` will be 100 and the loop will terminate.

While it's very common to use a block statement with control flow, it's not required. For example, if we wanted to simply count up to 100 by twos, we don't need a block statement:

```
let funds = 50;      // starting conditions

while(funds > 1 && funds < 100)
    funds = funds + 2;
```

## Whitespace

For the most part, JavaScript doesn't care about additional whitespace (including newlines[2]): 1 space is as good as 10, or 10 spaces and 10 newlines. This doesn't mean you should use whitespace capriciously. For example, the preceding `while` statement is equivalent to:

```
while(funds > 1 && funds < 100)

funds = funds + 2;
```

But this hardly makes it look as if the two statements are connected! Using this formatting is very misleading, and should be avoided. The following equivalents, however, are relatively common, and mostly unambiguous:

```
// no newline
while(funds > 1 && funds < 100) funds = funds + 2;

// no newline, block with one statement
while(funds > 1 && funds < 100) { funds = funds + 2; }
```

There are those who insist that control flow statement bodies—for the sake of consistency and clarity—should *always* be a block statement (even if they contain only one statement). While I do not fall in this camp, I should point out that careless indentation fuels the fire of this argument:

```
while(funds > 1 && funds < 100)
    funds = funds + 2;
    funds = funds - 1;
```

2 Newlines after `return` statements will cause problems; see Chapter 6 for more information.

At a glance, it looks like the body of the `while` loop is executing two statements (two steps forward and one step back), but because there's no block statement here, JavaScript interprets this as:

```
while(funds > 1 && funds < 100)
    funds = funds + 2;                // while loop body

funds = funds - 1;                    // after while loop
```

I side with those who say that omitting the block statement for single-line bodies is acceptable, but of course you should always be responsible with indentation to make your meaning clear. Also, if you're working on a team or an open source project, you should adhere to any style guides agreed upon by the team, regardless of your personal preferences.

While there is disagreement on the issue of using blocks for single-statement bodies, one syntactically valid choice is nearly universally reviled: mixing blocks and single statements in the same `if` statement:

```
// don't do this
if(funds > 1) {
    console.log("There's money left!");
    console.log("That means keep playing!");
} else
    console.log("I'm broke!  Time to quit.");

// or this
if(funds > 1)
    console.log("There's money left!  Keep playing!");
else {
    console.log("I'm broke"!);
    console.log("Time to quit.")
}
```

## Helper Functions

To follow along with the examples in this chapter, we'll need two *helper functions*. We haven't learned about functions yet (or pseudorandom number generation), but we will in upcoming chapters. For now, copy these two helper functions verbatim:

```
// returns a random integer in the range [m, n] (inclusive)
function rand(m, n) {
    return m + Math.floor((n - m + 1)*Math.random());
}

// randomly returns a string representing one of the six
// Crown and Anchor faces
function randFace() {
    return ["crown", "anchor", "heart", "spade", "club", "diamond"]
        [rand(0, 5)];
}
```

## if...else Statement

One of the shaded boxes in our flowchart is "place bets," which we'll fill out now. So how does Thomas place bets? Thomas has a ritual, as it turns out. He reaches into his right pocket and randomly pulls out a handful of coins (as few as one, or as many as all of them). That will be his funds for this round. Thomas is superstitious, however, and believes the number 7 is lucky. So if he happens to pull out 7 pence, he reaches back into his pocket and bets *all* his money on the "Heart" square. Otherwise, he randomly places the bet on some number of squares (which, again, we'll save for later). Let's look at the "place bets" flowchart in Figure 4-3.

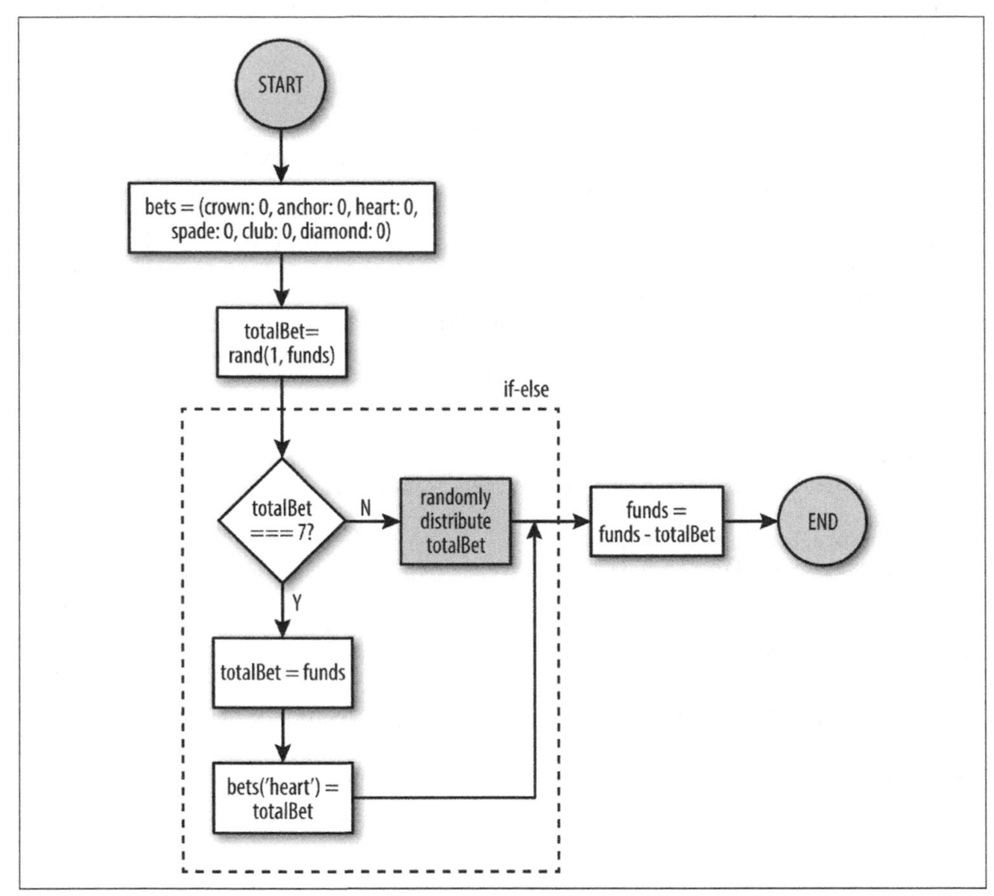


*Figure 4-3. Crown and Anchor simulation: place bets flowchart*

The decision node in the middle (`totalBet === 7`) here represents an `if...else` statement. Note that, unlike the `while` statement, it doesn't loop back on itself: the decision is made, and then you move on. We translate this flowchart into JavaScript:

```
const bets = { crown: 0, anchor: 0, heart: 0,
    spade: 0, club: 0, diamond: 0 };
let totalBet = rand(1, funds);
if(totalBet === 7) {
    totalBet = funds;
    bets.heart = totalBet;
} else {
    // distribute total bet
}
funds = funds - totalBet;
```

We'll see later that the `else` part of the `if...else` statement is optional.

## do...while Loop

When Thomas doesn't pull out 7 pence by chance, he randomly distributes the funds among the squares. He has a ritual for doing this: he holds the coins in his right hand, and with his left hand, selects a random number of them (as few as one, and as many as all of them), and places it on a random square (sometimes he places a bet on the same square more than once). We can now update our flowchart to show this random distribution of the total bet, as shown in Figure 4-4.

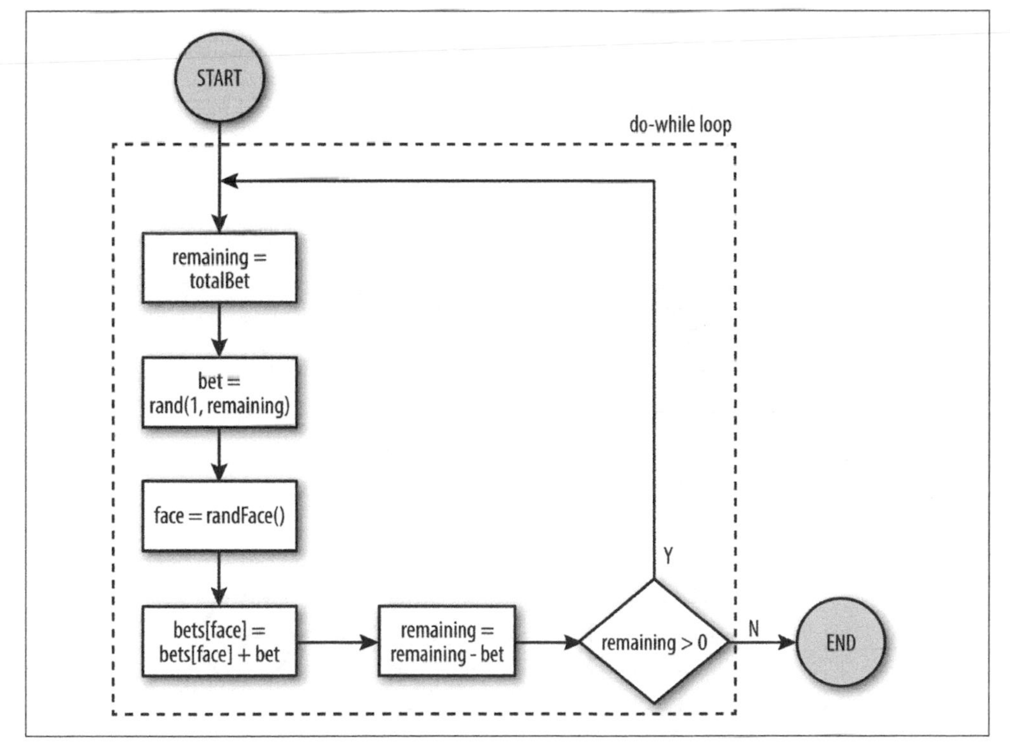


*Figure 4-4. Crown and Anchor simulation: distribute bets flowchart*

Note how this differs from the `while` loop: the decision comes at the end, not the beginning. `do...while` loops are for when you know you always want to execute the body of the loop *at least once* (if the condition in a `while` loop starts off as falsy, it won't even run once). Now in JavaScript:

```
let remaining = totalBet;
do {
    let bet = rand(1, remaining);
    let face = randFace();
    bets[face] = bets[face] + bet;
    remaining = remaining - bet;
} while(remaining > 0);
```

## for Loop

Thomas has now placed all his bets! Time to roll the dice.

The `for` loop is extremely flexible (it can even replace a `while` or `do...while` loop), but it's best suited for those times when you need to do things a fixed number of times (especially when you need to know which step you're on), which makes it ideal for rolling a fixed number of dice (three, in this case). Let's start with our "roll dice" flowchart, shown in Figure 4-5.

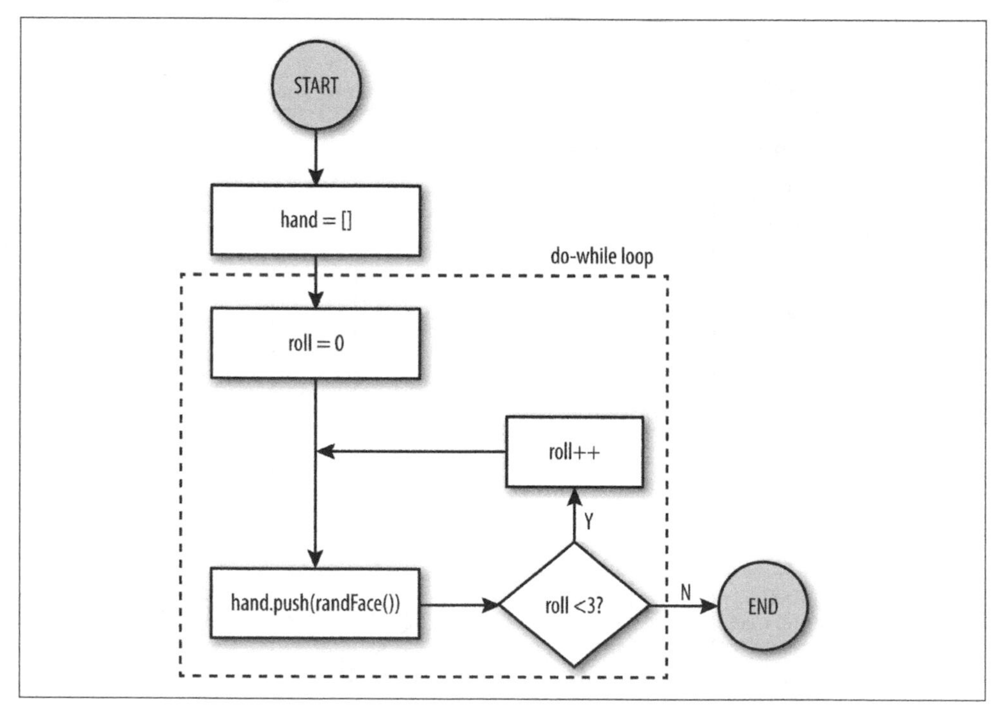


*Figure 4-5. Crown and Anchor simulation: roll dice flowchart*

A `for` loop consists of three parts: the *initializer* (`roll = 0`), the *condition* (`roll < 3`), and the *final expression* (`roll++`). It's nothing that can't be constructed with a `while` loop, but it conveniently puts all the loop information in one place. Here's how it looks in JavaScript:

```
const hand = [];
for(let roll = 0; roll < 3; roll++) {
    hand.push(randFace());
}
```

Programmers have a tendency to count from 0, which is why we start at roll 0 and stop at roll 2.

It has become a convention to use the variable `i` (shorthand for "index") in a `for` loop, no matter what you're counting, though you can use whatever variable name you wish. I chose `roll` here to be clear that we're counting the number of rolls, but I had to catch myself: when I first wrote out this example, I used `i` out of habit!

## if Statement

We're almost there! We've placed our bets and rolled our hand; all that's left is to collect any winnings. We have three random faces in the `hand` array, so we'll use another `for` loop to see if any of them are winners. To do that, we'll use an `if` statement (this time without an `else` clause). Our final flowchart is shown in Figure 4-6.

Notice the difference between an `if...else` statement and an `if` statement: only one of the `if` statement's branches lead to an action, whereas both of the `if...else` statement's do. We translate this into code for the final piece of the puzzle:

```
let winnings = 0;
for(let die=0; die < hand.length; die++) {
    let face = hand[die];
    if(bets[face] > 0) winnings = winnings + bets[face];
}
funds = funds + winnings;
```

Note that, instead of counting to 3 in the `for` loop, we count to `hand.length` (which happens to be 3). The goal of this part of the program is to calculate the winnings for *any hand*. While the rules of the game call for a hand of three dice, the rules could change...or perhaps more dice are given as a bonus, or fewer dice are given as a penalty. The point is, it costs us very little to make this code more *generic*. If we change the rules to allow more or fewer dice in a hand, we don't have to worry about changing this code: it will do the correct thing no matter how many dice there are in the hand.

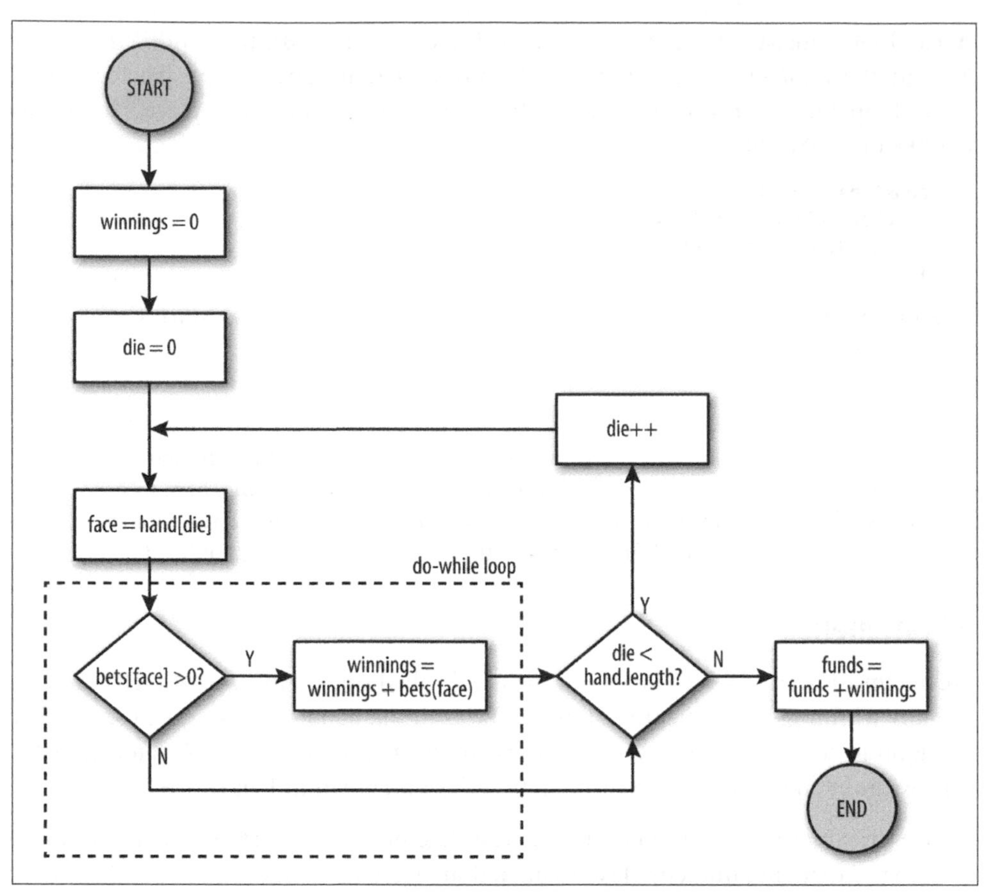


*Figure 4-6. Crown and Anchor simulation: collect winnings flowchart*

## Putting It All Together

We would need a large piece of paper to put all of the pieces of the flowchart together, but we can write the whole program out fairly easily.

In the following program listing (which includes the helper functions), there are also some calls to `console.log` so you can observe Thomas's progress (don't worry about understanding how the logging works: it's using some advanced techniques we'll learn about in later chapters).

We also add a `round` variable to count the number of rounds Thomas plays, for display purposes only:

```
// returns a random integer in the range [m, n] (inclusive)
function rand(m, n) {
    return m + Math.floor((n - m + 1)*Math.random());
}
```

```
// randomly returns a string representing one of the six
// Crown and Anchor faces
function randFace() {
    return ["crown", "anchor", "heart", "spade", "club", "diamond"]
        [rand(0, 5)];
}

let funds = 50;     // starting conditions
let round = 0;

while(funds > 1 && funds < 100) {
    round++;
    console.log(`round ${round}:`);
    console.log(`\tstarting funds: ${funds}p`);
    // place bets
    let bets = { crown: 0, anchor: 0, heart: 0,
        spade: 0, club: 0, diamond: 0 };
    let totalBet = rand(1, funds);
    if(totalBet === 7) {
        totalBet = funds;
        bets.heart = totalBet;
    } else {
        // distribute total bet
        let remaining = totalBet;
        do {
            let bet = rand(1, remaining);
            let face = randFace();
            bets[face] = bets[face] + bet;
            remaining = remaining - bet;
        } while(remaining > 0)
    }
    funds = funds - totalBet;
    console.log('\tbets: ' +
        Object.keys(bets).map(face => `${face}: ${bets[face]} pence`).join(', ') +
        ` (total: ${totalBet} pence)`);

    // roll dice
    const hand = [];
    for(let roll = 0; roll < 3; roll++) {
        hand.push(randFace());
    }
    console.log(`\thand: ${hand.join(', ')}`);

    // collect winnings
    let winnings = 0;
    for(let die=0; die < hand.length; die++) {
        let face = hand[die];
        if(bets[face] > 0) winnings = winnings + bets[face];
    }
    funds = funds + winnings;
    console.log(`\twinnings: ${winnings}`);
```

```
}
console.log(`\tending funs: ${funds}`);
```

## Control Flow Statements in JavaScript

Now that we've got a firm grasp on what control flow statements actually *do*, and some exposure to the most basic ones, we can get down to the details of JavaScript control flow statements.

We're also going to leave flowcharts behind. They are a great visualization tool (especially for those who are visual learners), but they would get very unwieldy past this point.

Broadly speaking, control flow can be broken into two subcategories: *conditional* (or *branching*) control flow and *loop* control flow. Conditional control flow (`if` and `if...else`, which we've seen, and `switch`, which we'll see shortly) represent a fork in the road: there are two or more paths to take, and we take one, but we don't double back. Loop control flow (`while`, `do...while`, and `for` loops) repeat their bodies until a condition is met.

### Control Flow Exceptions

There are four statements that can alter the normal processing of flow control. You can think of these as control flow "trump cards":

`break`
: Breaks out of loop early.

`continue`
: Skip to the next step in the loop.

`return`
: Exits the current function (regardless of control flow). See Chapter 6.

`throw`
: Indicates an *exception* that must be caught by an exception handler (even if it's outside of the current control flow statement). See Chapter 11.

The use of the statements will become clear as we go along; the important thing to understand now is that these four statements can override the behavior of the control flow constructs we'll be discussing.

Broadly speaking, control flow can be broken into two subcategories: *conditional* control flow and *loop* control flow.

## Chaining if...else Statements

Chaining `if...else` statements is not actually a special syntax: it's simply a series of `if...else` statements where each `else` clause contains another `if...else`. It's a common enough pattern that it deserves mention. For example, if Thomas's superstition extends to days of the week, and he'll only bet a single penny on a Wednesday, we could combine this logic in an `if...else` chain:

```
if(new Date().getDay() === 3) {   // new Date().getDay() returns the current
    totalBet = 1;                 // numeric day of the week, with 0 = Sunday
} else if(funds === 7) {
    totalBet = funds;
} else {
    console.log("No superstition here!");
}
```

By combining `if...else` statements this way, we've created a three-way choice, instead of simply a two-way choice. The astute reader may note that we're technically breaking the guideline we established (of not mixing single statements and block statements), but this is an exception to the rule: it is a common pattern, and is not confusing to read. We could rewrite this using block statements:

```
if(new Date().getDay() === 3) {
    totalBet = 1;
} else {
    if(funds === 7) {
        totalBet = funds;
    } else {
        console.log("No superstition here!");
    }
}
```

We haven't really gained any clarity, and we've made our code more verbose.

## Metasyntax

The term *metasyntax* means a syntax that, in turn, describes or communicates yet another syntax. Those with a computer science background will immediately think of "Extended Backus-Naur Form" (EBNF), which is an incredibly intimidating name for a simple concept.

For the rest of this chapter, I'll be using a metasyntax to concisely describe JavaScript flow control syntax. The metasyntax I'm using is simple and informal and—most importantly—used for JavaScript documentation on the Mozilla Developer Network (MDN) (*https://developer.mozilla.org/en-US/docs/Web/JavaScript*). Because the MDN is a resource you will undoubtedly find yourself using quite often, familiarity with it will be useful.

There are only two real elements to this metasyntax: something surrounded by square brackets is *optional*, and an ellipsis (three periods, technically) indicates "more goes here." Words are used as placeholders, and their meaning is clear from context. For example, `statement1` and `statement2` represent two different statements, `expression` is something that results in a value, and `condition` refers to an expression that is treated as truthy or falsy.

Remember that a block statement *is* a statement...so wherever you can use a statement, you can use a block statement.

Because we're already familiar with some control flow statements, let's see their metasyntax:

### while statement

```
while(condition)
    statement
```

While `condition` is truthy, `statement` will be executed.

### if...else statement

```
if(condition)
    statement1
[else
    statement2]
```

If `condition` is truthy, `statement1` will be executed; otherwise, `statement2` will be executed (assuming the `else` part is present).

### do...while statement

```
do
    statement
while(condition);
```

`statement` is executed at least once, and is repeatedly executed as long as `condition` is truthy.

### for statement

```
for([initialization]; [condition]; [final-expression])
    statement
```

Before the loop runs, `initialization` is executed. As long as `condition` is true, `statement` is executed, then `final-expression` is executed before testing `condition` again.

## Additional for Loop Patterns

By using the comma operator (which we'll learn more about in Chapter 5), we can combine multiple assignments and final expressions. For example, here's a `for` loop to print the first eight Fibonacci numbers:

```
for(let temp, i=0, j=1; j<30; temp = i, i = j, j = i + temp)
    console.log(j);
```

In this example, we're declaring multiple variables (`temp`, `i`, and `j`), and we're modifying each of them in the final expression. Just as we can do more with a `for` loop by using the comma operator, we can use nothing at all to create an infinite loop:

```
for(;;) console.log("I will repeat forever!");
```

In this `for` loop, the condition will simply evaluate to `undefined`, which is falsy, meaning the loop will never have cause to exit.

While the most common use of `for` loops is to increment or decrement integer indices, that is not a requirement: any expression will work. Here are some examples:

```
let s = '3';                          // string containing a number
for(; s.length<10; s = ' ' + s);      // zero pad string; note that we must
                                      // include a semicolon to terminate
                                      // this for loop!

for(let x=0.2; x<3.0; x += 0.2)       // increment using noninteger
    console.log(x);

for(; !player.isBroke;)               // use an object property as conditional
    console.log("Still playing!");
```

Note that a `for` loop can always be written as a `while` loop. In other words:

```
for([initialization]; [condition]; [final-expression])
    statement
```

is equivalent to:

```
[initialization]
while([condition]) {
    statement
    [final-expression]
}
```

However, the fact that you can write a `for` loop as a `while` loop doesn't mean you should. The advantage of the `for` loop is that all of the loop control information is right there on the first line, making it very clear what's happening. Also, with a `for` loop, initializing variables with `let` confines them to the body of the `for` loop (we'll learn more about this in Chapter 7); if you convert such a `for` statement to a `while` statement, the control variable(s) will, by necessity, be available outside of the `for` loop body.

## switch Statements

Where `if...else` statements allow you to take one of two paths, `switch` statements allow you to take multiple paths based on a single condition. It follows, then, that the condition must be something more varied than a truthy/falsy value: for a `switch` statement, the condition is an *expression* that evaluates to a value. The syntax of a `switch` statement is:

```
switch(expression) {
    case value1:
        // executed when the result of expression matches value1
        [break;]
    case value2:
        // executed when the result of expression matches value2
        [break;]
        ...
    case valueN:
        // executed when the result of expression matches valueN
        [break;]
    default:
        // executed when none of the values match the value of expression
        [break;]
}
```

JavaScript will evaluate `expression`, pick the first `case` that matches, and then execute statements until it sees a `break`, `return`, `continue`, `throw` or the end of the `switch` statement (we will learn about `return`, `continue`, and `throw` later). If that sounds complex to you, you're not alone: because of the nuances of the `switch` statement, it's received a lot of criticism as being a common source of programmer error. Often, beginning programmers are discouraged from using it at all. I feel that the `switch` statement is very useful in the right situation: it's a good tool to have in your toolbox, but like any tool, you should exercise caution, and use it when appropriate.

We'll start with a very straightforward example of a `switch` statement. If our fictional sailor has multiple numbers he's superstitious about, we can use a `switch` statement to handle them accordingly:

```
switch(totalBet) {
    case 7:
        totalBet = funds;
        break;
    case 11:
        totalBet = 0;
```

```
        break;
    case 13:
        totalBet = 0;
        break;
    case 21:
        totalBet = 21;
        break;
}
```

Note that the same action is being taken when the bet is 11 or 13. This is where we might want to take advantage of *fall-through execution*. Remember that we said the `switch` statement will keep executing statements until it sees a `break` statement. Using this to our advantage is called fall-through execution:

```
switch(totalBet) {
    case 7:
        totalBet = funds;
        break;
    case 11:
    case 13:
        totalBet = 0;
        break;
    case 21:
        totalBet = 21;
        break;
}
```

This is pretty straightforward so far: it's clear that Thomas won't bet anything if he happens to pull out 11 or 13 pence. But what if 13 is a far more ominous omen than 11, and requires not only forgoing the bet, but giving a penny to charity? With some clever rearranging, we can handle this:

```
switch(totalBet) {
    case 7:
        totalBet = funds;
        break;
    case 13:
        funds = funds - 1;  // give 1 pence to charity!
    case 11:
        totalBet = 0;
        break;
    case 21:
        totalBet = 21;
        break;
}
```

If `totalBet` is 13, we give a penny to charity, but because there's no `break` statement, we *fall through* to the next case (11), and additionally set `totalBet` to 0. This code is valid JavaScript, and furthermore, it is correct: it does what we intended it to do. However, it does have a weakness: it *looks* like a mistake (even though it's correct). Imagine if a colleague saw this code and thought "Ah, there's supposed to be a `break` statement there." They would add the break statement, and the code would no longer be correct. Many people feel that fall-through execution is more trouble than it's worth, but if you choose to utilize this feature, I recommend always including a comment to make it clear that your use of it is intentional.

You can also specify a special case, called default, that will be used if no other case matches. It is conventional (but not required) to put the default case last:

```
switch(totalBet) {
    case 7:
        totalBet = funds;
        break;
    case 13:
        funds = funds - 1;  // give 1 pence to charity!
    case 11:
        totalBet = 0;
        break;
    case 21:
        totalBet = 21;
        break;
    default:
        console.log("No superstition here!");
        break;
}
```

The break is unnecessary because no cases follow default, but always providing a break statement is a good habit to get into. Even if you're using fall-through execution, you should get into the habit of including break statements: you can always replace a break statement with a comment to enable fall-through execution, but omitting a break statement when it is correct can be a very difficult-to-locate defect. The one exception to this rule of thumb is if you are using a switch statement inside a function (see Chapter 6), you can replace break statements with return statements (because they immediately exit the function):

```
function adjustBet(totalBet, funds) {
    switch(totalBet) {
        case 7:
            return funds;
        case 13:
            return 0;
        default:
            return totalBet;
    }
}
```

As usual, JavaScript doesn't care how much whitespace you use, so it's quite common to put the break (or return) on the same line to make switch statements more compact:

```
switch(totalBet) {
    case 7: totalBet = funds; break;
    case 11: totalBet = 0; break;
    case 13: totalBet = 0; break;
    case 21: totalBet = 21; break;
}
```

Note that, in this example, we chose to repeat the same action for 11 and 13: omitting the newline is clearest when cases have single statements and no fall-through execution.

`switch` statements are extremely handy when you want to take many different paths based on a single expression. That said, you will find yourself using them less once you learn about dynamic dispatch in Chapter 9.

## for...in loop

The `for...in` loop is designed to loop over the *property keys of an object*. The syntax is:

```
for(variable in object)
    statement
```

Here is an example of its use:

```
const player = { name: 'Thomas', rank: 'Midshipman', age: 25 };
for(let prop in player) {
    if(!player.hasOwnProperty(prop)) continue;  // see explanation below
    console.log(prop + ': ' + player[prop]);
}
```

Don't worry if this seems confusing now; we'll learn more about this example in Chapter 9. In particular, the call to `player.hasOwnProperty` is not required, but its omission is a common source of errors, which will be covered in Chapter 9. For now, all you need to understand is that this is a type of looping control flow statement.

## for...of loop

New in ES6, the `for...of` operator provides yet another way to loop over the elements in a collection. Its syntax is:

```
for(variable of object)
    statement
```

The `for...of` loop can be used on arrays, but more generically, on any object that is *iterable* (see Chapter 9). Here is an example of its use for looping over the contents of an array:

```
const hand = [randFace(), randFace(), randFace()];
for(let face of hand)
    console.log(`You rolled...${face}!`);
```

for...of is a great choice when you need to loop over an array, but don't need to know the index number of each element. If you need to know the indexes, use a regular for loop:

```
const hand = [randFace(), randFace(), randFace()];
for(let i=0; i<hand.length; i++)
    console.log(`Roll ${i+1}: ${hand[i]}`);
```

# Useful Control Flow Patterns

Now that you know the basics of control flow constructs in JavaScript, we turn our attention to some of the common patterns that you'll encounter.

## Using continue to Reduce Conditional Nesting

Very often, in the body of a loop, you'll only want to continue to execute the body under certain circumstances (essentially combining a loop control flow with a conditional control flow). For example:

```
while(funds > 1 && funds < 100) {
    let totalBet = rand(1, funds);
    if(totalBet === 13) {
        console.log("Unlucky!  Skip this round....");
    } else {
        // play...
    }
}
```

This is an example of *nested control flow*; inside the body of the while loop, the bulk of the action is inside the else clause; all we do inside the if clause is to call console.log. We can use continue statements to "flatten" this structure:

```
while(funds > 1 && funds < 100) {
    let totalBet = rand(1, funds);
    if(totalBet === 13) {
        console.log("Unlucky!  Skip this round....");
        continue;
    }
    // play...
}
```

In this simple example, the benefits aren't immediately obvious, but imagine that the loop body consisted of not 1 line, but 20; by removing those lines from the nested control flow, we're making the code easier to read and understand.

## Using break or return to Avoid Unnecessary Computation

If your loop exists solely to find something and then stop, there's no point in executing every step if you find what you're looking for early.

For example, determining if a number is prime is relatively expensive, computationally speaking. If you're looking for the first prime in a list of thousands of numbers, a naive approach might be:

```
let firstPrime = null;
for(let n of bigArrayOfNumbers) {
    if(isPrime(n) && firstPrime === null) firstPrime = n;
}
```

If `bigArrayOfNumbers` has a million numbers, and only the last one is prime (unbeknownst to you), this approach would be fine. But what if the first one were prime? Or the fifth, or the fiftieth? You would be checking to see if a million numbers are prime when you could have stopped early! Sounds exhausting. We can use a `break` statement stop as soon as we've found what we're looking for:

```
let firstPrime = null;
for(let n of bigArrayOfNumbers) {
    if(isPrime(n)) {
        firstPrime = n;
        break;
    }
}
```

If this loop is inside a function, we could use a `return` statement instead of `break`.

## Using Value of Index After Loop Completion

Occasionally, the important output of a loop is the value of the index variable when the loop terminates early with a `break`. We can take advantage of the fact that when a `for` loop finishes, the index variable retains its value. If you employ this pattern, keep in mind the edge case where the loop completes successfully without a `break`. For example, we can use this pattern to find the index of the first prime number in our array:

```
let i = 0;
for(; i < bigArrayOfNumbers.length; i++) {
    if(isPrime(bigArrayOfNumbers[i])) break;
}
if(i === bigArrayOfNumbers.length) console.log('No prime numbers!');
else console.log(`First prime number found at position ${i}`);
```

## Using Descending Indexes When Modifying Lists

Modifying a list while you're looping over the elements of the list can be tricky, because by modifying the list, you could be modifying the loop termination conditions. At best, the output won't be what you expect; at worst, you could end up with an infinite loop. One common way to deal with this is to use *descending* indexes to start at the end of the loop and work your way toward the beginning. In this way, if you add or remove elements from the list, it won't affect the termination conditions of the loop.

For example, we might want to remove all prime numbers from `bigArrayOfNumbers`. We'll use an array method called `splice`, which can add or remove elements from an array (see Chapter 8). The following will *not* work as expected:

```
for(let i=0; i<bigArrayOfNumbers.length; i++) {
    if(isPrime(bigArrayOfNumbers[i])) bigArrayOfNumbers.splice(i, 1);
}
```

Because the index is increasing, and we're removing elements, there's a possibility that we might skip over primes (if they are adjacent). We can solve this problem by using descending indexes:

```
for(let i=bigArrayOfNumbers.length-1; i >= 0; i--) {
    if(isPrime(bigArrayOfNumbers[i])) bigArrayOfNumbers.splice(i, 1);
}
```

Note carefully the initial and test conditions: we have to start with one *less* than the length of the array, because arrays indexes are zero-based. Also, we continue the loop as long as `i` is greater than or *equal to* 0; otherwise, this loop won't cover the first element in the array (which would cause problems if the first element were a prime).

# Conclusion

Control flow is really what makes our programs tick. Variables and constants may contain all the interesting information, but control flow statements allow us to make useful choices based on that data.

Flowcharts are a useful way to describe control flow visually, and very often it can be helpful to describe your problem with a high-level flowchart before you start writing code. At the end of the day, however, flowcharts are not very compact, and code is a more efficient and (with practice) natural way to express control flow (many attempts have been made to construct programming languages that were visual only, yet text-based languages have never been threatened by this usurper).

CHAPTER 5

# Expressions and Operators

An *expression* is a special kind of statement that *evaluates to a value*. The distinction between an expression statement (which results in a value) and a non-expression statement (which does not) is critical: understanding the difference gives you the tools you need to combine language elements in useful ways.

You can think of a (nonexpression) statement as an *instruction*, and an expression statement as a *request for something*. Imagine it's your first day on the job, and the foreman comes over and says, "Your job is to screw widget A into flange B." That's a *nonexpression* statement: the foreman isn't asking for the assembled part, merely instructing you to do the assembly. If the foreman instead said, "Screw widget A into flange B, and give it to me for inspection," that would be equivalent to an *expression* statement: not only are you being given an instruction, you're also being asked to return something. You may be thinking that either way something gets made: the assembled part exists whether you set it back on the assembly line or give it to the foreman for inspection. In a programming language, it's similar: a nonexpression statement usually *does* produce something, but only an expression statement results in an explicit transfer of the thing that was produced.

Because expressions resolve to a value, we can combine them with other expressions, which in turn can be combined with other expressions, and so on. Nonexpression statements, on the other hand, might do something useful, but they cannot be combined in the same way.

Also because expressions resolve to a value, you can use them in assignments. That is, you can assign the result of the expression to a variable, constant, or property. Let's consider a common *operation expression*: multiplication. It makes sense that multiplication is an expression: when you multiply two numbers, you get a result. Consider two very simple statements:

```
let x;
x = 3 * 5;
```

The first line is a *declaration statement*; we are declaring the variable x. Of course we could have combined these two lines, but that would confuse this discussion. What's more interesting is the second line: there are actually two combined expressions in that line. The first expression is 3 * 5, a multiplication expression that resolves to the value 15. Then, there's an *assignment expression* that assigns the value 15 to the variable x. Note that the assignment is itself an expression, and we know that an expression resolves to a value. So what does the assignment expression resolve to? As it turns out, assignment expressions resolve quite reasonably to the value that was assigned. So not only is x assigned the value 15, but the *whole expression* also resolves to the value 15. Because the assignment is an expression that resolves to a value, we could in turn assign it to another variable. Consider the following (very silly) example:

```
let x, y;
y = x = 3 * 5;
```

Now we have two variables, x and y, that both contain the value 15. We are able to do this because multiplication and assignment are both expressions. When JavaScript sees combined expressions like this, it has to break the combination down and evaluate it in parts, like so:

```
let x, y;
y = x = 3 * 5;          // original statement
y = x = 15;             // multiplication expression evaluated
y = 15;                 // first assignment evaluated; x now has value 15,
                        // y is still undefined
15;                     // second assignment evaluated; y now has value 15,
                        // the result is 15, which isn't used or assigned to
                        // anything, so this final value is simply discarded
```

The natural question is "How did JavaScript know to execute the expressions in that order?" That is, it could have reasonably done the assignment y = x first, giving y the value undefined, and *then* evaluated the multiplication and the final assignment, leaving y as undefined and x as 15. The order in which JavaScript evaluates expressions is called *operator precedence*, and we'll cover it in this chapter.

Most expressions, such as multiplication and assignment, are *operator* expressions. That is, a multiplication expression consists of a *multiplication operator* (the asterisk) and two *operands* (the numbers you are trying to multiply, which are themselves expressions).

The two expressions that are not operator expressions are *identifier expressions* (variable and constant names) and *literal expressions*. These are self-explanatory: a variable or constant is itself an expression, and a literal is itself an expression. Understanding this allows you to see how expressions provide homogeneity: if everything that results in a value is an expression, it makes sense that variables, constants, and literals are all expressions.

## Operators

You can think of operators as the "verb" to an expression's "noun." That is, an expression is a *thing that results in a value*; an operator is something you *do* to produce a value. The outcome in both cases is a value. We'll start our discussion of operators with arithmetic operators: however you may feel about math, most people have some experience with arithmetic operators, so they are an intuitive place to start.

Operators take one or more *operands* to produce a result. For example, in the expression `1 + 2`, 1 and 2 are the operands and + is the operator. While *operand* is technically correct, you often see operands called *arguments*.

## Arithmetic Operators

JavaScript's arithmetic operators are listed in Table 5-1.

*Table 5-1. Arithmetic operators*

| Operator | Description | Example |
| --- | --- | --- |
| + | Addition (also string concatenation) | `3 + 2 // 5` |
| - | Subtraction | `3 - 2 // 1` |
| / | Division | `3/2 // 1.5` |
| * | Multiplication | `3*2 // 6` |
| % | Remainder | `3%2 // 1` |
| - | Unary negation | `-x // negative x; if x is 5, -x will be -5` |
| + | Unary plus | `+x // if x is not a number, this will attempt conversion` |
| ++ | Pre-increment | `++x // increments x by one, and evaluates to the new value` |
| ++ | Post-increment | `x++ // increments x by one, and evaluates to value of x before the increment` |

| Operator | Description | Example |
|---|---|---|
| -- | Pre-decrement | `--x // decrements x by one, and evaluates to the new value` |
| -- | Post-decrement | `x-- // decrements x by one, and evaluates to value of x before the decrement` |

Remember that all numbers in JavaScript are doubles, meaning that if you perform an arithmetic operation on an integer (such as `3/2`), the result will be a decimal number (1.5).

Subtraction and unary negation both use the same symbol (the minus sign), so how does JavaScript know how to tell them apart? The answer to this question is complex and beyond the scope of the book. What's important to know is that unary negation is evaluated before subtraction:

```
const x = 5;
const y = 3 - -x;      // y is 8
```

The same thing applies for unary plus. Unary plus is not an operator you see used very often. When it is, it is usually to force a string to be converted to a number, or to align values when some are negated:

```
const s = "5";
const y = 3 + +s;    // y is 8; without the unary plus,
                     // it would be the result of string
                     // concatenation: "35"

// using unnecessary unary pluses so that expressions line up
const x1 = 0, x2 = 3, x3 = -1.5, x4 = -6.33;
const p1 = -x1*1;
const p2 = +x2*2;
const p3 = +x3*3;
const p3 = -x4*4;
```

Note that in these examples, I specifically used variables in conjunction with unary negation and unary plus. That's because if you use them with numeric literals, the minus sign actually becomes part of the numeric literal, and is therefore technically not an operator.

The remainder operator returns the remainder after division. If you have the expression `x % y`, the result will be the remainder when dividing the *dividend* (`x`) by the *divisor* (`y`). For example, `10 % 3` will be `1` (3 goes into 10 three times, with 1 left over). Note that for negative numbers, the result takes on the sign of the dividend, not the divisor, preventing this operator from being a true modulo operator. While the remainder operator is usually only used on integer operands, in JavaScript, it works on fractional operands as well. For example, `10 % 3.6` will be `3` (3.6 goes into 10 twice, with 2.8 left over).

The increment operator (++) is effectively an assignment and addition operator all rolled into one. Likewise, the decrement operator (--) is an assignment and subtraction operator. They are useful shortcuts, but should be used with caution: if you bury one of these deep in an expression, it might be hard to see the "side effect" (the change in a variable). Understanding the difference between the *prefix* and *postfix* operators is important as well. The prefix version modifies the variable and then evaluates to the *new* value; the postfix operator modifies the variable and then evaluates to the value *before* modification. See if you can predict what the following expressions evaluate to (hint: increment and decrement operators are evaluated before addition, and we evaluate from left to right in this example):

```
let x = 2;
const r1 = x++ + x++;
const r2 = ++x + ++x;
const r3 = x++ + ++x;
const r4 = ++x + x++;
let y = 10;
const r5 = y-- + y--;
const r6 = --y + --y;
const r7 = y-- + --y;
const r8 = --y + y--;
```

Go ahead and run this example in a JavaScript console; see if you can anticipate what `r1` through `r8` will be, and what the value of `x` and `y` is at each step. If you have problems with this exercise, try writing the problem down on a piece of paper, and adding parentheses according to the order of operations, then doing each operation in order. For example:

```
let x = 2;
const r1 = x++  +  x++;
//        ((x++) + (x++))
//        (  2   + (x++))   eval left to right; x now has value 3
//        (  2   +   3  )   x now has value 4
//               5          result is 5; x has value 4
const r2 = ++x  +  ++x;
//        ((++x) + (++x))
//        (  5   + (++x))   eval left to right; x now has value 5
//        (  5   +   6  )   x now has value 6
//               11         result is 11; x has value 6
const r3 = x++  +  ++x;
//        ((x++) + (++x))
//        (  6   + (++x))   eval left to right; x now has value 7
//        (  6   +   8  )   x now has value 8
//               14         result is 14; x has value 8
//
// ... and so on
```

## Operator Precedence

Second in importance to understanding that every expression resolves to a value is understanding operator precedence: it is a vital step to following how a JavaScript program works.

Now that we've covered arithmetic operators, we're going to pause our discussion of JavaScript's many operators and review operator precedence—if you've had an elementary education, you've already been exposed to operator precedence, even if you aren't aware of it.

See if you remember enough from elementary school to solve this problem (I apologize in advance to those who suffer from math anxiety):

$$8 \div 2 + 3 \times (4 \times 2 - 1)$$

If you answered 25, you correctly applied operator precedence. You knew to start inside the parentheses, then move on to multiplication and division, then finish with addition and subtraction.

JavaScript uses a similar set of rules to determine how to evaluate any expression—not just arithmetic expressions. You'll be pleased to know that arithmetic expressions in JavaScript use the same order of operations you learned in elementary school—perhaps with the aid of the mnemonic "PEMDAS" or "Please Excuse My Dear Aunt Sally."

In JavaScript, there are many more operators than just arithmetic ones, so the bad news is that you have a much larger order to memorize. The good news is that, just like in mathematics, parentheses trump everything: if you're ever unsure about the order of operations for a given expression, you can always put parentheses around the operations you want to happen first.

Currently, JavaScript has 56 operators grouped into 19 *precedence levels*. Operators with a higher precedence are performed before operators with a lower precedence. Although I have gradually memorized this table over the years (without making a conscious effort to do so), I still sometimes consult it to refresh my memory or see where new language features fit into the precedence levels. See Appendix B for the operator precedence table.

Operators at the same precedence level are either evaluated *right to left* or *left to right*. For example, multiplication and division have the same precedence level (14) and are evaluated left to right, and assignment operators (precedence level 3) are evaluated right to left. Armed with that knowledge, we can evaluate the order of operations in this example:

```
let x = 3, y;
x += y = 6*5/2;
// we'll take this in order of precedence, putting parentheses around
// the next operation:
//
// multiplication and division (precedence level 14, left to right):
//     x += y = (6*5)/2
//     x += y = (30/2)
//     x += y = 15
// assignment (precedence level 3, right to left):
//     x += (y = 15)
//     x += 15            (y now has value 15)
//     18                 (x now has value 18)
```

Understanding operator precedence may seem daunting at first, but it quickly becomes second nature.

## Comparison Operators

Comparison operators, as the name implies, are used to compare two different values. Broadly speaking, there are three types of comparison operator: strict equality, abstract (or loose) equality, and relational. (We don't consider inequality as a different type: inequality is simply "not equality," even though it has its own operator for convenience.)

The most difficult distinction for beginners to understand is the difference between *strict equality* and *abstract equality*. We'll start with strict equality because I recommend you generally prefer strict equality. Two values are considered strictly equal if they refer to the same object, or if they are the same type and have the same value (for primitive types). The advantage of strict equality is that the rules are very simple and straightforward, making it less prone to bugs and misunderstandings. To determine if values are strictly equal, use the `===` operator or its opposite, the not strictly equal operator (`!==`). Before we see some examples, let's consider the abstract equality operator.

Two values are considered abstractly equal if they refer to the same object (so far, so good) or *if they can be coerced into having the same value*. It's this second part that causes so much trouble and confusion. Sometimes this is a helpful property. For example, if you want to know if the number `33` and the string `"33"` are equal, the abstract equality operator will says yes, but the strict equality operator will say no (because they aren't the same type). While this may make abstract equality seem convenient, you are getting a lot of undesirable behavior along with this convenience. For this reason, I recommend converting strings into numbers early, so you can compare them with the strict equality operator instead. The abstract equality operator is `==` and the abstract inequality operator is `!=`. If you want more information about the problems and pitfalls with the abstract equality operator, I recommend Douglas Crockford's book, *JavaScript: The Good Parts* (O'Reilly).

Most of the problematic behavior of the abstract equality operators surrounds the values `null`, `undefined`, the empty string, and the number 0. For the most part, if you are comparing values that you know not to be one of these values, it's generally safe to use the abstract equality operator. However, don't underestimate the power of rote habit. If you decide, as I recommend, to use the strict equality operator by default, then you *never have to think about it*. You don't have to interrupt your thought flow to wonder whether it's safe or advantageous to use the abstract equality operator; you just use the strict equality operator and move on. If you later find that the strict equality operator isn't producing the right result, you can do the appropriate type conversion instead of switching to the problematic abstract equality operator. Programming is hard enough: do yourself a favor, and avoid the problematic abstract equality operator.

Here are some examples of strict and abstract equality operators in use. Note that even though objects `a` and `b` contain the same information, *they are distinct objects*, and are neither strictly or abstractly equal:

```
const n = 5;
const s = "5";
n === s;            // false -- different types
n !== s;            // true
n === Number(s);    // true -- "5" converted to numeric 5
n !== Number(s);    // false
n == s;             // true; not recommended
n != s;             // false; not recommended

const a = { name: "an object" };
const b = { name: "an object" };
a === b;            // false -- distinct objects
a !== b;            // true
a == b;             // false; not recommended
a != b;             // true; not recommended
```

Relational operators compare values in *relation* to one another, and they only make sense for data types that have a natural ordering, such as strings ("a" comes before "b") and numbers (0 comes before 1). The relational operators are less than (<), less than or equal to (<=), greater than (>), and greater than or equal to (>=):

```
3 > 5;      // false
3 >= 5;     // false
3 < 5;      // true
3 <= 5;     // true
```

```
5 > 5;      // false
5 >= 5;     // true
5 < 5;      // false
5 <= 5;     // true
```

## Comparing Numbers

When doing identity or equality comparisons on numbers, you must take special care.

First, note that the special numeric value `NaN` is not equal to anything, including itself (that is, `NaN === NaN` and `NaN == NaN` are both `false`). If you want to test to see if a number is `NaN`, use the built-in `isNaN` function: `isNaN(x)` will return `true` if `x` is `NaN` and `false` otherwise.

Recall that all numbers in JavaScript are doubles: because doubles are (by necessity) approximations, you can run into nasty surprises when comparing them.

If you're comparing integers (between `Number.MIN_SAFE_INTEGER` and `Number.MAX_SAFE_INTEGER`, inclusive), you can safely use identity to test for equality. If you're using fractional numbers, you are better off using a relational operator to see if your test number is "close enough" to the target number. What's close enough? That depends on your application. JavaScript does make a special numeric constant available, `Number.EPSILON`. It's a very small value (about `2.22e-16`), and generally represents the difference required for two numbers to be considered distinct. Consider this example:

```
let n = 0;
while(true) {
    n += 0.1;
    if(n === 0.3) break;
}
console.log(`Stopped at ${n}`);
```

If you try to run this program, you will be in for a rude surprise: instead of stopping at 0.3, this loop will skip right past it and execute forever. This is because 0.1 is a well-known value that can't be expressed exactly as a double, as it falls between two binary fraction representations. So the third pass through this loop, `n` will have the value `0.30000000000000004`, the test will be `false`, and the only chance to break the loop will have passed.

You can rewrite this loop to use `Number.EPSILON` and a relational operator to make this comparison "softer" and successfully halt the loop:

```
let n = 0;
while(true) {
    n += 0.1;
    if(Math.abs(n - 0.3) < Number.EPSILON) break;
}
console.log(`Stopped at ${n}`);
```

Notice we subtract our target (0.3) from our test number (`n`) and take the absolute value (using `Math.abs`, which we'll cover in Chapter 16). We could have done an easier calculation here (for example, we could have just tested to see if `n` was greater than 0.3), but this is the general way to determine if two doubles are close enough to be considered equal.

# String Concatenation

In JavaScript, the + operator doubles as numeric addition and string concatenation (this is quite common; Perl and PHP are notable counterexamples of languages that *don't* use + for string concatenation).

JavaScript determines whether to attempt addition or string concatenation by the types of operands. Both addition and concatenation are evaluated from left to right. JavaScript examines each pair of operands from left to right, and if either operand is a string, it assumes string concatenation. If both values are numeric, it assumes addition. Consider the following two lines:

```
3 + 5 + "8"          // evaluates to string "88"
"3" + 5 + 8          // evaluates to string "358"
```

In the first case, JavaScript evaluated `(3 + 5)` as addition first. Then it evaluated `(8 + "8")` as string concatenation. In the second case, it evaluated `("3" + 5)` as concatenation, then `("35" + 8)` as concatenation.

# Logical Operators

Whereas the arithmetic operators we're all familiar with operate on numbers that can take on an infinite number of values (or at least a very large number of values, as computers have finite memory), logical operators concern themselves only with boolean values, which can take on only one of two values: true or false.

In mathematics—and many other programming languages—logical operators operate only on boolean values and return only boolean values. JavaScript allows you to operate on values that are not boolean, and even more surprising, can return values that aren't boolean. That is not to say JavaScript's implementation of logical operators is somehow wrong or not rigorous: if you use only boolean values, you will get results that are only boolean values.

Before we discuss the operators themselves, we need to acquaint ourselves with JavaScript's mechanism for mapping nonboolean values to boolean values.

## Truthy and Falsy Values

Many languages have a concept of "truthy" and "falsy" values; C, for example, doesn't even have a boolean type: numeric 0 is false, and all other numeric values are true. JavaScript does something similar, except it includes all data types, effectively allowing you to partition any value into truthy or falsy buckets. JavaScript considers the following values to be falsy:

- `undefined`
- `null`
- `false`
- `0`
- `NaN`
- `''` (an empty string)

Everything else is truthy. Because there are a great number of things that are truthy, I won't enumerate them all here, but I will point out some you should be conscious of:

- Any object (including an object whose `valueOf()` method returns `false`)
- Any array (even an empty array)
- Strings containing only whitespace (such as " ")
- The string "`false`"

Some people stumble over the fact that the string "`false`" is `true`, but for the most part, these partitions make sense, and are generally easy to remember and work with. One notable exception might be the fact that an empty array is truthy. If you want an array `arr` to be falsy if it's empty, use `arr.length` (which will be 0 if the array is empty, which is falsy).

# AND, OR, and NOT

The three logical operators supported by JavaScript are AND (`&&`), OR (`||`), and NOT (`!`). If you have a math background, you might know AND as conjunction, OR as disjunction, and NOT as negation.

Unlike numbers, which have infinite possible values, booleans can take on only two possible values, so these operations are often described with *truth tables*, which completely describe their behavior (see Tables 5-2 through 5-4).

*Table 5-2. Truth table for AND (&&)*

| x | y | x && y |
|---|---|---|
| false | false | false |
| false | true | false |
| true | false | false |
| true | true | true |

*Table 5-3. Truth table for OR (||)*

| x | y | x \|\| y |
|---|---|---|
| false | false | false |
| false | true | true |
| true | false | true |
| true | true | true |

*Table 5-4. Truth table for NOT (!)*

| x | !x |
|---|---|
| false | true |
| true | false |

Looking over these tables, you'll see that AND is `true` only if both of its operands are `true`, and OR is `false` only if both of its operands are `false`. NOT is straightforward: it takes its only operand and inverts it.

The OR operator is sometimes called "inclusive OR" because if both operands are `true`, the result is `true`. There is also an "exclusive OR" (or XOR), which is `false` if both operands are `true`. JavaScript doesn't have a logical operator for XOR, but it does have a bitwise XOR, which will be discussed later.

If you need the exclusive OR (XOR) of two variables `x` and `y`, you can use the equivalent expression `(x || y) && x !== y`.

## Short-Circuit Evaluation

If you look at the truth table for AND (Table 5-2), you'll notice you can take a shortcut: if `x` is falsy, you don't even need to consider the value of `y`. Similarly, if you're evaluating `x || y`, and `x` is truthy, you don't need to evaluate `y`. JavaScript does exactly this, and it's known as *short-circuit evaluation*.

Why is short-circuit evaluation important? Because if the second operand has *side effects*, they will not happen if the evaluation is short-circuited. Very often, the term "side effect" is taken to be a bad thing in programming, but it isn't always: if the side effect is intentional and clear, then it's not a bad thing.

In an expression, side effects can arise from incrementing, decrementing, assignment, and function calls. We've already covered increment and decrement operators, so let's see an example:

```
const skipIt = true;
let x = 0;
const result = skipIt || x++;
```

The second line in that example has a direct result, stored in the variable `result`. That value will be `true` because the first operand (`skipIt`) is `true`. What's interesting, though, is because of the short-circuit evaluation, the increment expression isn't evaluated, leaving the value of `x` at `0`. If you change `skipIt` to `false`, then both parts of the expression have to be evaluated, so the increment will execute: the increment is the side effect. The same thing happens in reverse with AND:

```
const doIt = false;
let x = 0;
const result = doIt && x++;
```

Again, JavaScript will not evaluate the second operand, which contains the increment, because the first operand to AND is `false`. So `result` will be `false`, and `x` will not be incremented. What happens if you change `doIt` to `true`? JavaScript has to evaluate both operands, so the increment will happen, and `result` will be `0`. Wait, what? Why is `result` `0` and not `false`? The answer to that question brings us neatly to our next subject.

## Logical Operators with Nonboolean Operands

If you are using boolean operands, the logical operators always return booleans. If you're not, however, the value that *determined the outcome* gets returned, as Tables 5-5 and 5-6 show.

*Table 5-5. Truth table for AND (`&&`) with nonboolean operands*

| x | y | x && y |
|---|---|---|
| falsy | falsy | x (falsy) |
| falsy | truthy | x (falsy) |
| truthy | falsy | y (falsy) |
| truthy | truthy | y (truthy) |

*Table 5-6. Truth table for OR (`||`) with nonboolean operands*

| x | y | x \|\| y |
|---|---|---|
| falsy | falsy | y (falsy) |
| falsy | truthy | y (truthy) |
| truthy | falsy | x (truthy) |
| truthy | truthy | x (truthy) |

Note that if you convert the result to a boolean, it will be correct according to the boolean definitions of AND and OR. This behavior of the logical operators allows you to take certain convenient shortcuts. Here's one that you will see a lot:

```
const options = suppliedOptions || { name: "Default" }
```

Remember that objects (even if they are empty) always evaluate to truthy. So if `suppliedOptions` is an object, `options` will refer to `suppliedOptions`. If no options were supplied—in which case, `suppliedOptions` will be `null` or `undefined`—`options` will get some default values.

In the case of NOT, there's no reasonable way to return anything other than a boolean, so the NOT operator (`!`) always returns a boolean for an operand of any type. If the operand is truthy, it returns `false`, and if the operand is falsy, it returns `true`.

## Conditional Operator

The conditional operator is JavaScript's sole *ternary* operator, meaning it takes three operands (all other operands take one or two). The conditional operator is the expression equivalent of an `if...else` statement. Here's an example of the conditional operator:

```
const doIt = false;
const result = doIt ? "Did it!" : "Didn't do it.";
```

If the first operand (which comes before the question mark—`doIt`, in this example) is truthy, the expression evaluates to the second operand (between the question mark and colon), and if it's falsy, it evaluates to the third operand (after the colon). Many beginning programmers see this as a more confusing version of an `if...else` statement, but the fact that it's an expression and not a statement gives it a very useful property: it can be combined with other expressions (such as the assignment to `result` in the last example).

## Comma Operator

The comma operator provides a simple way to combine expressions: it simply evaluates two expressions and returns the result of the second one. It is convenient when you want to execute more than one expression, but the only value you care about is the result of the final expression. Here is a simple example:

```
let x = 0, y = 10, z;
z = (x++, y++);
```

In this example, `x` and `y` are both incremented, and `z` gets the value `10` (which is what `y++` returns). Note that the comma operator has the lowest precedence of any operator, which is why we enclosed it in parentheses here: if we had not, `z` would have received `0` (the value of `x++`), and *then* `y` would have been incremented. You most commonly see this used to combine expressions in a `for` loop (see Chapter 4) or to combine multiple operations before returning from a function (see Chapter 6).

# Grouping Operator

As mentioned already, the grouping operator (parentheses) has no effect other than to modify or clarify operator precedence. Thus, the grouping operator is the "safest" operator in that it has no effect other than on order of operations.

## Bitwise Operators

Bitwise operators allow you to perform operations on all the individual bits in a number. If you've never had any experience with a low-level language such as C, or have never had any exposure to how numbers are stored internally in a computer, you may want to read up on these topics first (you are also welcome to skip or skim this section: very few applications require bitwise operators anymore). Bitwise operators treat their operands as 32-bit signed integers in two's complement format. Because all numbers in JavaScript are doubles, JavaScript converts the numbers to 32-bit integers before performing bitwise operators, and then converts them back to doubles before returning the result.

Bitwise operators are related to the logical operators in that they perform logical operations (AND, OR, NOT, XOR), but they perform them on every individual bit in an integer. As Table 5-7 shows, they also include additional *shift* operators to shift bits into different positions.

*Table 5-7. Bitwise operators*

| Operator | Description | Example |
| --- | --- | --- |
| & | Bitwise AND | `0b1010 & 0b1100 // result: 0b1000` |
| \| | Bitwise OR | `0b1010 \| 0b1100 // result: 0b1110` |
| ^ | Bitwise XOR | `0b1010 ^ 0b1100 // result: 0b0110` |
| ~ | Bitwise NOT | `~0b1010 // result: 0b0101` |
| << | Left shift | `0b1010 << 1 // result:  0b10100` |
| | | `0b1010 << 2 // result: 0b101000` |
| >> | Sign-propagating right shift | (See below) |
| >>> | Zero-fill right shift | (See below) |

Note that left shifting is effectively multiplying by two, and right shifting is effectively dividing by two and rounding down.

In two's complement, the leftmost bit is 1 for negative numbers, and 0 for positive numbers, hence the two ways to perform a right shift. Let's take the number –22, for example. If we want to get its binary representation, we start with positive 22, take the complement (one's complement), and then add one (two's complement):

```
let n = 22      // 32-bit binary:     00000000000000000000000000010110
n >> 1          //                    00000000000000000000000000001011
n >>> 1         //                    00000000000000000000000000001011
n = ~n          // one's complement:  11111111111111111111111111101001
n++             // two's complement:  11111111111111111111111111101010
n >> 1          //                    11111111111111111111111111110101
n >>> 1         //                    01111111111111111111111111110101
```

Unless you are interfacing with hardware, or getting a better grasp on how numbers are represented by a computer, you'll probably have little call to use bitwise operators (often playfully called "bit twiddling"). One nonhardware use you may see is using bits to efficiently store "flags" (boolean values).

For example, consider Unix-style file permissions: read, write, and execute. A given user can have any combination of these three settings, making them ideal for flags. Because we have three flags, we need three bits to store the information:

```
const FLAG_READ 1        // 0b001
const FLAG_WRITE 2       // 0b010
const FLAG_EXECUTE 4     // 0b100
```

With bitwise operators, we can combine, toggle, and detect individual flags in a single numeric value:

```
let p = FLAG_READ | FLAG_WRITE;        // 0b011
let hasWrite = p & FLAG_WRITE;         // 0b010 - truthy
let hasExecute = p & FLAG_EXECUTE;     // 0b000 - falsy
p = p ^ FLAG_WRITE;                    // 0b001 -- toggle write flag (now off)
p = p ^ FLAG_WRITE;                    // 0b011 -- toggle write flag (now on)

// we can even determine multiple flags in one expression:
const hasReadAndExecute = p & (FLAG_READ | FLAG_EXECUTE);
```

Note that for `hasReadAndExecute` we had to use the grouping operator; AND has a higher precedence than OR, so we had to force the OR to evaluate before the AND.

## typeof Operator

The `typeof` operator returns a string representing the type of its operand. Unfortunately, this operator doesn't exactly map to the seven data types in JavaScript (`undefined`, `null`, boolean, number, string, symbol, and object), which has caused no end of criticism and confusion.

The `typeof` operator has one quirk that's usually referred to as a bug: `typeof null` returns `"object"`. `null` is not, of course, an object (it is a primitive). The reasons are historical and not particularly interesting, and it has been suggested many times that it be fixed, but too much existing code is already built on this behavior, so it's now immortalized in the language specification.

`typeof` is also often criticized for not being able to distinguish arrays and nonarray objects. It correctly identifies functions (which are also special types of objects), but `typeof []` results in `"object"`.

Table 5-8 lists the possible return values of `typeof`.

*Table 5-8. typeof return values*

| Expression | Return value | Notes |
|---|---|---|
| `typeof undefined` | `"undefined"` | |
| `typeof null` | `"object"` | Unfortunate, but true |
| `typeof {}` | `"object"` | |
| `typeof true` | `"boolean"` | |
| `typeof 1` | `"number"` | |
| `typeof ""` | `"string"` | |
| `typeof Symbol()` | `"symbol"` | New in ES6 |
| `typeof function() {}` | `"function"` | |

Because `typeof` is an operator, parentheses are not required. That is, if you have a variable `x`, you can use `typeof x` instead of `typeof(x)`. The latter is valid syntax—the parentheses just form an unnecessary expression group.

## void Operator

The `void` operator has only one job: to evaluate its operand and then return `undefined`. Sound useless? It is. It can be used to force expression evaluation where you want a return value of `undefined`, but I have never run across such a situation in the wild. The only reason I include it in this book is that you will occasionally see it used as the URI for an HTML `<a>` tag, which will prevent the browser from navigating to a new page:

```
<a href="javascript:void 0">Do nothing.</a>
```

This is not a recommended approach, but you do see it from time to time.

## Assignment Operators

The assignment operator is straightforward: it assigns a value to a variable. What's on the lefthand side of the equals sign (sometimes called the *lvalue*) *must* be a variable, property, or array element. That is, it must be something that can hold a value (assigning a value to a constant is technically part of the declaration, not an assignment operator).

Recall from earlier in this chapter that assignment is itself an expression, so the value that's returned is the value that's being assigned. This allows you to chain assignments, as well as perform assignments within other expressions:

```
let v, v0;
v = v0 = 9.8;        // chained assignment; first v0 gets
                     // the value 9.8, and then v gets the
                     // value 9.8

const nums = [ 3, 5, 15, 7, 5 ];
let n, i=0;
// note the assignment in the while condition; n
// takes on the value of nums[i], and the whole
// expression also evalutes to that value, allowing
// a numeric comparison:
while((n = nums[i]) < 10, i++ < nums.length) {
    console.log(`Number less than 10: ${n}.`);
}
console.log(`Number greater than 10 found: ${n}.`);
console.log(`${nums.length} numbers remain.`);
```

Notice in the second example, we have to use a grouping operator because assignment has a lower precedence than relational operators.

In addition to the ordinary assignment operators, there are convenience assignment operators that perform an operation and assignment in one step. Just as with the ordinary assignment operator, these operators evaluate to the final assignment value. Table 5-9 summarizes these convenience assignment operators.

*Table 5-9. Assignment with operation*

| Operator | Equivalent |
|---|---|
| `x += y` | `x = x + y` |
| `x -= y` | `x = x - y` |
| `x *= y` | `x = x * y` |
| `x /= y` | `x = x / y` |
| `x %= y` | `x = x % y` |
| `x <<= y` | `x = x << y` |
| `x >>= y` | `x = x >> y` |
| `x >>>= y` | `x = x >>> y` |

| Operator | Equivalent |
|---|---|
| x &= y | x = x & y |
| x \|= y | x = x \| y |
| x ^= y | x = x ^ y |

# Destructuring Assignment

New in ES6 is a welcome feature called *destructuring assignment* that allows you to take an object or an array, and "destructure" it into individual variables. We'll start with object destructuring:

```
// a normal object
const obj = { b: 2, c: 3, d: 4 };

// object destructuring assignment
const {a, b, c} = obj;
a;                  // undefined: there was no property "a" in obj
b;                  // 2
c;                  // 3
d;                  // reference error: "d" is not defined
```

When you destructure an object, the variable names must match property names in the object (array destructuring can only assign property names that are identifiers). In this example, `a` didn't match any property in the object, so it received the value `undefined`. Also, because we didn't specify `d` in the declaration, it was not assigned to anything.

In this example, we're doing declaration and assignment in the same statement. Object destructuring can be done on assignment alone, but it must be surrounded by parentheses; otherwise, JavaScript interprets the lefthand side as a block:

```
const obj = { b: 2, c: 3, d: 4 };
let a, b, c;

// this produces an error:
{a, b, c} = obj;

// this works:
({a, b, c} = obj);
```

With array destructuring, you can assign any names you want (in order) to the elements of the array:

```
// a normal array
const arr = [1, 2, 3];

// array destructuring assignment
```

```
let [x, y] = arr;
x;                  // 1
y;                  // 2
z;                  // error: z hasn't been defined
```

In this example, x is assigned the value of the first element in the array, and y is assigned the value of the second element; all elements past that are discarded. It's possible to take all the remaining elements and put those in a new array with the spread operator (...), which we'll cover in Chapter 6:

```
const arr = [1, 2, 3, 4, 5];

let [x, y, ...rest] = arr;
x;                        // 1
y;                        // 2
rest;                     // [3, 4, 5]
```

In this example, x and y receive the first two elements, and the variable rest receives the rest (you don't have to name the variable rest; you can use whatever name you want). Array destructuring makes it easy to swap the values of variables (something that previously required a temporary variable):

```
let a = 5, b = 10;
[a, b] = [b, a];
a;                  // 10
b;                  // 5
```

Array destructuring doesn't only work on arrays; it works on any iterable object (which we'll cover in Chapter 9).

In these simple examples, it would have been easier to simply assign the variables directly instead of using destructuring. Where destructuring comes in handy is when you get an object or array from elsewhere, and can easily pick out certain elements. We'll see this used to great effect in Chapter 6.

# Object and Array Operators

Objects, arrays, and functions have a collection of special operators. Some we have already seen (such as the member access and computed member access operator), and the rest will be covered in Chapters 6, 8, and 9. For completeness, they are summarized in Table 5-10.

*Table 5-10. Object and array operators*

| Operator | Description | Chapter |
| --- | --- | --- |
| `.` | Member access | Chapter 3 |
| `[]` | Computed member access | Chapter 3 |
| `in` | Property existence operator | Chapter 9 |
| `new` | Object instantiation operator | Chapter 9 |
| `instanceof` | Prototype chain test operator | Chapter 9 |
| `...` | Spread operator | Chapter 6, Chapter 8 |
| `delete` | Delete operator | Chapter 3 |

# Expressions in Template Strings

Template strings, which we introduced in Chapter 3, can be used to inject the value of *any expression* into a string. The example in Chapter 3 used a template string to display the current temperature. What if we wanted to display the temperature difference or display the temperature in degrees Fahrenheit instead of Celsius? We can use expressions in template strings:

```
const roomTempC = 21.5;
let currentTempC = 19.5;
const message = `The current temperature is ` +
    `${currentTempC-roomTempC}\u00b0C different than room temperature.`;
const fahrenheit =
   `The current temperature is ${currentTempC * 9/5 + 32}\u00b0F`;
```

Again we see the pleasing symmetry that expressions bring. We can use variables by themselves in a template string because a variable is simply a type of expression.

# Expressions and Control Flow Patterns

In Chapter 4, we covered some common control flow patterns. Now that we've seen some expressions that can affect control flow (ternary expressions and short-circuit evaluation), we can cover some additional control flow patterns.

## Converting if...else Statements to Conditional Expressions

Whenever an `if...else` statement is used to resolve a value—either as part of assignment, a smaller part of an expression, or the return value of a function—it is generally preferable to use the conditional operator instead of `if...else`. It produces more compact code that is easier to read. For example:

```
if(isPrime(n)) {
   label = 'prime';
} else {
   label = 'non-prime';
}
```

would be better written as:

```
label = isPrime(n) ? 'prime' : 'non-prime';
```

## Converting if Statements to Short-Circuited Logical OR Expressions

Just as `if...else` statements that resolve to a value can easily be translated to conditional expressions, `if` statements that resolve to a value can easily be translated to short-circuited logical OR expressions. This technique is not as obviously superior as conditional operators over `if...else` statements, but you will see it quite often, so it's good to be aware of. For example,

```
if(!options) options = {};
```

can be easily translated to:

```
options = options || {};
```

# Conclusion

JavaScript, like most modern languages, has an extensive and useful collection of operators, which will form the basic building blacks for manipulating data. Some, like the bitwise operators, you will probably use very seldom. Others, such as the member access operators, you won't even normally think about as operators (where it can come in handy is when you're trying to untangle a difficult operator precedence problem).

Assignment, arithmetic, comparison, and boolean operators are the most common operators, and you'll be using them frequently, so make sure you have a good understanding of them before proceeding.

CHAPTER 6

# Functions

A *function* is a self-contained collection of statements that run as a single unit: essentially, you can think of it as a subprogram. Functions are central to JavaScript's power and expressiveness, and this chapter introduces you to their basic usage and mechanics.

Every function has a *body*; this is the collection of statements that compose the function:

```
function sayHello() {
  // this is the body; it started with an opening curly brace...

  console.log("Hello world!");
  console.log("¡Hola mundo!");
  console.log("Hallo wereld!");
  console.log("Привет мир!");

  // ...and ends with a closing curly brace
}
```

This is an example of a *function declaration*: we're declaring a function called `sayHello`. Simply declaring a function does *not* execute the body: if you try this example, you will not see our multilingual "Hello, World" messages printed to the console. To *call* a function (also called *running*, *executing*, *invoking*, or *dispatching*), you use the name of the function followed by parentheses:

```
sayHello();         // "Hello, World!" printed to the
                    // console in different languages
```

The terms *call*, *invoke*, and *execute* (as well as *run*) are interchangeable, and I will use each in this book to get you comfortable with them all. In certain contexts and languages, there may be subtle differences between these terms, but in general use, they are equivalent.

## Return Values

Calling a function is an expression, and as we know, expressions resolve to a value. So what value does a function call resolve to? This is where *return values* come in. In the body of a function, the `return` keyword will *immediately terminate the function and return the specified value*, which is what the function call will resolve to. Let's modify our example; instead of writing to the console, we'll return a greeting:

```
function getGreeting() {
  return "Hello world!";
}
```

Now when we call that function, it will resolve to the return value:

```
getGreeting();          // "Hello, World!"
```

If you don't explicitly call `return`, the return value will be `undefined`. A function can return any type of value; as a reader's exercise, try creating a function, `getGreetings`, to return an array containing "Hello, World" in different languages.

## Calling Versus Referencing

In JavaScript, functions are objects, and as such, can be passed around and assigned just like any other object. It's important to understand the distinction between *calling* a function and simply *referencing* it. When you follow a function identifier with parentheses, JavaScript knows that you're calling it: it executes the body of the function, and the expression resolves to the return value. When you *don't* provide the parentheses, you're simply referring to the function just like any other value, and it's *not* invoked. Try the following in a JavaScript console:

```
getGreeting();          // "Hello, World!"
getGreeting;            // function getGreeting()
```

Being able to reference a function like any other value (without calling it) allows a lot of flexibility in the language. For example, you can assign a function to a variable, which allows you to call the function by another name:

```
const f = getGreeting;
f();                    // "Hello, World!"
```

Or assign a function to an object property:

```
const o = {};
o.f = getGreeting;
o.f();                  // "Hello, World!"
```

Or even add a function to an array:

```
const arr = [1, 2, 3];
arr[1] = getGreeting;   // arr is now [1, function getGreeting(), 2]
arr[1]();               // "Hello, World!"
```

This last example should make clear the role of the parentheses: if JavaScript encounters parentheses that follow a value, the value is assumed to be a function, and that function is called. In the preceding example, `arr[1]` is an expression that resolves to a value. That value is followed by parentheses, which is a signal to JavaScript that the value is a function and should be called.

If you try to add parentheses to a value that is not a function, you will get an error. For example, `"whoops"()` will result in the error `TypeError: "whoops" is not a function`.

## Function Arguments

We've now seen how to call functions and get values *out* of them; how about getting information *into* them? The primary mechanism to pass information to a function call is function *arguments* (sometimes called *parameters*). Arguments are like variables that don't exist until the function is called. Let's consider a function that takes two numeric arguments and returns the average of those numbers:

```
function avg(a, b) {
   return (a + b)/2;
}
```

In this function declaration, `a` and `b` are called *formal arguments*. When a function is called, formal arguments receive values and become *actual arguments*:

```
avg(5, 10);        // 7.5
```

In this example, the formal arguments `a` and `b` receive the values `5` and `10`, and become actual arguments (which are very much like variables, but specific to the function body).

One thing that beginners often stumble over is that the arguments *exist only in the function*, even if they have the same name as variables outside of the function. Consider:

```
const a = 5, b = 10;
avg(a, b);
```

The variables a and b here are separate, distinct variables from the *arguments* a and b in the function avg, even though they share the same name. When you call a function, the function arguments receive the *values* that you pass in, not the variables themselves. Consider the following code:

```
function f(x) {
   console.log(`inside f: x=${x}`);
   x = 5;
   console.log(`inside f: x=${x} (after assignment)`);
}

let x = 3;
console.log(`before calling f: x=${x}`);
f(x);
console.log(`after calling f: x=${x}`);
```

If you run this example, you will see:

```
before calling f: x=3
inside f: x=3
inside f: x=5 (after assignment)
after calling f: x=3
```

The important takeaway here is that assigning a value to x inside the function doesn't affect the variable x that's outside the function; that's because they're two distinct entities that happen to have the same name.

Whenever we assign to an argument inside a function, there will be no effect on any variables outside of the function. It is, however, possible to modify an *object type* in a function in such a way that the object itself changes, which will be visible outside of the function:

```
function f(o) {
   o.message = `set in f (previous value: '${o.message}')`;
}
let o = {
   message: "initial value"
};
console.log(`before calling f: o.message="${o.message}"`);
f(o);
console.log(`after calling f: o.message="${o.message}"`);
```

This results in the following output:

```
before calling f: o.message="initial value"
after calling f: o.message="set in f (previous value: 'initial value')"
```

In this example, we see that f modified o within the function, and those changes affected the object o outside of the function. This highlights the key difference between primitives and objects. Primitives can't be modified (we can change the value of a primitive variable, but the primitive *value* itself doesn't change). Objects, on the other hand, can be modified.

Let's be clear here: the o inside the function is separate and distinct from the o outside of the function, but they both *refer to the same object*. We can see that difference again with assignment:

```
function f(o) {
   o.message = "set in f";
   o = {
      message: "new object!"
   };
   console.log(`inside f: o.message="${o.message}" (after assignment)`);
}
let o = {
   message: 'initial value'
};
console.log(`before calling f: o.message="${o.message}"`);
f(o);
console.log(`after calling f: o.message="${o.message}"`);
```

If you run this example, you will see:

```
before calling f: o.message="initial value"
inside f: o.message="new object!" (after assignment)
after calling f: o.message="set in f"
```

The key to understanding what's going on here is understanding that the *argument* o (inside the function) is different than the variable o (outside the function). When f is called, both point to the same object, but when o is assigned inside f, it points to a *new, distinct* object. The o outside the function still points to the original object.

Primitives in JavaScript are considered *value types* in computer science parlance, because when they are passed around, the value is *copied*. Objects are called *reference types* because when they are passed around, both variables refer to the *same object* (that is, they both hold a reference to the same object).

## Do Arguments Make the Function?

In many languages, a function's *signature* includes its arguments. For example, in C, f() (no arguments) is a different function than f(x) (one argument), which is a different function than f(x, y) (two arguments). JavaScript makes no such distinction, and when you have a function named f, you can call it with 0 or 1 or 10 arguments, and you're calling the same function.

The implication of this is that you can call any function with any number of arguments. If you fail to provide arguments, they will implicitly receive the value `undefined`:

```
function f(x) {
   return `in f: x=${x}`;
}
f();     // "in f: x=undefined"
```

Later in this chapter, we'll see how to handle the situation where you pass more arguments than the function defines.

## Destructuring Arguments

Just as we can have destructured assignment (see Chapter 5), we can have *destructured arguments* (arguments are, after all, very much like variable definition). Consider destructuring an object into individual variables:

```
function getSentence({ subject, verb, object }) {
   return `${subject} ${verb} ${object}`;
}

const o = {
   subject: "I",
   verb: "love",
   object: "JavaScript",
};

getSentence(o);          // "I love JavaScript"
```

As with destructuring assignment, property names must be identifier strings, and a variable that doesn't have a matching property in the incoming object will receive the value `undefined`.

You can also destructure arrays:

```
function getSentence([ subject, verb, object ]) {
   return `${subject} ${verb} ${object}`;
}

const arr = [ "I", "love", "JavaScript" ];
getSentence(arr);          // "I love JavaScript"
```

Finally, you can use the spread operator (`...`) to collect any additional arguments:

```
function addPrefix(prefix, ...words) {
   // we will learn a better way to do this later!
   const prefixedWords = [];
   for(let i=0; i<words.length; i++) {
      prefixedWords[i] = prefix + words[i];
   }
   return prefixedWords;
```

```
}

addPrefix("con", "verse", "vex");    // ["converse", "convex"]
```

Note that if you use the spread operator in a function declaration, it *must be the last argument*. If you put arguments after it, JavaScript wouldn't have a reasonable way to distinguish between what should go in the spread argument and what should go in the remaining arguments.

In ES5, similar functionality can be accomplished with a special variable that exists only within function bodies: `arguments`. This variable was not actually an array, but an "array-like" object, which often required special handling, or conversion to a proper array. Spread arguments in ES6 address this weakness, and should be preferred over using the `arguments` variable (which is still available).

## Default Arguments

New in ES6 is the ability to specify *default values* for arguments. Normally, when values for arguments aren't provided, they get a value of `undefined`. Default values allow you to specify some other default value:

```
function f(a, b = "default", c = 3) {
   return `${a} - ${b} - ${c}`;
}

f(5, 6, 7);     // "5 - 6 - 7"
f(5, 6);        // "5 - 6 - 3"
f(5);           // "5 - default - 3"
f();            // "undefined - default - 3"
```

# Functions as Properties of Objects

When a function is a property of an object, it is often called a *method* to distinguish it from a normal function (we'll learn a more nuanced distinction between *function* and *method* shortly). We already saw in Chapter 3 how we could add a function to an existing object. We can also add a method in the object literal:

```
const o = {
   name: 'Wallace',                          // primitive property
   bark: function() { return 'Woof!'; },  // function property (method)
}
```

ES6 introduces a new shorthand syntax for methods. The following is functionally equivalent to the preceding example:

```
const o = {
   name: 'Wallace',                    // primitive property
   bark() { return 'Woof!'; },         // function property (method)
}
```

## The this Keyword

Inside a function body, a special read-only value called `this` is available. This keyword is normally associated with object-oriented programming, and we will be learning more about its use in that context in Chapter 9. However, in JavaScript, it can be used in multiple ways.

Normally, the `this` keyword relates to functions that are properties of objects. When methods are called, the `this` keyword takes on the value of the specific object it was called on:

```
const o = {
   name: 'Wallace',
   speak() { return `My name is ${this.name}!`; },
}
```

When we call `o.speak()`, the `this` keyword is bound to `o`:

```
o.speak();      // "My name is Wallace!
```

It's important to understand that `this` is bound according to *how the function is called, not where the function is declared.* That is, `this` is bound to `o` not because `speak` is a property of `o`, but because we called it directly on `o` (`o.speak`). Consider what happens if we assign that same function to a variable:

```
const speak = o.speak;
speak === o.speak;    // true; both variables refer to the same function
speak();              // "My name is !"
```

Because of the way we called the function, JavaScript didn't know that the function was originally declared in `o`, so `this` was bound to `undefined`.

If you call a function in such a way that it's not clear how to bind `this` (such as calling the function variable `speak` as we did previously), what `this` gets bound to is complex. It depends on whether you're in strict mode or not, and where the function is being called from. We are intentionally glossing over these details because it's best to avoid this situation. If you want to know more, see the MDN documentation for code formatting (*https://developer.mozilla.org/en-US/docs/Web/JavaScript/Reference/Operators/this*).

The term *method* is traditionally associated with object-oriented programming, and in this book, we'll use it to mean a function that is a property of an object and is designed to be called directly from an object instance (such as `o.speak()`) above. If a function doesn't use `this`, we will generally refer to it as a function, no matter where it's declared.

One detail about the `this` variable that often trips people up is when you need to access it in a nested function. Consider the following example, where we use a helper function inside a method:

```
const o = {
   name: 'Julie',
   greetBackwards: function() {
      function getReverseName() {
         let nameBackwards = '';
         for(let i=this.name.length-1; i>=0; i--) {
            nameBackwards += this.name[i];
         }
         return nameBackwards;
      }
      return `${getReverseName()} si eman ym ,olleH`;
   },
};
o.greetBackwards();
```

Here we're using a nested function, `getReverseName`, to reverse the name. Unfortunately, `getReverseName` won't work as we expect it to: when we call `o.greetBackwards()`, JavaScript binds `this` as we expect. However, when we call `getReverseName` from inside `greetBackwards`, `this` will be bound to something else.[1] A common solution to this problem is to assign a second variable to `this`:

```
const o = {
   name: 'Julie',
   greetBackwards: function() {
      const self = this;
      function getReverseName() {
         let nameBackwards = '';
         for(let i=self.name.length-1; i>=0; i--) {
            nameBackwards += self.name[i];
         }
         return nameBackwards;
      }
      return `${getReverseName()} si eman ym ,olleH`;
   },
};
o.greetBackwards();
```

1 It will either get bound to the global object or it will be `undefined`, depending on whether or not you are in strict mode. We're not covering all the details here because you should avoid this situation.

This is a common technique, and you will see `this` get assigned to `self` or `that`. Arrow functions, which we'll see later in this chapter, are another way of addressing this problem.

## Function Expressions and Anonymous Functions

So far, we've been dealing exclusively with *function declarations*, which give functions both a body (which defines what the function does) and an identifier (so we can call it later). JavaScript also supports *anonymous functions*, which don't necessarily have an identifier.

You might reasonably be wondering what use is a function without an identifier. Without an identifier, how are we to call it? The answer lies in understanding *function expressions*. We know that an expression is something that evaluates to a value, and we also know that functions are values like any other in JavaScript. A function expression is simply a way to declare a (possibly unnamed) function. A function expression can be assigned to something (thereby giving it an identifier), or called immediately.[2]

Function expressions are syntactically identical to function declarations except that you can omit the function name. Let's consider the example where we use a function expression and assign the result to a variable (which is effectively equivalent to a function declaration):

```
const f = function() {
    // ...
};
```

The outcome is the same as if we had declared the function in the usual way: we're left with an identifier `f` that refers to a function. Just as with regular function declaration, we can call the function with `f()`. The only difference is that we are creating an anonymous function (by using a function expression) and assigning it to a variable.

Anonymous functions are used all the time: as arguments to other functions or methods, or to create function properties in an object. We will see these uses throughout the book.

I said that the function name is *optional* in a function expression...so what happens when we give the function a name *and* assign it to a variable (and why would we want to do this)? For example:

```
const g = function f() {
    // ...
}
```

2 A so-called "immediately invoked function expression" (IIFE), which we will cover in Chapter 7.

When a function is created this way, the name g takes priority, and to refer to the function (from outside of the function), we use g; trying to access f will give you an undefined variable error. Taking this into account, why would we want to do this? It can be necessary if we want to refer to the function from within the function itself (called *recursion*):

```
const g = function f(stop) {
    if(stop) console.log('f stopped');
    f(true);
};
g(false);
```

From inside the function, we use f to reference the function, and from outside we use g. There's no particularly good reason to give a function two separate names, but we do so here to make it clear how named function expressions work.

Because function declaration and function expressions look identical, you might be wondering how JavaScript tells the two apart (or if there's even any difference). The answer is *context*: if the function declaration is used as an expression, it is a function expression, and if it isn't, it's a function declaration.

The difference is mostly academic, and you don't normally have to think about it. When you're defining a named function that you intend to call later, you'll probably use a function declaration without thinking about it, and if you need to create a function to assign to something or pass into another function, you'll use a function expression.

## Arrow Notation

ES6 introduces a new and welcome syntax called *arrow notation* (also called "fat arrow" notation because the arrow uses an equals sign instead of a dash). It is essentially syntactic sugar (with one major functional difference we'll get to shortly) that reduces the number of times you have to type the word function, as well as the number of curly braces you have to type.

Arrow functions allow you to simplify syntax in three ways:

- You can omit the word function.
- If the function takes a single argument, you can omit the parentheses.
- If the function body is a single expression, you can omit curly braces and the return statement.

Arrow functions are always anonymous. You can still assign them to a variable, but you can't create a named function like you can with the function keyword.

Consider the following equivalent function expressions:

```
const f1 = function() { return "hello!"; }
// OR
const f1 = () => "hello!";

const f2 = function(name) { return `Hello, ${name}!`; }
// OR
const f2 = name => `Hello, ${name}!`;

const f3 = function(a, b) { return a + b; }
// OR
const f3 = (a,b) => a + b;
```

These examples are a bit contrived; usually, if you need a named function, you would simply use a regular function declaration. Arrow functions are most useful when you're creating and passing around anonymous functions, which we'll see quite often starting in Chapter 8.

Arrow functions do have one major difference from regular functions: `this` is bound lexically, just like any other variable. Recall our `greetBackwards` example from earlier in the chapter. With an arrow function, we can use `this` inside the inner function:

```
const o = {
   name: 'Julie',
   greetBackwards: function() {
      const getReverseName = () => {
         let nameBackwards = '';
         for(let i=this.name.length-1; i>=0; i--) {
            nameBackwards += this.name[i];
         }
         return nameBackwards;
      };
      return `${getReverseName()} si eman ym ,olleH`;
   },
};
o.greetBackwards();
```

Arrow functions have two additional minor differences from regular functions: they can't be used as object constructors (see Chapter 9), and the special `arguments` variable isn't available in arrow functions (which is no longer necessary thanks to the spread operator).

## call, apply, and bind

We've already seen the "normal" way `this` is bound (which is consistent with other object-oriented languages). However, JavaScript allows you to specify what `this` is bound to no matter how or where the function in question is called. We'll start with `call`, which is a method available on all functions that allows you to call the function with a specific value of `this`:

```
const bruce = { name: "Bruce" };
const madeline = { name: "Madeline" };

// this function isn't associated with any object, yet
// it's using 'this'!
function greet() {
   return `Hello, I'm ${this.name}!`;
}

greet();                  // "Hello, I'm !" - 'this' not bound
greet.call(bruce);        // "Hello, I'm Bruce!" - 'this' bound to 'bruce'
greet.call(madeline);     // "Hello, I'm Madeline!" - 'this' bound to 'madeline'
```

You can see that `call` allows us to call a function as if it were a method by providing it an object to bind `this` to. The first argument to `call` is the value you want `this` bound to, and any remaining arguments become arguments to the function you're calling:

```
function update(birthYear, occupation) {
   this.birthYear = birthYear;
   this.occupation = occupation;
}

update.call(bruce, 1949, 'singer');
   // bruce is now { name: "Bruce", birthYear: 1949,
   //     occupation: "singer" }
update.call(madeline, 1942, 'actress');
   // madeline is now { name: "Madeline", birthYear: 1942,
   //     occupation: "actress" }
```

`apply` is identical to `call` except the way it handles function arguments. `call` takes arguments directly, just like a normal function. `apply` takes its arguments as an array:

```
update.apply(bruce, [1955, "actor"]);
   // bruce is now { name: "Bruce", birthYear: 1955,
   //     occupation: "actor" }
update.apply(madeline, [1918, "writer"]);
   // madeline is now { name: "Madeline", birthYear: 1918,
   //     occupation: "writer" }
```

`apply` is useful if you've got an array and you want to use its values as arguments to a function. The classic example is finding the minimum or maximum number in an array. The built-in `Math.min` and `Math.max` functions take any number of arguments and return the minimum or maximum, respectively. We can use `apply` to use these functions with an existing array:

```
const arr = [2, 3, -5, 15, 7];
Math.min.apply(null, arr);    // -5
Math.max.apply(null, arr);    // 15
```

Note that we simply pass `null` in for the value of `this`. That's because `Math.min` and `Math.max` don't use `this` at all; it doesn't matter what we pass in here.

With the ES6 spread operator (`...`), we can accomplish the same result as `apply`. In the instance of our `update` method, where we do care about the `this` value, we still have to use `call`, but for `Math.min` and `Math.max`, where it doesn't matter, we can use the spread operator to call these functions directly:

```
const newBruce = [1940, "martial artist"];
update.call(bruce, ...newBruce);    // equivalent to apply(bruce, newBruce)
Math.min(...arr);                   // -5
Math.max(...arr);                   // 15
```

There's one final function that allows you to specify the value for `this`: `bind`. `bind` allows you to *permanently* associate a value for `this` with a function. Imagine we're passing our `update` method around, and we want to make sure that it *always* gets called with `bruce` as the value for `this`, no matter how it's called (even with `call`, `apply`, or another `bind`). `bind` allows us to do that:

```
const updateBruce = update.bind(bruce);

updateBruce(1904, "actor");
   // bruce is now { name: "Bruce", birthYear: 1904, occupation: "actor" }
updateBruce.call(madeline, 1274, "king");
   // bruce is now { name: "Bruce", birthYear: 1274, occupation: "king" };
   // madeline is unchanged
```

The fact that the action of `bind` is permanent makes it potentially a source of difficult-to-find bugs: in essence, you are left with a function that cannot be used effectively with `call`, `apply`, or `bind` (a second time). Imagine passing around a function that gets invoked with `call` or `apply` in some distant location, fully expecting `this` to get bound accordingly. I'm not suggesting that you avoid the use of `bind`; it's quite useful, but be mindful of the way bound functions will be used.

You can also provide parameters to `bind`, which has the effect of creating a new function that's always invoked with specific parameters. For example, if you wanted an `update` function that always set the birth year of `bruce` to `1949`, but still allowed you to change the occupation, you could do this:

```
const updateBruce1949 = update.bind(bruce, 1949);
updateBruce1949("singer, songwriter");
   // bruce is now { name: "Bruce", birthYear: 1949,
   //    occupation: "singer, songwriter" }
```

# Conclusion

Functions are a vital part of JavaScript. They do far more than just modularize code: they allow for the construction of incredibly powerful algorithmic units. This chapter has mainly been about the mechanics of functions—a dry but important introduction. Armed with this foundation, we'll see the power of functions unlocked in coming chapters.

CHAPTER 7

# Scope

*Scope* determines when and where variables, constants, and arguments are considered to be defined. We've already had some exposure to scope: we know that the arguments of a function exist only in the body of the function. Consider the following:

```
function f(x) {
    return x + 3;
}
f(5);           // 8
x;              // ReferenceError: x is not defined
```

We know that `x` lived very briefly (otherwise, how would it have successfully calculated `x + 3`?), but we can see that outside of the function body, it's as if `x` doesn't exist. Thus, we say the *scope* of `x` is the function `f`.

When we say that the scope of a variable is a given function, we must remember that the formal arguments in the function body don't exist until the function is called (thereby becoming actual arguments). A function may be called multiple times: each time the function is called, its arguments come into existence, and then go out of scope when the function returns.

We have also taken it for granted that variables and constants do not exist before we create them. That is, they aren't in scope until we declare them with `let` or `const` (`var` is a special case we'll cover later in this chapter).

In some languages, there's an explicit distinction between *declaration* and *definition*. Typically, declaring a variable means that you are announcing its existence by giving it an identifier. Definition, on the other hand, usually means declaring it *and* giving it a value. In JavaScript, the two terms are interchangeable, as all variables are given a value when they're declared (if not explicitly, they implicitly get the value `undefined`).

## Scope Versus Existence

It's intuitively obvious that if a variable doesn't exist, it's not in scope. That is, variables that have not yet been declared, or variables that have ceased to exist because a function exits, are clearly not in scope.

What about the converse? If a variable is not in scope, does that mean it doesn't exist? Not necessarily, and this is where we must make a distinction between *scope* and *existence*.

Scope (or *visibility*) refers to the identifiers that are currently visible and accessible by the currently executing part of the program (called the *execution context*). Existence, on the other hand, refers to identifiers that hold something for which memory has been allocated (reserved). We'll soon see examples of variables that exist but are not in scope.

When something ceases to exist, JavaScript doesn't necessarily reclaim the memory right away: it simply notes that the item no longer needs to be kept around, and the memory is periodically reclaimed in a process called *garbage collection*. Garbage collection in JavaScript is automatic, and outside of certain highly demanding applications, isn't something you'll need to concern yourself with.

## Lexical Versus Dynamic Scoping

When you look at the source code for a program, you are looking at its *lexical structure*. When the program actually runs, execution can jump around. Consider this program with two functions:

```
function f1() {
    console.log('one');
}
function f2() {
    console.log('two');
}

f2();
f1();
f2();
```

Lexically, this program is simply a series of statements that we generally read from top to bottom. However, when we run this program, execution jumps around: first to the body of function `f2`, then to the body of function `f1` (even though it's defined before `f2`), then back to the body of function `f2`.

Scoping in JavaScript is *lexical*, meaning we can determine what variables are in scope simply by looking at the source code. That's not to say that scope is aways immediately *obvious* from the source code: we'll see some examples in this chapter that require close examination to determine scope.

Lexical scoping means whatever variables are in scope where you *define* a function from (as opposed to when you *call* it) are in scope in the function. Consider this example:

```
const x = 3;
function f() {
     console.log(x); // this will work
     console.log(y); // this will cause a crash
}

const y = 3;
f();
```

The variable x exists when we define the function f, but y doesn't. Then we declare y and call f, and see that x is in scope inside the body of f when it's called, but y isn't. This is an example of lexical scoping: the function f has access to the identifiers that were available when it was *defined*, not when it was *called*.

Lexical scoping in JavaScript applies to *global scope*, *block scope*, and *function scope*.

## Global Scope

Scope is hierarchical, and there has to be something at the base of the tree: the scope that you're implicitly in when you start a program. This is called *global scope*. When a JavaScript program starts—before any functions are called—it is executing in global scope. The implication is, then, that anything you declare in global scope will be available to all scopes in your program.

Anything declared in global scope is called a *global*, and globals have a bad reputation. It's hard to crack open a book about programming without being warned that using globals will cause the very earth to split open and swallow you whole. So why are globals so bad?

Globals are not bad—as a matter of fact, they are a necessity. What's bad is the *abuse* of the global scope. We already mentioned that anything available in global scope is therefore available in *all* scopes. The lesson there is to use globals judiciously.

The clever reader might think "well, I will create a single function in the global scope, and therefore reduce my globals to one!" Clever, except you've now just moved the problem one level down. Anything declared in the scope of that function will be available to anything called from that function…which is hardly better than global scope!

The bottom line is this: you will probably have things that live in global scope, and that's not necessarily bad. What you should try to avoid is things that *rely* on global scope. Let's consider a simple example: keeping track of information about a user. Your program keeps track of a user's name and age, and there are some functions that operate on that information. One way to do this is with global variables:

```
let name = "Irena";     // global
let age = 25;           // global

function greet() {
    console.log(`Hello, ${name}!`);
}
function getBirthYear() {
    return new Date().getFullYear() - age;
}
```

The problem with this approach is that our functions are highly dependent on the context (or scope) that they're called from. Any function—anywhere in your entire program—could change the value of `name` (accidentally or intentionally). And "name" and "age" are generic names that might reasonably be used elsewhere, for other reasons. Because `greet` and `getBirthYear` rely on global variables, they are basically relying on the rest of the program using `name` and `age` correctly.

A better approach would be to put user information in a single object:

```
let user = {
    name = "Irena",
    age = 25,
};

function greet() {
    console.log(`Hello, ${user.name}!`);
}
function getBirthYear() {
    return new Date().getFullYear() - user.age;
}
```

In this simple example, we've only reduced the number of identifiers in the global scope by one (we got rid of `name` and `age`, and added `user`), but imagine if we had 10 pieces of information about the user...or 100.

We could do better still, though: our functions `greet` and `getBirthYear` are still dependent on the global `user`, which can be modified by anything. Let's improve those functions so they're not dependent on global scope:

```
function greet(user) {
    console.log(`Hello, ${user.name}!`);
}
function getBirthYear(user) {
    return new Date().getFullYear() - user.age;
}
```

Now our functions can be called from *any* scope, and explicitly passed a user (when we learn about modules and object-oriented programming, we'll see better ways still of handling this).

If all programs were this simple, it would hardly matter if we used global variables or not. When your program is a thousand lines long—or a hundred thousand—and you can't keep all scopes in your mind at once (or even on your screen), it becomes critically important not to rely on global scope.

## Block Scope

`let` and `const` declare identifiers in what's known as *block scope*. You'll recall from Chapter 5 that a block is a list of statements surrounded by curly braces. Block scope, then, refers to identifiers that are only in scope within the block:

```
console.log('before block');
{
    console.log('inside block');
    const x = 3;
    console.log(x):                    // logs 3
}
console.log(`outside block; x=${x}`);  // ReferenceError: x is not defined
```

Here we have a *standalone block*: usually a block is part of a control flow statement such as `if` or `for`, but it's valid syntax to have a block on its own. Inside the block, x is defined, and as soon as we leave the block, x goes out of scope, and is considered undefined.

You might remember from Chapter 4 that there's little practical use for standalone blocks; they can be used to control scope (as we'll see in this chapter), but that's rarely necessary. It is very convenient for explaining how scope works, which is why we're using them in this chapter.

## Variable Masking

A common source of confusion is variables or constants with the same name in different scopes. It's relatively straightforward when scopes come one after another:

```
{
    // block 1
    const x = 'blue';
    console.log(x);         // logs "blue"
}
console.log(typeof x);      // logs "undefined"; x out of scope
{
    // block 2
```

```
    const x = 3;
    console.log(x);          // logs "3"
}
console.log(typeof x);       // logs "undefined"; x out of scope
```

It's easy enough to understand here that there are two distinct variables, both named x in different scopes. Now consider what happens when the scopes are *nested*:

```
{
    // outer block
    let x = 'blue';
    console.log(x);          // logs "blue"
    {
        // inner block
        let x = 3;
        console.log(x);      // logs "3"
    }
    console.log(x);          // logs "blue"
}
console.log(typeof x);       // logs "undefined"; x out of scope
```

This example demonstrates *variable masking*. In the inner block, x is a distinct variable from the outer block (with the same name), which in effect *masks* (or hides) the x that's defined in the outer scope.

What's important to understand here is that, when execution enters the inner block, and a new variable x is defined, *both variables are in scope*; we simply have no way of accessing the variable in the outer scope (because it has the same name). Contrast this with the previous example where one x came into scope and then exited scope before the second variable named x did the same.

To drive this point home, consider this example:

```
{
    // outer block
    let x = { color: "blue" };
    let y = x;                    // y and x refer to the same object
    let z = 3;
    {
        // inner block
        let x = 5;                // outer x now masked
        console.log(x);           // logs 5
        console.log(y.color);     // logs "blue"; object pointed to by
                                  // y (and x in the outer scope) is
                                  // still in scope
        y.color = "red";
        console.log(z);           // logs 3; z has not been masked
    }
    console.log(x.color);         // logs "red"; object modified in
                                  // inner scope
    console.log(y.color);         // logs "red"; x and y point to the
                                  // same object
```

```
    console.log(z);             // logs 3
}
```

Variable masking is sometimes called variable *shadowing* (that is, a variable with the same name will *shadow* the variable in the outer scope). I've never cared for this term because shadows don't usually completely obscure things, just make them darker. When a variable is masked, the masked variable is completely inaccessible using that name.

By now, it should be clear that scope is hierarchical: you can enter a new scope without leaving the old one. This establishes a *scope chain* that determines what variables are in scope: all variables in the current scope chain are in scope, and (as long as they're not masked), can be accessed.

## Functions, Closures, and Lexical Scope

So far, we've only been dealing with blocks, which make it simple to see lexical scope, especially if you indent your blocks. Functions, on the other hand, can be defined in one place and used in another, meaning you might have to do some hunting to understand their scope.

In a "traditional" program, all of your functions might be defined in global scope, and if you avoid referencing global scope in your functions (which I recommend), you don't even need to think about what scope your functions have access to.

In modern JavaScript development, however, functions are often defined wherever they're needed. They're assigned to variables or object properties, added to arrays, passed into other functions, passed out of functions, and sometimes not given a name at all.

It's quite common to intentionally define a function in a specific scope so that it explicitly has access to that scope. This is usually called a *closure* (you can think of closing the scope around the function). Let's look at an example of a closure:

```
let globalFunc;                 // undefined global function
{
    let blockVar = 'a';         // block-scoped variable
    globalFunc = function() {
        console.log(blockVar);
    }
}
globalFunc();                   // logs "a"
```

`globalFunc` is assigned a value within a block: that block (and its parent scope, the global scope) form a closure. No matter where you call `globalFunc` from, it will have access to the identifiers in that closure.

Consider the important implications of this: when we call `globalFunc`, it has access to `blockVar` *despite the fact that we've exited that scope*. Normally, when a scope is exited, the variables declared in that scope can safely cease to exist. Here, JavaScript notes that a function is defined in that scope (and that function can be referenced outside of the scope), so it has to keep the scope around.

So defining a function within a closure can affect the closure's lifetime; it *also* allows us to access things we wouldn't normally have access to. Consider this example:

```
let f;                              // undefined function
{
    let o = { note: 'Safe' };
    f = function() {
        return o;
    }
}
let oRef = f();
oRef.note = "Not so safe after all!";
```

Normally, things that are out of scope are strictly inaccessible. Functions are special in that they allow us a window into scopes that are otherwise inaccessible. We'll see the importance of this in upcoming chapters.

## Immediately Invoked Function Expressions

In Chapter 6, we covered function expressions. Function expressions allow us to create something called an *immediately invoked function expression* (IIFE). An IIFE declares a function and then runs it immediately. Now that we have a solid understanding of scope and closures, we have the tools we need to understand why we might want to do such a thing. An IIFE looks like this:

```
(function() {
   // this is the IIFE body
})();
```

We create an anonymous function using a function expression, and then immediately call (invoke) that function. The advantage of the IIFE is that anything inside it has its own scope, and because it is a function, it can pass something out of the scope:

```
const message = (function() {
   const secret = "I'm a secret!";
   return `The secret is ${secret.length} characters long.`;
})();
console.log(message);
```

The variable `secret` is safe inside the scope of the IIFE, and can't be accessed from outside. You can return anything you want from an IIFE, and it's quite common to return arrays, objects, and functions. Consider a function that can report the number of times it's been called in a way that can't be tampered with:

```
const f = (function() {
   let count = 0;
   return function() {
      return `I have been called ${++count} time(s).`;
   }
})();
f();  // "I have been called 1 time(s)."
f();  // "I have been called 2 time(s)."
//...
```

Because the variable `count` is safely ensconced in the IIFE, there's no way to tamper with it: `f` will always have an accurate count of the number of times it's been called.

While block-scoped variables in ES6 have somewhat reduced the need for IIFEs, they are still quite commonly used, and are useful when you want to create a closure and return something out of it.

## Function Scope and Hoisting

Prior to ES6's introduction of `let`, variables were declared with `var` and had something called *function scope* (global variables declared with `var`, while not in an explicit function, share the same behavior).

When you declare a variable with `let`, it doesn't spring into existence until you declare it. When you declare a variable with `var`, it's available *everywhere in the current scope*...even before it's declared. Before we see an example, remember that there's a difference between a variable being undeclared and a variable that has the value `undefined`. Undeclared variables will result in an error, whereas variables that exist but have the value `undefined` will not:

```
let var1;
let var2 = undefined;
var1;                    // undefined
var2;                    // undefined
undefinedVar;            // ReferenceError: notDefined is not defined
```

With `let`, you will get an error if you try to use a variable before it's been declared:

```
x;              // ReferenceError: x is not defined
let x = 3;      // we'll never get here -- the error stops execution
```

Variables declared with `var`, on the other hand, can be referenced before they're declared:

```
x;              // undefined
var x = 3;
x;              // 3
```

So what's going on here? On the surface, it doesn't make sense that you should be able to access a variable before it's declared. Variables declared with `var` employ a mechanism called *hoisting*. JavaScript scans the entire scope (either a function or the global scope), and any variables declared with `var` are *hoisted* to the top. What's important to understand is that only the declaration—*not the assignment*—is hoisted. So JavaScript would interpret the previous example as:

```
var x;          // declaration (but not assignment) hoisted
x;              // undefined
x = 3;
x;              // 3
```

Let's look at a more complicated example, side by side with the way JavaScript interprets it:

```
// what you write                  // how JavaScript interprets it
                                   var x;
                                   var y;
if(x !== 3) {                      if(x !== 3) {
    console.log(y);                    console.log(y);
    var y = 5;                         y = 5;
    if(y === 5) {                      if(y === 5) {
        var x = 3;                         x = 3;
    }                                  }
    console.log(y);                    console.log(y);
}                                  }
if(x === 3) {                      if(x === 3) {
    console.log(y);                    console.log(y);
}                                  }
```

I'm not suggesting that this is well-written JavaScript—it's needlessly confusing and error-prone to use variables before you declare them (and there's no practical reason to do so). But this example does make clear how hoisting works.

Another aspect of variables declared with `var` is that JavaScript doesn't care if you repeat the definition:

```
// what you write            // how JavaScript interprets it
                             var x;
var x = 3;                   x = 3;
if(x === 3) {                if(x === 3) {
    var x = 2;                   x = 2;
    console.log(x);              console.log(x):
}                            }
console.log(x);              console.log(x);
```

This example should make it clear that (within the same function or global scope), `var` can't be used to create new variables, and variable masking doesn't happen as it does with `let`. In this example, there's only *one* variable `x`, even though there's a second `var` definition inside a block.

Again, this is not something I'm suggesting that you do: it only serves to confuse. The casual reader (especially one familiar with other languages) may glance at this example and reasonably assume that the author intended to create a new variable x whose scope is the block formed by the if statement, which is not what will happen.

If you are thinking "Why does var allow you to do these things that are confusing and useless?", you now understand why let came about. You can certainly use var in a responsible and clear fashion, but it's painfully easy to write code that is confusing and unclear. ES6 could not simply "fix" var, as that would break existing code; hence, let was introduced.

I cannot think of an example that uses var that could not be written better or more clearly using let. In other words, var offers no advantage over let, and many in the JavaScript community (including myself) believe that let will eventually completely replace var (it's even possible that var definitions will eventually become deprecated).

So why understand var and hoisting? For two reasons. First, ES6 will not be ubiquitous for some time, meaning code will have to be transcompiled to ES5, and of course much existing code is written in ES5. So for some time to come, it will still be important to understand how var works. Second, function declarations are also hoisted, which brings us to our next topic.

## Function Hoisting

Like variables declared with var, function declarations are hoisted to the top of their scope, allowing you to call functions before they're declared:

```
f();                         // logs "f"
function f() {
    console.log('f');
}
```

Note that function expressions that are assigned to variables are *not* hoisted; rather, they are subject to the scoping rules of variables. For example:

```
f();                         // TypeError: f is not a function
let f = function() {
    console.log('f');
}
```

## The Temporal Dead Zone

The *temporal dead zone* (TDZ) is a dramatic expression for the intuitive concept that variables declared with let don't exist until you declare them. Within a scope, the TDZ for a variable is the code before the variable is declared.

For the most part, this should cause no confusion or problems, but there is one aspect of the TDZ that will trip up people who are familiar with JavaScript prior to ES6.

The typeof operator is commonly used to determine if a variable has been declared, and is considered a "safe" way to test for existence. That is, prior to let and the TDZ, for any identifier x, this was always a safe operation that would not result in an error:

```
if(typeof x === "undefined") {
    console.log("x doesn't exist or is undefined");
} else {
    // safe to refer to x....
}
```

This code is no longer safe with variables declared with let. The following will result in an error:

```
if(typeof x === "undefined") {
    console.log("x doesn't exist or is undefined");
} else {
    // safe to refer to x....
}
let x = 5;
```

Checking whether or not variables are defined with typeof will be less necessary in ES6, so in practice, the behavior of typeof in the TDZ should not cause a problem.

## Strict Mode

The syntax of ES5 allowed for something called *implicit globals*, which have been the source of many frustrating programming errors. In short, if you forgot to declare a variable with var, JavaScript would merrily assume you were referring to a global variable. If no such global variable existed, it would create one! You can imagine the problems this caused.

For this (and other) reasons, JavaScript introduced the concept of *strict mode*, which would prevent implicit globals. Strict mode is enabled with the string "use strict" (you can use single or double quotes) on a line by itself, before any other code. If you do this in global scope, the entire script will execute in strict mode, and if you do it in a function, the function will execute in strict mode.

Because strict mode applies to the entire script if used in the global scope, you should use it with caution. Many modern websites combine various scripts together, and strict mode in the global scope of one will enable strict mode in all of them. While it would be nice if all scripts worked correctly in strict mode, not all of them do. So it's generally inadvisable to use strict mode in global scope. If you don't want to enable strict mode in every single function you write (and who would?), you can wrap all of your code in one function that's executed immediately (something we'll learn more about in Chapter 13):

```
(function() {
    'use strict';

    // all of your code goes here...it
    // is executed in strict mode, but
    // the strict mode won't contaminate
    // any other scripts that are combined
    // with this one

})();
```

Strict mode is generally considered a good thing, and I recommend you use it. If you're using a linter (and you should be), it will save you from many of the same problems, but doubling up can't hurt!

To learn more about what strict mode does, see the MDN article on strict mode (*https://developer.mozilla.org/en-US/docs/Web/JavaScript/Reference/Strict_mode*).

## Conclusion

Understanding scope is an important part of learning any programming language. The introduction of `let` brings JavaScript in line with most other modern languages. While JavaScript is not the first language to support closures, it is one of the first *popular* (nonacademic) languages to do so. The JavaScript community has used closures to great effect, and it's an important part of modern JavaScript development.

CHAPTER 8

# Arrays and Array Processing

JavaScript's array methods are among my favorite features of the language. So many programming problems involve the manipulation of collections of data, and fluency with JavaScript's array methods will make that easy. Getting comfortable with these methods is also a great way to attain the next level of JavaScript mastery.

## A Review of Arrays

Before we dive in, let's remind ourselves of the basics of arrays. Arrays (unlike objects) are inherently ordered, with zero-based numeric indices. Arrays in JavaScript can be *nonhomogeneous*, meaning the elements in an array do not need to be the same type (it follows from this that arrays can have other arrays as elements, or objects). Literal arrays are constructed with square brackets, and the same square brackets are used to access elements by index. Every array has a `length` property, which tells you how many elements are in the array. Assigning to an index that's larger than the array will automatically make the array larger, with unused indexes getting the value `undefined`. You can also use the `Array` constructor to create arrays, though this is seldom necessary. Make sure all of the following makes sense to you before you proceed:

```
// array literals
const arr1 = [1, 2, 3];                            // array of numbers
const arr2 = ["one", 2, "three"];                  // nonhomogeneous array
const arr3 = [[1, 2, 3], ["one", 2, "three"]];     // array containing arrays
const arr4 = [                                     // nonhomogeneous array
   { name: "Fred", type: "object", luckyNumbers = [5, 7, 13] },
   [
      { name: "Susan", type: "object" },
      { name: "Anthony", type: "object" },
   ],
   1,
```

```
    function() { return "arrays can contain functions too"; },
    "three",
];

// accessing elements
arr1[0];                    // 1
arr1[2];                    // 3
arr3[1];                    // ["one", 2, "three"]
arr4[1][0];                 // { name: "Susan", type: "object" }

// array length
arr1.length;                // 3
arr4.length;                // 5
arr4[1].length;             // 2

// increasing array size
arr1[4] = 5;
arr1;                       // [1, 2, 3, undefined, 5]
arr1.length;                // 5

// accessing (not assigning) an index larger than the array
// does *not* change the size of the array
arr2[10];                   // undefined
arr2.length;                // 3

// Array constructor (rarely used)
const arr5 = new Array();           // empty array
const arr6 = new Array(1, 2, 3);    // [1, 2, 3]
const arr7 = new Array(2);          // array of length 2 (all elements undefined)
const arr8 = new Array("2");        // ["2"]
```

## Array Content Manipulation

Before we get into the exciting methods, let's first consider the (very useful) methods for manipulating arrays. One aspect of array methods that is unfortunately confusing is the difference between methods that modify the array "in place" and those that return a new array. There's no convention, and this is just one of these things you have to memorize (for example, that `push` modifies an array in place but `concat` returns a new array).

Some languages, like Ruby, have conventions that make it easy to tell if a method modifies something in place or returns a copy. For example, in Ruby, if you have a string `str`, and you call `str.downcase`, it will return a lowercased version, but `str` will remain unchanged. On the other hand, if you call `str.downcase!`, it will modify `str` in place. The fact that the standard libraries in JavaScript offer no clue about which methods return a copy and which modify in place is, in my opinion, one of the language's shortcomings, requiring unnecessary memorization.

## Adding or Removing Single Elements at the Beginning or End

When we refer to the *beginning* (or *front*) of an array, we're referring to the first element (element 0). Likewise, the *end* (or *back*) of an array is the largest element (if our array is `arr`, element `arr.length-1`). `push` and `pop` add and remove, respectively, elements to the end of the array (in place). `shift` and `unshift` remove and add, respectively, elements to the beginning of the array (in place).

The names of these methods come from computer science terminology. `push` and `pop` are actions on a *stack*, where the important elements were the most recent ones added. `shift` and `unshift` treat the array like a *queue*, where the important elements are the oldest ones added.

`push` and `unshift` return the new length of the array after the new element has been added, and `pop` and `shift` return the element that was removed. Here are examples of these methods in action:

```
const arr = ["b", "c", "d"];
arr.push("e");                  // returns 4; arr is now ["b", "c", "d", "e"]
arr.pop();                      // returns "e"; arr is now ["b", "c", "d"]
arr.unshift("a");               // returns 4; arr is now ["a", "b", "c", "d"]
arr.shift();                    // returns "a"; arr is now ["b", "c", "d"]
```

## Adding Multiple Elements at the End

The `concat` method adds multiple elements to the array and returns a copy. If you pass `concat` arrays, it will break apart those arrays and add their elements to the original array. Examples:

```
const arr = [1, 2, 3];
arr.concat(4, 5, 6);           // returns [1, 2, 3, 4, 5, 6]; arr unmodified
arr.concat([4, 5, 6]);         // returns [1, 2, 3, 4, 5, 6]; arr unmodified
arr.concat([4, 5], 6);         // returns [1, 2, 3, 4, 5, 6]; arr unmodified
arr.concat([4, [5, 6]]);       // returns [1, 2, 3, 4, [5, 6]]; arr unmodified
```

Note that `concat` only breaks apart arrays you provide it directly; it does not break apart arrays inside those arrays.

## Getting a Subarray

If you want to get a subarray from an array, use `slice`. `slice` takes up to two arguments. The first argument is where the subarray begins, and the second argument is where the subarray ends (which does not include the specified character). If you omit the end argument, it returns everything up to the end of the string. This method allows you to use negative indices to refer to elements with respect to the end of the string, which is handy. Examples:

```
const arr = [1, 2, 3, 4, 5];
arr.slice(3);                 // returns [4, 5]; arr unmodified
arr.slice(2, 4);              // returns [3, 4]; arr unmodified
arr.slice(-2);                // returns [4, 5]; arr unmodified
arr.slice(1, -2);             // returns [2, 3]; arr unmodified
arr.slice(-2, -1);            // returns [4]; arr unmodified
```

## Adding or Removing Elements at Any Position

`splice` allows you to do in-place modification of the string, adding and/or removing elements from any index. The first argument is the index you want to start modifying; the second argument is the number of elements to remove (use `0` if you don't want to remove any elements), and the remaining arguments are the elements to be added. Examples:

```
const arr = [1, 5, 7];
arr.splice(1, 0, 2, 3, 4);    // returns []; arr is now [1, 2, 3, 4, 5, 7]
arr.splice(5, 0, 6);          // returns []; arr is now [1, 2, 3, 4, 5, 6, 7]
arr.splice(1, 2);             // returns [2, 3]; arr is now [1, 4, 5, 6, 7]
arr.splice(2, 1, 'a', 'b');   // returns [5]; arr is now [1, 4, 'a', 'b', 6, 7]
```

## Cutting and Replacing Within an Array

ES6 brings a new method, `copyWithin`, that takes a sequence of elements from an array and copies them, in place, to a different part of the array, overwriting whatever elements are there. The first argument is where to copy to (the target), the second argument is where to start copying from, and the final (optional) argument is where to stop copying from. As with `slice`, you can use negative numbers for the start and end indexes, and they count backward from the end of the array. Examples:

```
const arr = [1, 2, 3, 4];
arr.copyWithin(1, 2);         // arr is now [1, 3, 4, 4]
arr.copyWithin(2, 0, 2);      // arr is now [1, 3, 1, 3]
arr.copyWithin(0, -3, -1);    // arr is now [3, 1, 1, 3]
```

## Filling an Array with a Specific Value

ES6 brings a welcome new method, `fill`, which allows you to set any number of elements with a fixed value (in place). This is particularly useful when used with the `Array` constructor (which allows you to specify the initial size of the array). You can optionally specify a start and end index if you only want to fill part of the array (negative indexes work as expected). Examples:

```
const arr = new Array(5).fill(1);   // arr initialized to [1, 1, 1, 1, 1]
arr.fill("a");                      // arr is now ["a", "a", "a", "a", "a"]
arr.fill("b", 1);                   // arr is now ["a", "b", "b", "b", "b"]
arr.fill("c", 2, 4);                // arr is now ["a", "b", "c", "c", "b"]
arr.fill(5.5, -4);                  // arr is now ["a", 5.5, 5.5, 5.5, 5.5]
arr.fill(0, -3, -1);                // arr is now ["a", 5.5, 0, 0, 5.5]
```

## Reversing and Sorting Arrays

`reverse` is as simple as it gets; it reverses the order of the array in place:

```
const arr = [1, 2, 3, 4, 5];
arr.reverse();                      // arr is now [5, 4, 3, 2, 1]
```

`sort` sorts an array in place:

```
const arr = [5, 3, 2, 4, 1];
arr.sort();                         // arr is now [1, 2, 3, 4, 5]
```

`sort` also allows you to specify a *sort function*, which can come in quite handy. For example, there's no meaningful way to sort objects:

```
const arr = [{ name: "Suzanne" }, { name: "Jim" },
   { name: "Trevor" }, { name: "Amanda" }];
arr.sort();                                   // arr unchanged
arr.sort((a, b) => a.name > b.name);          // arr sorted alphabetically
                                              // by name property
arr.sort((a, b) => a.name[1] < b.name[1]); // arr sorted reverse alphabetically
                                              // by second letter of name property
```

In this example of `sort`, we're returning a boolean. However, `sort` accepts a number as a return value. If you return a `0`, `sort` will consider the two elements "equal," and leave their order intact. This would allow you, for example, to sort alphabetically except for words starting with the letter *k*; everything would be sorted alphabetically, with all *k* words coming after all *j* words, and before all *l* words, but the *k* words would be in their original order.

## Array Searching

If you want to find something in an array, you have a few choices. We'll start with the humble indexOf, which has been available in JavaScript for some time. indexOf simply returns the index of the first element it finds that is strictly equal to what you're looking for (there is a corresponding lastIndexOf that searches in the other direction, and returns the last index that matches what you're looking for). If you only want to search a portion of an array, you can specify an optional start index. If indexOf (or lastIndexOf) returns -1, it wasn't able to find a match:

```
const o = { name: "Jerry" };
const arr = [1, 5, "a", o, true, 5, [1, 2], "9"];
arr.indexOf(5);                    // returns 1
arr.lastIndexOf(5);                // returns 5
arr.indexOf("a");                  // returns 2
arr.lastIndexOf("a");              // returns 2
arr.indexOf({ name: "Jerry" });    // returns -1
arr.indexOf(o);                    // returns 3
arr.indexOf([1, 2]);               // returns -1
arr.indexOf("9");                  // returns 7
arr.indexOf(9);                    // returns -1

arr.indexOf("a", 5);               // returns -1
arr.indexOf(5, 5);                 // returns 5
arr.lastIndexOf(5, 4);             // returns 1
arr.lastIndexOf(true, 3);          // returns -1
```

Next up is findIndex, which is similar to indexOf in that it returns an index (or -1 if there's no match). findIndex is more flexible, though, in that you can provide a function that determines if an element is a match (findIndex doesn't have an option to start at an arbitrary index, nor is there a corresponding findLastIndex):

```
const arr = [{ id: 5, name: "Judith" }, { id: 7, name: "Francis" }];
arr.findIndex(o => o.id === 5);                // returns 0
arr.findIndex(o => o.name === "Francis");      // returns 1
arr.findIndex(o => o === 3);                   // returns -1
arr.findIndex(o => o.id === 17);               // returns -1
```

find and findIndex are great if you're looking for the index of an element. But what if you don't care about the index of the element, but just want the element itself? find is like findIndex in that it allows you to specify a function to find what you're looking for, but it returns the element itself instead of the index (or null if no such element was found):

```
const arr = [{ id: 5, name: "Judith" }, { id: 7, name: "Francis" }];
arr.find(o => o.id === 5);          // returns object { id: 5, name: "Judith" }
arr.find(o => o.id === 2);          // returns null
```

The functions that you pass to `find` and `findIndex`, in addition to receiving each element as their first argument, also receive the index of the current element and the whole array itself as arguments. This allows you to do things, for example, such as finding square numbers past a certain index:

```
const arr = [1, 17, 16, 5, 4, 16, 10, 3, 49];
arr.find((x, i) => i > 2 && Number.isInteger(Math.sqrt(x)));    // returns 4
```

`find` and `findIndex` also allow you to specify what to use for the `this` variable during the function invocation. This can be handy if you want to invoke a function as if it were a method of an object. Consider the following equivalent techniques for searching for a `Person` object by ID:

```
class Person {
   constructor(name) {
      this.name = name;
      this.id = Person.nextId++;
   }
}
Person.nextId = 0;
const jamie = new Person("Jamie"),
   juliet = new Person("Juliet"),
   peter = new Person("Peter"),
   jay = new Person("Jay");
const arr = [jamie, juliet, peter, jay];

// option 1: direct comparison of ID:
arr.find(p => p.id === juliet.id);          // returns juliet object

// option 2: using "this" arg:
arr.find(p => p.id === this.id, juliet);  // returns juliet object
```

You'll probably find limited use for specifying the `this` value in `find` and `findIndex`, but it's a technique that you'll see later, where it is more useful.

Just as we don't always care about the index of an element within an array, sometimes we don't care about the index *or* the element itself: we just want to know if it's there or isn't. Obviously we can use one of the preceding functions and check to see if it returns `-1` or `null`, but JavaScript provides two methods just for this purpose: `some` and `every`.

`some` returns `true` if it finds an element that meets the criteria (all it needs is one; it'll stop looking after it finds the first one), and `false` otherwise. Example:

```
const arr = [5, 7, 12, 15, 17];
arr.some(x => x%2===0);                        // true; 12 is even
arr.some(x => Number.isInteger(Math.sqrt(x)));  // false; no squares
```

every returns true if every element in the array passes the criteria, and false otherwise. every will stop looking and return false if it finds an element that doesn't match the criteria; otherwise, it will have to scan the entire array:

```
const arr = [4, 6, 16, 36];
arr.every(x => x%2===0);                          // true; no odd numbers
arr.every(x => Number.isInteger(Math.sqrt(x)));   // false; 6 is not square
```

Like all of the methods in this chapter that accept a method, some and every accept a second parameter that allows you to specify the value of this when the function is invoked.

## The Fundamental Array Operations: map and filter

Of all the array operations, the ones you'll find the most useful are map and filter. It's really quite remarkable what you can accomplish with these two methods.

map *transforms* the elements in the array. To what? That's the beauty: it's up to you. Do you have objects that contain numbers, but you really just need the numbers? Easy. Does your array contain functions, and you need promises? Easy. *Whenever the array is in one format and you need it in another, use* map. Both map and filter return copies, and do not modify the original array. Let's see some examples:

```
const cart = [ { name: "Widget", price: 9.95 }, { name: "Gadget", price: 22.95 }];
const names = cart.map(x => x.name);              // ["Widget", "Gadget"]
const prices = cart.map(x => x.price);            // [9.95, 22.95]
const discountPrices = prices.map(x => x*0.8);    // [7.96, 18.36]
const lcNames = names.map(String.toLowerCase);    // ["widget", "gadget"]
```

You may be wondering how lcNames is working: it doesn't look like the others. All of the methods we're discussing that take functions, including map, don't care how you pass the function in. In the case of names, prices, and discountPrices, we're constructing our own custom function (using the arrow notation). For lcNames, we're using a function that already exists, String.toLowerCase. This function takes a single string argument and returns the lowercased string. We could as easily have written names.map(x ⇒ x.toLowerCase()), but it's important to understand that a function is a function, no matter what form it takes.

When the function you provide gets called, it gets called for each element with three arguments: the element itself, the index of the element, and the array itself (which is seldom useful). Consider this example where we have our items and corresponding prices in two separate arrays, and we want to combine them:

```
const items = ["Widget", "Gadget"];
const prices = [9.95, 22.95];
const cart = items.map((x, i) => ({ name: x, price: prices[i]}));
// cart: [{ name: "Widget", price: 9.95 }, { name: "Gadget", price: 22.95 }]
```

This example is a little more sophisticated, but it demonstrates the power of the `map` function. Here, we're using not just the element itself (`x`), but its index (`i`). We need the index because we want to correlate elements in `items` with elements in `prices` according to their index. Here, `map` is converting an array of strings to an array of objects, by pulling in information from a separate array. (Note that we had to surround the object in parentheses; without the parentheses, the arrow notation will take the curly braces to denote a block.)

`filter`, as the name implies, is designed to remove unwanted things from an array. Like `map`, it returns a new array with elements removed. What elements? Again, that's completely up to you. If you guessed that we're providing a function to determine which elements to remove, you're catching on. Let's see some examples:

```
// create a deck of playing cards
const cards = [];
for(let suit of ['H', 'C', 'D', 'S']) // hearts, clubs, diamonds, spades
   for(let value=1; value<=13; value++)
      cards.push({ suit, value });

// get all cards with value 2:
cards.filter(c => c.value === 2);    // [
                                     //    { suit: 'H', value: 2 },
                                     //    { suit: 'C', value: 2 },
                                     //    { suit: 'D', value: 2 },
                                     //    { suit: 'S', value: 2 }
                                     // ]

// (for the following, we will just list length, for compactness)

// get all diamonds:
cards.filter(c => c.suit === 'D');                // length: 13

// get all face cards
cards.filter(c => c.value > 10);                  // length: 12

// get all face cards that are hearts
cards.filter(c => c.value > 10 && c.suit === 'H'); // length: 3
```

Hopefully you can start to see how `map` and `filter` can be combined to great effect. For example, let's say we want to create short string representation of the cards in our deck. We'll use the Unicode code points for the suits, and we'll use "A," "J," "Q," and "Q" for ace and the face cards. Because the function that constructs this is a bit long, we'll go ahead and create it as a separate function instead of trying to use an anonymous function:

```
function cardToString(c) {
   const suits = { 'H': '\u2665', 'C': '\u2663', 'D': '\u2666', 'S': '\u2660' };
   const values = { 1: 'A', 11: 'J', 12: 'Q', 13: 'K' };
   // constructing values each time we call cardToString is not very
   // efficient; a better solution is a reader's exercise
```

```
    for(let i=2; i<=10; i++) values[i] = i;
    return values[c.value] + suits[c.suit];
}

// get all cards with value 2:
cards.filter(c => c.value === 2)
    .map(cardToString);    // [ "2♥", "2♣", "2♦", "2♠" ]

// get all face cards that are hearts
cards.filter(c => c.value > 10 && c.suit === 'H')
    .map(cardToString);    // [ "J♥", "Q♥", "K♥" ]
```

## Array Magic: reduce

Of all the array methods, my favorite is `reduce`. Where `map` transforms each element in the array, `reduce` transforms the *entire array*. It's called `reduce` because it's often used to reduce the array to a single value. For example, summing the numbers in an array or calculating the average is a way of reducing the array to a single value. However, the single value `reduce` provides can be an object or another array—as a matter of fact, `reduce` is capable of reproducing the functionality of `map` and `filter` (or, for that matter, any other array function we've discussed).

`reduce`—like `map` and `filter`—allows you to provide a function that controls the outcome. In the callbacks we've dealt with heretofore, the first element passed into the callback is always the current array element. Not so with `reduce`: the first value is an *accumulator*, which is what the array is being reduced to. The rest of the arguments are what you would expect: the current array element, the current index, and the array itself.

In addition to taking a callback, `reduce` takes an (optional) initial value for the accumulator. Let's look at a simple example—summing the numbers in an array:

```
const arr = [5, 7, 2, 4];
const sum = arr.reduce((a, x) => a += x, 0);
```

The function being passed into `reduce` takes two parameters: the accumulator (`a`) and the current array element (`x`). In this example, we're starting the accumulator off with a value of `0`. Because this is our first experience with `reduce`, let's walk through the steps JavaScript takes so we understand how it's working:

1. The (anonymous) function is called for the first array element (`5`). `a` has the initial value `0`, and `x` has the value `5`. The function returns the sum of `a` and `x` (`5`), which will become the value of `a` in the next step.
2. The function is called for the second array element (`7`). `a` has the initial value `5` (passed in from the previous step), and `x` has the value `7`. The function returns the sum of `a` and `x` (`12`), which will become the value of `a` in the next step.

3. The function is called for the third array element (`2`). `a` has the initial value `12`, and `x` has the value `2`. The function returns the sum of `a` and `x` (`14`).
4. The function is called for the fourth and final array element (`4`). `a` has the value `14`, and `x` has the value `4`. The function returns the sum of `a` and `x` (`18`), which is the return value of `reduce` (which is then assigned to `sum`).

The astute reader might realize that—in this very simple example—we don't even need to assign to `a`; what's important is what's returned from the function (remember that the arrow notation doesn't require an explicit `return` statement), so we could have just returned `a + x`. However, in more sophisticated examples, you might want to do more with the accumulator, so it's a good habit to get into to modify the accumulator inside the function.

Before we move on to more interesting applications of `reduce`, let's consider what happens if the initial accumulator is `undefined`. In this case, `reduce` takes the first array element as the initial value and starts calling the function with the second element. Let's revisit our example, and omit the initial value:

```
const arr = [5, 7, 2, 4];
const sum = arr.reduce((a, x) => a += x);
```

1. The (anonymous) function is called for the *second* array element (`7`). `a` has the initial value `5` (the first array element), and `x` has the value `7`. The function returns the sum of `a` and `x` (`12`), which will become the value of `a` in the next step.
2. The function is called for the third array element (`2`). `a` has the initial value `12`, and `x` has the value `2`. The function returns the sum of `a` and `x` (`14`).
3. The function is called for the fourth and final array element (`4`). `a` has the value `14`, and `x` has the value `4`. The function returns the sum of `a` and `x` (`18`), which is the return value of `reduce` (which is then assigned to `sum`).

You can see that there is one fewer step, but the outcome is the same. In this example (and in any case where the first element can serve as the initial value of the accumulator), we can benefit from omitting the initial value.

Using an atomic value (a number or string) as the accumulator is a common use for `reduce`, but using an object as an accumulator is a very powerful (and often overlooked) method. For example, if you have an array of strings, and you want to group the strings into alphabetic arrays (*A* words, *B* words, etc.), you can use an object:

```
const words = ["Beachball", "Rodeo", "Angel",
    "Aardvark", "Xylophone", "November", "Chocolate",
    "Papaya", "Uniform", "Joker", "Clover", "Bali"];
const alphabetical = words.reduce((a, x) => {
    if(!a[x[0]]) a[x[0]] = [];
    a[x[0]].push(x);
    return a; }, {});
```

This example is a little more involved, but the principle is the same. For every element in the array, the function checks the accumulator to see if it has a property for the first letter in the word; if not, it adds an empty array (when it sees `"Beachball"`, there is no property `a.B`, so it creates one whose value is an empty array). It then adds the word to the appropriate array (which may have just been created), and finally, the accumulator (`a`) is returned (remember the value you *return* is used as the accumulator for the next element in the array).

Another example is computational statistics. For example, to calculate the mean and variation of a data set:

```
const data = [3.3, 5, 7.2, 12, 4, 6, 10.3];
// Donald Knuth's algorithm for calculating variance:
// Art of Computer Programming, Vol. 2: Seminumerical Algorithms, 3rd Ed., 1998
const stats = data.reduce((a, x) => {
        a.N++;
        let delta = x - a.mean;
        a.mean += delta/a.N;
        a.M2 += delta*(x - a.mean);
        return a;
    }, { N: 0, mean: 0, M2: 0 });
if(stats.N > 2) {
    stats.variance = stats.M2 / (stats.N - 1);
    stats.stdev = Math.sqrt(stats.variance);
}
```

Again, we're leveraging an object as the accumulator because we need multiple variables (`mean` and `M2`, specifically: we could have used the index argument—minus one—in place of `N` if we had wanted to).

We'll see one last (and very silly) example to drive home the flexibility of `reduce` by using an accumulator type we haven't used yet—a string:

```
const words = ["Beachball", "Rodeo", "Angel",
    "Aardvark", "Xylophone", "November", "Chocolate",
    "Papaya", "Uniform", "Joker", "Clover", "Bali"];
const longWords = words.reduce((a, w) => w.length>6 ? a+" "+w : a, "").trim();
// longWords: "Beachball Aardvark Xylophone November Chocolate Uniform"
```

Here we're using a string accumulator to get a single string containing all words longer than six letters. As a reader's exercise, try rewriting this using `filter` and `join` (a string method) instead of `reduce`. (Start by asking yourself why we need to call `trim` after the `reduce`.)

Hopefully the power of `reduce` is dawning on you. Of all the array methods, it's the most general and powerful.

## Array Methods and Deleted or Never-Defined Elements

One behavior of the `Array` methods that often trips people up is the way they treat elements that have never been defined or have been deleted. `map`, `filter`, and `reduce` *do not invoke the function for elements that have never been assigned or have been deleted.* For example, before ES6, if you tried to be clever and initialize an array this way, you would be disappointed:

```
const arr = Array(10).map(function(x) { return 5 });
```

`arr` would still be an array with 10 elements, all `undefined`. Similarly, if you delete an element from the middle of an array, and then call `map`, you'll get an array with a "hole" in it:

```
const arr = [1, 2, 3, 4, 5];
delete arr[2];
arr.map(x => 0);     // [0, 0, <1 empty slot>, 0, 0]
```

In practice, this is seldom a problem because you're normally working with arrays whose elements have been explicitly set (and unless you explicitly want a gap in an array, which is rare, you won't use `delete` on an array), but it's good to be aware of.

## String Joining

Very often, you simply want to join the (string) value of the elements in an array together with some separator. `Array.prototype.join` takes a single argument, the separator (which defaults to a comma if you omit it), and returns a string with the elements joined together (including never-defined and deleted elements, which become empty strings; `null` and `undefined` also become empty strings):

```
const arr = [1, null, "hello", "world", true, undefined];
delete arr[3];
arr.join();         // "1,,hello,,true,"
arr.join('');       // "1hellotrue"
arr.join(' -- '); // "1 -- -- hello -- -- true --"
```

If used cleverly—and combined with string concatenation—`Array.prototype.join` can be used to create things like HTML `<ul>` lists:

```
const attributes = ["Nimble", "Perceptive", "Generous"];
const html = '<ul><li>' + attributes.join('</li><li>') + '</li></ul>';
// html: "<ul><li>Nimble</li><li>Perceptive</li><li>Generous</li></ul>";
```

Be careful you don't do this on an empty array: you'll end up with a single empty `<li>` element!

## Conclusion

There's a lot of power and flexibility built into the JavaScript's `Array` class, but it can sometimes be daunting to know which method to use when. Tables 8-1 through 8-4 summarize `Array` functionality.

For `Array.prototype` methods that take a function (`find`, `findIndex`, `some`, `every`, `map`, `filter`, and `reduce`), the function that you provide receives the arguments shown in Table 8-1 for each element in the array.

*Table 8-1. Array function arguments (in order)*

| Method | Description |
|---|---|
| `reduce` only | Accumulator (initial value, or return value of last invocation) |
| all | Element (value of current element) |
| all | Index of current element |
| all | Array itself (rarely useful) |

All `Array.prototype` methods that take a function also take an (optional) value of `this` to be used when the functions are invoked, allowing you to invoke the function as if it were a method.

*Table 8-2. Array content manipulation*

| When you need to… | Use… | In-place or copy |
|---|---|---|
| Create a stack (last-in, first-out [LIFO]) | `push` (returns new length), `pop` | In-place |
| Create a queue (first-in, first-out [FIFO]) | `unshift` (returns new length), `shift` | In-place |
| Add multiple elements at end | `concat` | Copy |
| Get subarray | `slice` | Copy |
| Add or remove elements at any position | `splice` | In-place |
| Cut and replace within an array | `copyWithin` | In-place |
| Fill an array | `fill` | In-place |

| When you need to... | Use... | In-place or copy |
| --- | --- | --- |
| Reverse an array | `reverse` | In-place |
| Sort an array | `sort` (pass in function for custom sort) | In-place |

*Table 8-3. Array searching*

| When you want to know/find... | Use... |
| --- | --- |
| The index of an item | `indexOf` (simple values), `findIndex` (complex values) |
| The last index of an item | `lastIndexOf` (simple values) |
| The item itself | `find` |
| Whether the array has an item that matches some criteria | `some` |
| Whether all elements in the array matches some criteria | `every` |

*Table 8-4. Array transformation*

| When you want to... | Use... | In-place or copy |
| --- | --- | --- |
| Transform every element in an array | `map` | Copy |
| Eliminate elements from an array based on some criteria | `filter` | Copy |
| Transform an entire array into another data type | `reduce` | Copy |
| Convert elements to strings and join together | `join` | Copy |

CHAPTER 9

# Objects and Object-Oriented Programming

We covered the basics of objects in Chapter 3, but now it's time to take a deeper look at objects in JavaScript.

Like arrays, objects in JavaScript are *containers* (also called *aggregate* or *complex data types*). Objects have two primary differences from arrays:

- Arrays contain values, indexed numerically; objects contain properties, indexed by string or symbol.
- Arrays are ordered (`arr[0]` always comes before `arr[1]`); objects are not (you can't guarantee `obj.a` comes before `obj.b`).

These differences are pretty esoteric (but important), so let's think about the property (no pun intended) that makes objects really special. A *property* consists of a *key* (a string or symbol) and a *value*. What makes objects special is that you can access properties by their key.

## Property Enumeration

In general, if you want to list out the contents of the container (called *enumeration*), you probably want an array, not an object. But objects are containers, and do support property enumeration; you just need to be aware of the special complexities involved.

The first thing you need to remember about property enumeration is that *order isn't guaranteed*. You might do some testing and find that you get properties out in the order in which you put them in, and that may be true for many implementations *most of the time*. However, JavaScript explicitly offers no guarantee on this, and implementations may change at any time for reasons of efficiency. So don't be lulled into a false sense of security by anecdotal testing: *never* assume a given order of enumeration for properties.

With that warning out of the way, let's now consider the primary ways to enumerate an object's properties.

## for...in

The traditional way to enumerate the properties of an object is `for...in`. Consider an object that has some string properties and a lone symbol property:

```
const SYM = Symbol();

const o = { a: 1, b: 2, c: 3, [SYM]: 4 };

for(let prop in o) {
  if(!o.hasOwnProperty(prop)) continue;
  console.log(`${prop}: ${o[prop]}`);
}
```

This seems pretty straightforward...except you are probably reasonably wondering what `hasOwnProperty` does. This addresses a danger of the `for...in` loop that won't be clear until later in this chapter: inherited properties. In this example, you could omit it, and it wouldn't make a difference. However, if you're enumerating the properties of other types of objects—especially objects that originated elsewhere—you may find properties you didn't expect. I encourage you to make it a habit to use `hasOwnProperty`. We'll soon learn why it's important, and you'll have the knowledge to determine when it's safe (or desirable) to omit.

Note that the `for...in` loop doesn't include properties with symbol keys.

While it's possible to use `for...in` to iterate over an array, it's generally considered a bad idea. I recommend using a regular `for` loop or `forEach` for arrays.

## Object.keys

`Object.keys` gives us a way to get all of the enumerable string properties of an object as an array:

```
const SYM = Symbol();

const o = { a: 1, b: 2, c: 3, [SYM]: 4 };

Object.keys(o).forEach(prop => console.log(`${prop}: ${o[prop]}`));
```

This example produces the same result as a `for...in` loop (and we don't have to check `hasOwnProperty`). It's handy whenever you need the property keys of an object as an array. For example, it makes it easy to list all the properties of an object that start with the letter *x*:

```
const o = { apple: 1, xochitl: 2, balloon: 3, guitar: 4, xylophone: 5, };

Object.keys(o)
  .filter(prop => prop.match(/^x/))
  .forEach(prop => console.log(`${prop}: ${o[prop]}`));
```

# Object-Oriented Programming

Object-oriented programming (OOP) is an old paradigm in computer science. Some of the concepts we now know as OOP begin to appear in the 1950s, but it wasn't until the introduction of Simula 67 and then Smalltalk that a recognizable form of OOP emerged.

The basic idea is simple and intuitive: an *object* is a logically related collection of data and functionality. It's designed to reflect our natural understanding of the world. A *car* is an object that has data (make, model, number of doors, VIN, etc.) and functionality (accelerate, shift, open doors, turn on headlights, etc.). Furthermore, OOP makes it possible to think about things abstractly (*a* car) and concretely (a *specific* car).

Before we dive in, let's cover the basic vocabulary of OOP. A *class* refers to a generic thing (*a* car). An *instance* (or *object instance*) refers to a specific thing (a *specific* car, such as "My Car"). A piece of functionality (accelerate) is called a *method*. A piece of functionality that is related to the class, but doesn't refer to a specific instance, is called a *class method* (for example, "create new VIN" might be a class method: it doesn't yet refer to a specific new car, and certainly we don't expect a specific car to have the knowledge or ability to create a new, valid VIN). When an instance is first created, its *constructor* runs. The constructor initializes the object instance.

OOP also gives us a framework for hierarchically categorizing classes. For example, there could be a more generic *vehicle* class. A vehicle may have a *range* (the distance it can go without refueling or recharging), but unlike a car, it might not have wheels (a boat is an example of a vehicle that probably doesn't have wheels). We say that vehicle is a *superclass* of car, and that car is a *subclass* of vehicle. The vehicle class may have multiple subclasses: cars, boats, planes, motorcycles, bicycles, and so on. And subclasses may, in turn, have additional subclasses. For example, the boat subclass may have further subclasses of sailboat, rowboat, canoe, tugboat, motorboat, and so on.

We'll use the example of a car throughout this chapter, as it's a real-world object we can probably all relate to (even if we don't participate in the car culture).

## Class and Instance Creation

Prior to ES6, creating a class in JavaScript was a fussy, unintuitive affair. ES6 introduces some convenient new syntax for creating classes:

```
class Car {
   constructor() {
   }
}
```

This establishes a new class called `Car`. No instances (specific cars) have been created yet, but we have the ability to do so now. To create a specific car, we use the `new` keyword:

```
const car1 = new Car();
const car2 = new Car();
```

We now have two instances of class `Car`. Before we make the `Car` class more sophisticated, let's consider the `instanceof` operator, which can tell you if a given object is an instance of a given class:

```
car1 instanceof Car        // true
car1 instanceof Array      // false
```

From this we can see that `car1` is an instance of `Car`, not `Array`.

Let's make the `Car` class a little more interesting. We'll give it some data (make, model), and some functionality (shift):

```
class Car {
   constructor(make, model) {
      this.make = make;
      this.model = model;
      this.userGears = ['P', 'N', 'R', 'D'];
      this.userGear = this.userGears[0];
   }
   shift(gear) {
      if(this.userGears.indexOf(gear) < 0)
         throw new Error(`Invalid gear: ${gear}`);
      this.userGear = gear;
   }
}
```

Here the `this` keyword is used for its intended purpose: to refer to the instance the method was invoked on. You can think of it as a placeholder: when you're writing your class—which is abstract—the `this` keyword is a placeholder for a *specific* instance, which will be known by the time the method is invoked. This constructor allows us to specify the make and model of the car when we create it, and it also sets up some defaults: the valid gears (`userGears`) and the current gear (`gear`), which we initialize to the first valid gear. (I chose to call these *user* gears because if this car has an automatic transmission, when the car is in drive, there will be an actual mechanical gear, which may be different.) In addition to the constructor—which is called implicitly when we create a new object—we also created a method `shift`, which allows us to change to a valid gear. Let's see it in action:

```
const car1 = new Car("Tesla", "Model S");
const car2 = new Car("Mazda", "3i");
car1.shift('D');
car2.shift('R');
```

In this example, when we invoke `car1.shift('D')`, `this` is bound to `car1`. Similarly, in `car2.shift('R')`, it's bound to `car2`. We can verify that `car1` is in drive (D) and `car2` is in reverse (R):

```
> car1.userGear      // "D"
> car2.userGear      // "R"
```

## Dynamic Properties

It may seem very clever that the `shift` method of our `Car` class prevents us from inadvertently selecting an invalid gear. However, this protection is limited because there's nothing to stop you from setting it directly: `car1.userGear = 'X'`. Most OO languages go to great lengths to provide mechanisms to protect against this kind of abuse by allowing you to specify the access level of methods and properties. JavaScript has no such mechanism, which is a frequent criticism of the language.

Dynamic properties[1] can help mitigate this weakness. They have the semantics of a property with the functionality of a method. Let's modify our `Car` class to take advantage of that:

```
class Car {
   constructor(make, model) {
      this.make = make;
      this.model = model;
      this._userGears = ['P', 'N', 'R', 'D'];
      this._userGear = this._userGears[0];
   }

   get userGear() { return this._userGear; }
   set userGear(value) {
      if(this._userGears.indexOf(value) < 0)
         throw new Error(`Invalid gear: ${value}`);
      this._userGear = vaule;
   }

   shift(gear) { this.userGear = gear; }
}
```

1 Dynamic properties are more correctly called *accessor properties*, which we'll learn more about in Chapter 21.

The astute reader will note that we haven't eliminated the problem as we can still set _userGear directly: car1._userGear = 'X'. In this example, we're using "poor man's access restriction"—prefixing properties we consider private with an underscore. This is protection by convention only, allowing you to quickly spot code that's accessing properties that it shouldn't be.

If you really need to enforce privacy, you can use an instance of WeakMap (see Chapter 10) that's protected by scope (if we don't use WeakMap, our private properties will never go out of scope, even if the instances they refer to do). Here's how we can modify our Car class to make the underlying current gear property truly private:

```
const Car = (function() {

   const carProps = new WeakMap();

   class Car {
      constructor(make, model) {
         this.make = make;
         this.model = model;
         this._userGears = ['P', 'N', 'R', 'D'];
         carProps.set(this, { userGear: this._userGears[0] });
      }

      get userGear() { return carProps.get(this).userGear; }
      set userGear(value) {
         if(this._userGears.indexOf(value) < 0)
            throw new Error(`Invalid gear: ${value}`);
         carProps.get(this).userGear = value;
      }

      shift(gear) { this.userGear = gear; }
   }

   return Car;
})();
```

Here we're using an immediately invoked function expression (see Chapter 13) to ensconce our WeakMap in a closure that can't be accessed by the outside world. That WeakMap can then safely store any properties that we don't want accessed outside of the class.

Another approach is to use symbols as property names; they also provide a measure of protection from accidental use, but the symbol properties in a class can be accessed, meaning even this approach can be circumvented.

## Classes Are Functions

Prior to the class keyword introduced in ES6, to create a class you would create a function that served as the class constructor. While the class syntax is much more intuitive and straightforward, under the hood the nature of classes in JavaScript hasn't changed (`class` just adds some syntactic sugar), so it's important to understand how a class is represented in JavaScript.

A class is really just a function. In ES5, we would have started our `Car` class like this:

```
function Car(make, model) {
   this.make = make;
   this.model = model;
   this._userGears = ['P', 'N', 'R', 'D'];
   this._userGear = this.userGears[0];
}
```

We can still do this in ES6: the outcome is exactly the same (we'll get to methods in a bit). We can verify that by trying it both ways:

```
class Es6Car {}          // we'll omit the constructor for brevity
function Es5Car {}
> typeof Es6Car          // "function"
> typeof Es5Car          // "function"
```

So nothing's really new in ES6; we just have some handy new syntax.

## The Prototype

When you refer to methods that are available on instances of a class, you are referring to *prototype* methods. For example, when talking about the `shift` method that's available on `Car` instances, you're referring to a prototype method, and you will often see it written `Car.prototype.shift`. (Similarly, the `forEach` function of `Array` would be written `Array.prototype.forEach`.) Now it's time to actually learn what the prototype *is*, and how JavaScript performs *dynamic dispatch* using the *prototype chain*.

Using a number sign (#) has emerged as a popular convention for describing prototype methods. For example, you will often see `Car.prototype.shift` written simply as `Car#shift`.

Every function has a special property called `prototype`. (You can vary this for any function `f` by typing **`f.prototype`** at the console.) For regular functions, the prototype isn't used, but it's critically important for functions that act as object constructors.

By convention, object constructors (aka classes) are always named with a capital letter—for example, `Car`. This convention is not enforced in any way, but many linters will warn you if you try to name a function with a capital letter, or an object constructor with a lowercase letter.

A function's `prototype` property becomes important when you create a new instance with the `new` keyword: the newly created object has access to its constructor's `prototype` object. The object instance stores this in its `__proto__` property.

The `__proto__` property is considered part of JavaScript's plumbing—as is any property that's surrounded by double underscores. You can do some very, very wicked things with these properties. Occasionally, there is a clever and valid use for them, but until you have a thorough understanding of JavaScript, I highly recommend you look at but don't touch these properties.

What's important about the prototype is a mechanism called *dynamic dispatch* ("dispatch" is another word for method invocation). When you attempt to access a property or method on an object, if it doesn't exist, JavaScript *checks the object's prototype* to see if it exists there. Because all instances of a given class share the same prototype, if there is a property or method on the prototype, all instances of that class have access to that property or method.

Setting data properties in a class's prototype is generally not done. All instances share that property's value, but if that value is *set* on any instance, it's set on that instance—not on the prototype, which can lead to confusion and bugs. If you need instances to have initial data values, it's better to set them in the constructor.

Note that defining a method or property on an instance will override the version in the prototype; remember that JavaScript first checks the instance before checking the prototype. Let's see all of this in action:

```
// class Car as defined previously, with shift method
const car1 = new Car();
const car2 = new Car();
car1.shift === Car.prototype.shift;      // true
car1.shift('D');
car1.shift('d');                         // error
car1.userGear;                           // 'D'
car1.shift === car2.shift                // true

car1.shift = function(gear) { this.userGear = gear.toUpperCase(); }
car1.shift === Car.prototype.shift;      // false
car1.shift === car2.shift;               // false
car1.shift('d');
car1.userGear;                           // 'D'
```

This example clearly demonstrates the way JavaScript performs dynamic dispatch. Initially, the object `car1` doesn't have a method `shift`, but when you call `car1.shift('D')`, JavaScript looks at the prototype for `car1` and finds a method of that name. When we replace `shift` with our own home-grown version, both `car1` and its prototype have a method of this name. When we invoke `car1.shift('d')`, we are now invoking the method on `car1`, not its prototype.

Most of the time, you won't have to understand the mechanics of the prototype chain and dynamic dispatch, but every once in a while, you'll run into a problem that will require you to dig deeper—and then it's good to know the details about what's going on.

## Static Methods

So far, the methods we've considered are *instance methods*. That is, they are designed to be useful against a specific instance. There are also *static methods* (or *class methods*), which do not apply to a specific instance. In a static method, `this` is bound to the class itself, but it's generally considered best practice to use the name of the class instead of `this`.

Static methods are used to perform generic tasks that are related to the class, but not any specific instance. We'll use the example of car VINs (vehicle identification numbers). It doesn't make sense for an individual car to be able to generate its own VIN: what would stop a car from using the same VIN as another car? However, assigning a VIN is an abstract concept that is related to the idea of cars in general; hence, it's a candidate to be a static method. Also, static methods are often used for methods that operate on multiple vehicles. For example, we may wish to have a method called `areSimilar` that returns `true` if two cars have the same make and model and `areSame` if two cars have the same VIN. Let's see these static methods implemented for `Car`:

```
class Car {
   static getNextVin() {
      return Car.nextVin++;     // we could also use this.nextVin++
                                // but referring to Car emphasizes
                                // that this is a static method
   }
   constructor(make, model) {
      this.make = make;
      this.model = model;
      this.vin = Car.getNextVin();
   }
   static areSimilar(car1, car2) {
      return car1.make===car2.make && car1.model===car2.model;
   }
   static areSame(car1, car2) {
      return car1.vin===car2.vin;
   }
}
Car.nextVin = 0;

const car1 = new Car("Tesla", "S");
```

```
const car2 = new Car("Mazda", "3");
const car3 = new Car("Mazda", "3");

car1.vin;       // 0
car2.vin;       // 1
car3.vin        // 2

Car.areSimilar(car1, car2);      // false
Car.areSimilar(car2, car3);      // true
Car.areSame(car2, car3);         // false
Car.areSame(car2, car2);         // true
```

## Inheritance

In understanding the prototype, we've already seen an inheritance of a sort: when you create an instance of a class, it inherits whatever functionality is in the class's prototype. It doesn't stop there, though: if a method isn't found on an object's prototype, it checks the *prototype's* prototype. In this way, a *prototype chain* is established. JavaScript will walk up the prototype chain until it finds a prototype that satisfies the request. If it can find no such prototype, it will finally error out.

Where this comes in handy is being able to create class hierarchies. We've already discussed how a car is generically a type of vehicle. The prototype chain allows us to assign functionality where it's most appropriate. For example, a car might have a method called `deployAirbags`. We could consider this a method of a generic vehicle, but have you ever been on a boat with an airbag? On the other hand, almost all vehicles can carry passengers, so a vehicle might have an `addPassenger` method (which could throw an error if the passenger capacity is exceeded). Let's see how this scenario is written in JavaScript:

```
class Vehicle {
   constructor() {
      this.passengers = [];
      console.log("Vehicle created");
   }
   addPassenger(p) {
      this.passengers.push(p);
   }
}

class Car extends Vehicle {
   constructor() {
      super();
      console.log("Car created");
   }
   deployAirbags() {
      console.log("BWOOSH!");
   }
}
```

The first new thing we see is the `extends` keyword; this syntax marks `Car` as a subclass of `Vehicle`. The second thing that you haven't seen before is the call to `super()`. This is a special function in JavaScript that invokes the superclass's constructor. This is required for subclasses; you will get an error if you omit it.

Let's see this example in action:

```
const v = new Vehicle();
v.addPassenger("Frank");
v.addPassenger("Judy");
v.passengers;                   // ["Frank", "Judy"]
const c = new Car();
c.addPassenger("Alice");
c.addPassenger("Cameron");
c.passengers;                   // ["Alice", "Cameron"]
v.deployAirbags();              // error
c.deployAirbags();              // "BWOOSH!"
```

Note that we can call `deployAirbags` on `c`, but not on `v`. In other words, inheritance works only one way. Instances of the `Car` class can access all methods of the `Vehicle` class, but not the other way around.

## Polymorphism

The intimidating word *polymorphism* is OO parlance for treating an instance as a member of not only its own class, but also any superclasses. In many OO languages, polymorphism is something special that OOP brings to the table. In JavaScript, which is not typed, any object can be used anywhere (though that doesn't guarantee correct results), so in a way, JavaScript has the ultimate polymorphism.

Very often in JavaScript, the code you write employs some form of *duck typing*. This technique comes from the expression "if it walks like a duck, and quacks like a duck...it's probably a duck." To use our `Car` example, if you have an object that has a `deployAirbags` method, you might reasonably conclude that it's an instance of `Car`. That may or may not be true, but it's a pretty strong hint.

JavaScript does provide the `instanceof` operator, which will tell you if an object is an instance of a given class. It can be fooled, but as long as you leave the `prototype` and `__proto__` properties alone, it can be relied upon:

```
class Motorcycle extends Vehicle {}
const c = new Car();
const m = new Motorcyle();
c instanceof Car;           // true
c instanceof Vehicle;       // true
m instanceof Car;           // false
m instanceof Motorcycle;    // true
m instanceof Vehicle;       // true
```

All objects in JavaScript are instances of the root class `Object`. That is, for any object `o`, `o instanceof Object` will be true (unless you explicitly set its `__proto__` property, which you should avoid). This has little practical consequence to you; it's primarily to provide some important methods that all objects must have, such as `toString`, which is covered later in this chapter.

## Enumerating Object Properties, Revisited

We've already seen how we can enumerate the properties in an object with `for...in`. Now that we understand prototypal inheritance, we can fully appreciate the use of `hasOwnProperty` when enumerating the proprties of an object. For an object `obj` and a property `x`, `obj.hasOwnProperty(x)` will return `true` if `obj` has the property `x`, and `false` if the property isn't defined or is defined in the prototype chain.

If you use ES6 classes as they're intended to be used, data properties will always be defined on instances, not in the prototype chain. However, because there's nothing to prevent adding properties directly to the prototype, it's always best to use `hasOwnProperty` to be sure. Consider this example:

```
class Super {
   constructor() {
      this.name = 'Super';
      this.isSuper = true;
   }
}

// this is valid, but not a good idea...
Super.prototype.sneaky = 'not recommended!';

class Sub extends Super {
   constructor() {
      super();
      this.name = 'Sub';
      this.isSub = true;
   }
}

const obj = new Sub();

for(let p in obj) {
   console.log(`${p}: ${obj[p]}` +
      (obj.hasOwnProperty(p) ? '' : ' (inherited)'));
}
```

If you run this program, you will see:

```
name: Sub
isSuper: true
isSub: true
sneaky: not recommended! (inherited)
```

The properties `name`, `isSuper`, and `isSub` are all defined on the instance, not in the prototype chain (note that properties declared in the superclass constructor are defined on the subclass instance as well). The property `sneaky`, on the other hand, was manually added to the superclass's prototype.

You can avoid this issue altogether by using `Object.keys`, which includes only properties defined on the prototype.

## String Representation

Every object ultimately inherits from `Object`, so the methods available on `Object` are by default available for all objects. One of those methods is `toString`, whose purpose is to provide a default string representation of an object. The default behavior of `toString` is to return `"[object Object]"`, which isn't particularly useful.

Having a `toString` method that says something descriptive about an object can be useful for debugging, allowing you to get important information about the object at a glance. For example, we might modify our `Car` class from earlier in this chapter to have a `toString` method that returns the make, model, and VIN:

```
class Car {
   toString() {
      return `${this.make} ${this.model}: ${this.vin}`;
   }
   //...
```

Now calling `toString` on a `Car` instance gives some identifying information about the object.

# Multiple Inheritance, Mixins, and Interfaces

Some OO languages support something called *multiple inheritance*, where one class can have two direct superclasses (as opposed to having a superclass that in turn has a superclass). Multiple inheritance introduces the risk of *collisions*. That is, if something inherits from two parents, and both parents have a `greet` method, which does the subclass inherit from? Many languages prefer single inheritance to avoid this thorny problem.

However, when we consider real-world problems, multiple inheritance often makes sense. For example, cars might inherit from both vehicles and "insurable" (you can insure a car or a house, but a house is clearly not a vehicle). Languages that don't support multiple inheritance often introduce the concept of an *interface* to get around this problem. A class (`Car`) can inherit from only one parent (`Vehicle`), but it can have multiple interfaces (`Insurable`, `Container`, etc.).

JavaScript is an interesting hybrid. It is technically a single inheritance language because the prototype chain does not look for multiple parents, but it does provide ways that are sometimes superior to either multiple inheritance or interfaces (and sometimes inferior).

The primary mechanism for the problem of multiple inheritance is the concept of the *mixin*. A mixin refers to functionality that's "mixed in" as needed. Because JavaScript is an untyped, extremely permissive language, you can mix in almost any functionality to any object at any time.

Let's create an "insurable" mixin that we could apply to cars. We'll keep this simple. In addition to the insurable mixin, we'll create a class called `InsurancePolicy`. An insurable mixin needs the methods `addInsurancePolicy`, `getInsurancePolicy`, and (for convenience) `isInsured`. Let's see how that would work:

```
class InsurancePolicy() {}
function makeInsurable(o) {
   o.addInsurancePolicy = function(p) { this.insurancePolicy = p; }
   o.getInsurancePolicy = function() { return this.insurancePolicy; }
   o.isInsured = function() { return !!this.insurancePolicy; }
}
```

Now we can make any object insurable. So with `Car`, what are we going to make insurable? Your first thought might be this:

```
makeInsurable(Car);
```

But you'd be in for a rude surprise:

```
const car1 = new Car();
car1.addInsurancePolicy(new InsurancePolicy());        // error
```

If you're thinking "of course; `addInsurancePolicy` isn't in the prototype chain," go to the head of the class. It does no good to make `Car` insurable. It also doesn't make sense: the abstract concept of a car isn't insurable, but specific cars are. So our next take might be this:

```
const car1 = new Car();
makeInsurable(car1);
car1.addInsurancePolicy(new InsurancePolicy());        // works
```

This works, but now we have to remember to call `makeInsurable` on every car we make. We could add this call in the `Car` constructor, but now we're duplicating this functionality for every car created. Fortunately, the solution is easy:

```
makeInsurable(Car.prototype);
const car1 = new Car();
car1.addInsurancePolicy(new InsurancePolicy());        // works
```

Now it's as if our methods have always been part of class Car. And, from JavaScript's perspective, they *are*. From the development perspective, we've made it easier to maintain these two important classes. The automotive engineering group manages and develops the Car class, and the insurance group manages the InsurancePolicy class and the makeInsurable mixin. Granted, there's still room for the two groups to interfere with each other, but it's better than having everyone working on one giant Car class.

Mixins don't eliminate the problem of collisions: if the insurance group were to create a method called shift in their mixin for some reason, it would break Car. Also, we can't use instanceof to identify objects that are insurable: the best we can do is duck typing (if it has a method called addInsurancePolicy, it must be insurable).

We can ameliorate some of these problems with symbols. Let's say the insurance group is constantly adding very generic methods that are inadvertently trampling Car methods. You could ask them to use symbols for all of their keys. Their mixin would then look like this:

```
class InsurancePolicy() {}
const ADD_POLICY = Symbol();
const GET_POLICY = Symbol();
const IS_INSURED = Symbol();
const _POLICY = Symbol();
function makeInsurable(o) {
   o[ADD_POLICY] = function(p) { this[_POLICY] = p; }
   o[GET_POLICY] = function() { return this[_POLICY]; }
   o[IS_INSURED] = function() { return !!this[_POLICY]; }
}
```

Because symbols are unique, this ensures that the mixin will never interfere with existing Car functionality. It makes it a little more awkward to use, but it's much safer. A middle-ground approach might have been to use regular strings for methods, but symbols (such as _POLICY) for data properties.

# Conclusion

Object-oriented programming is a tremendously popular paradigm, and for good reason. For many real-world problems, it encourages organization and encapsulation of code in a way that makes it easy to maintain, debug, and fix. JavaScript's implementation of OOP has many critics—some even go so far as to say that it doesn't even meet the definition of an OO language (usually because of the lack of data access controls). There is some merit to that argument, but once you get accustomed to JavaScript's take on OOP, you'll find it's actually quite flexible and powerful. And it allows you to do things that other OO languages would balk at.

# CHAPTER 10
# Maps and Sets

ES6 introduces two welcome data structures: *maps* and *sets*. Maps are similar to objects in that they can map a key to a value, and sets are similar to arrays except that duplicates are not allowed.

## Maps

Prior to ES6, when you needed to map keys to values, you would turn to an object, because objects allow you to map string keys to object values of any type. However, using objects for this purpose has many drawbacks:

- The prototypal nature of objects means that there could be mappings that you didn't intend.
- There's no easy way to know how many mappings there are in an object.
- Keys must be strings or symbols, preventing you from mapping objects to values.
- Objects do not guarantee any order to their properties.

The `Map` object addresses these deficiencies, and is a superior choice for mapping keys to values (even if the keys are strings). For example, imagine you have user objects you wish to map to roles:

```
const u1 = { name: 'Cynthia' };
const u2 = { name: 'Jackson' };
const u3 = { name: 'Olive' };
const u4 = { name: 'James' };
```

You would start by creating a map:

```
const userRoles = new Map();
```

Then you can use the map to assign users to roles by using its `set()` method:

```
userRoles.set(u1, 'User');
userRoles.set(u2, 'User');
userRoles.set(u3, 'Admin');
// poor James...we don't assign him a role
```

The `set()` method is also chainable, which can save some typing:

```
userRoles
   .set(u1, 'User')
   .set(u2, 'User')
   .set(u3, 'Admin');
```

You can also pass an array of arrays to the constructor:

```
const userRoles = new Map([
   [u1, 'User'],
   [u2, 'User'],
   [u3, 'Admin'],
]);
```

Now if we want to determine what role `u2` has, you can use the `get()` method:

```
userRoles.get(u2);        // "User"
```

If you call `get` on a key that isn't in the map, it will return `undefined`. Also, you can use the `has()` method to determine if a map contains a given key:

```
userRoles.has(u1);        // true
userRoles.get(u1);        // "User"
userRoles.has(u4);        // false
userRoles.get(u4);        // undefined
```

If you call `set()` on a key that's already in the map, its value will be replaced:

```
userRoles.get(u1);               // 'User'
userRoles.set(u1, 'Admin');
userRoles.get(u1);               // 'Admin'
```

The `size` property will return the number of entries in the map:

```
userRoles.size;           // 3
```

Use the `keys()` method to get the keys in a map, `values()` to return the values, and `entries()` to get the entries as arrays where the first element is the key and the second is the value. All of these methods return an iterable object, which can be iterated over by a `for...of` loop:

```
for(let u of userRoles.keys())
   console.log(u.name);

for(let r of userRoles.values())
   console.log(r);

for(let ur of userRoles.entries())
   console.log(`${ur[0].name}: ${ur[1]}`);
```

```
// note that we can use destructuring to make
// this iteration even more natural:
for(let [u, r] of userRoles.entries())
   console.log(`${u.name}: ${r}`);

// the entries() method is the default iterator for
// a Map, so you can shorten the previous example to:
for(let [u, r] of userRoles)
   console.log(`${u.name}: ${r}`);
```

If you need an array (instead of an iterable object), you can use the spread operator:

```
[...userRoles.values()];      // [ "User", "User", "Admin" ]
```

To delete a single entry from a map, use the `delete()` method:

```
userRoles.delete(u2);
userRoles.size;          // 2
```

Lastly, if you want to remove all entries from a map, you can do so with the `clear()` method:

```
userRoles.clear();
userRoles.size;          // 0
```

# Weak Maps

A `WeakMap` is identical to `Map` except:

- Its keys must be objects.
- Keys in a `WeakMap` can be garbage-collected.
- A `WeakMap` cannot be iterated or cleared.

Normally, JavaScript will keep an object in memory as long as there is a reference to it somewhere. For example, if you have an object that is a key in a `Map`, JavaScript will keep that object in memory as long as the `Map` is in existence. Not so with a `WeakMap`. Because of this, a `WeakMap` can't be iterated (there's too much danger of the iteration exposing an object that's in the process of being garbage-collected).

Thanks to these properties of `WeakMap`, it can be used to store private keys in object instances:

```
const SecretHolder = (function() {
   const secrets = new WeakMap();
   return class {
      setSecret(secret) {
         secrets.set(this, secret);
      }
      getSecret() {
```

```
            return secrets.get(this);
        }
    }
})();
```

Here we've put our `WeakMap` inside an IIFE, along with a class that uses it. Outside the IIFE, we get a class that we call `SecretHolder` whose instances can store secrets. We can only set a secret through the `setSecret` method, and only get the secret through the `getSecret` method:

```
const a = new SecretHolder();
const b = new SecretHolder();

a.setSecret('secret A');
b.setSecret('secret B');

a.getSecret();    // "secret A"
b.getSecret();    // "secret B"
```

We could have used a regular `Map`, but then the secrets we tell instances of `SecretHolder` could never be garbage-collected!

# Sets

A *set* is a collection of data where duplicates are not allowed (consistent with sets in mathematics). Using our previous example, we may want to be able to assign a user to multiple roles. For example, all users might have the `"User"` role, but administrators have both the `"User"` and `"Admin"` role. However, it makes no logical sense for a user to have the same role multiple times. A set is the ideal data structure for this case.

First, create a `Set` instance:

```
const roles = new Set();
```

Now if we want to add a user role, we can do so with the `add()` method:

```
roles.add("User");    // Set [ "User" ]
```

To make this user an administrator, call `add()` again:

```
roles.add("Admin");   // Set [ "User", "Admin" ]
```

Like `Map`, `Set` has a `size` property:

```
roles.size;      // 2
```

Here's the beauty of sets: we don't have to check to see if something is already in the set before we add it. If we add something that's already in the set, nothing happens:

```
roles.add("User");    // Set [ "User", "Admin" ]
roles.size;           // 2
```

To remove a role, we simply call `delete()`, which returns `true` if the role was in the set and `false` otherwise:

```
roles.delete("Admin");  // true
roles;                  // Set [ "User" ]
roles.delete("Admin");  // false
```

## Weak Sets

Weak sets can only contain objects, and the objects they contain may be garbage-collected. As with `WeakMap`, the values in a `WeakSet` can't be iterated, making weak sets very rare; there aren't many use cases for them. As a matter of fact, the only use for weak sets is determining whether or not a given object is in a set or not.

For example, Santa Claus might have a `WeakSet` called `naughty` so he can determine who to deliver the coal to:

```
const naughty = new WeakSet();

const children = [
   { name: "Suzy" },
   { name: "Derek" },
];

naughty.add(children[1]);

for(let child of children) {
   if(naughty.has(child))
      console.log(`Coal for ${child.name}!`);
   else
      console.log(`Presents for ${child.name}!`);
}
```

## Breaking the Object Habit

If you're an experienced JavaScript programmer who's new to ES6, chances are objects are your go-to choice for mapping. And no doubt you've learned all of the tricks to avoiding the pitfalls of objects as maps. But now you have real maps, and you should use them! Likewise, you're probably accustomed to using objects with boolean values as sets, and you don't have to do that anymore, either. When you find yourself creating an object, stop and ask yourself, "Am I using this object only to create a map?" If the answer is "Yes," consider using a `Map` instead.

CHAPTER 11

# Exceptions and Error Handling

As much as we would all like to live in an error-free world, we don't have that luxury. Even the most trivial applications are subject to errors arising from conditions you didn't anticipate. The first step to writing robust, high-quality software is acknowledging that it will have errors. The second step is anticipating those errors and handling them in a reasonable fashion.

*Exception handling* is a mechanism that came about to deal with errors in a controlled fashion. It's called *exception* handling (as opposed to *error* handling) because it's meant to deal with exceptional circumstances—that is, not the errors you anticipate, but the ones you don't.

The line between anticipated errors and unanticipated errors (exceptions) is a blurry one that is very much situational. An application that is designed to be used by the general, untrained public may anticipate a lot more unpredictable behavior than an application designed to be used by trained users.

An example of an anticipated error is someone providing an invalid email address on a form: people make typos *all the time*. An unanticipated error might be running out of disk space, or a usually reliable service being unavailable.

## The Error Object

JavaScript has a built-in `Error` object, which is convenient for any kind of error handling (exceptional or anticipated). When you create an instance of `Error`, you can provide an error message:

```
const err = new Error('invalid email');
```

Creating an `Error` instance doesn't, by itself, do anything. What it does is give you something that can be used to communicate errors. Imagine a function that validates an email address. If the function is successful, it returns the email address as a string. If it isn't, it returns an instance of `Error`. For the sake of simplicity, we'll treat anything that has an at sign (`@`) in it as a valid email address (see Chapter 17):

```
function validateEmail(email) {
   return email.match(/@/) ?
      email :
      new Error(`invalid email: ${email}`);
}
```

To use this, we can use the `typeof` operator to determine if an instance of `Error` has been returned. The error message we provided is available in a property `message`:

```
const email = "jane@doe.com";

const validatedEmail = validateEmail(email);
if(validatedEmail instanceof Error) {
   console.error(`Error: ${validatedEmail.message});
} else {
   console.log(`Valid email: ${validatedEmail}`);
}
```

While this is a perfectly valid and useful way to use the `Error` instance, it is more often used in exception handling, which we'll cover next.

# Exception Handling with try and catch

Exception handling is accomplished with a `try...catch` statement. The idea is that you "try" things, and if there were any exceptions, they are "caught." In our previous example, `validateEmail` handles the anticipated error of someone omitting an at-sign in their email address, but there is also the possibility of an unanticipated error: a wayward programmer setting `email` to something that is not a string. As written, our previous example setting `email` to `null`, or a number, or an object—anything but a string—will cause an error, and your program will halt in a very unfriendly fashion. To safeguard against this unanticipated error, we can wrap our code in a `try...catch` statement:

```
const email = null; // whoops

try {
   const validatedEmail = validateEmail(email);
   if(validatedEmail instanceof Error) {
      console.error(`Error: ${validatedEmail.message});
   } else {
      console.log(`Valid email: ${validatedEmail}`);
   }
} catch(err) {
   console.error(`Error: ${err.message}`);
}
```

Because we caught the error, our program will not halt—we log the error and continue. We may still be in trouble—if a valid email is required, our program might not be able to meaningfully continue, but at least we can now handle the error more gracefully.

Note that control shifts to the `catch` block as soon as an error occurs; that is, the `if` statement that follows the call to `validateEmail` won't execute. You can have as many statements as you wish inside the `try` block; the first one that results in an error will transfer control to the `catch` block. If there are no errors, the `catch` block is not executed, and the program continues.

## Throwing Errors

In our previous example, we used a `try...catch` statement to catch an error that JavaScript itself generated (when we tried to call the `match` method of something that's not a string). You can also "throw" (or "raise") errors yourself, which initiates the exception handling mechanism.

Unlike other languages with exception handling, in JavaScript, you can throw any value: a number or a string, or any other type. However, it's conventional to throw an instance of `Error`. Most `catch` blocks expect an instance of `Error`. Keep in mind that you can't always control where the errors you throw are caught (functions you write might be used by another programmer, who would reasonbly expect any errors thrown to be instances of `Error`).

For example, if you're writing a bill-pay feature for a banking application, you might throw an exception if the account balance can't cover the bill (this is exceptional because this situation should have been checked before bill pay was initiated):

```
function billPay(amount, payee, account) {
   if(amount > account.balance)
      throw new Error("insufficient funds");
   account.transfer(payee, amount);
}
```

When you call `throw`, the current function immediately stops executing (so, in our example, `account.transfer` won't get called, which is what we want).

## Exception Handling and the Call Stack

A typical program will call functions, and those functions will in turn call other functions, and those functions even more functions, and so on. The JavaScript interpreter has to keep track of all of this. If function `a` calls function `b` and function `b` calls function `c`, when function `c` finishes, control is returned to function `b`, and when `b` finishes, control is returned to function a. When c is executing, therefore, neither a nor b is "done." This nesting of functions that are not done is called the *call stack*.

If an error occurs in c, then, what happens to a and b? As it happens, it causes an error in b (because b may rely on the return of c), which in turn causes an error in a (because a may rely on the return of b). Essentially, the error propagates up the call stack until it's caught.

Errors can be caught at any level in the call stack; if they aren't caught, the JavaScript interpreter will halt your program unceremoniously. This is called an *unhandled exception* or an *uncaught exception*, and it causes a program to crash. Given the number of places errors can occur, it's difficult and unwieldy to catch all possible errors, which is why programs crash.

When an error *is* caught, the call stack provides useful information in diagnosing the problem. For example, if function a calls function b, which calls function c, and the error occurs in c, the call stack tells you that not only did the error occur in c, it occurred when it was called by b when b was called by a. This is helpful information if function c is called from many different places in your program.

In most implementations of JavaScript, instances of Error contain a property stack, which is a string representation of the stack (it is a nonstandard feature of JavaScript, but it is available in most environments). Armed with this knowledge, we can write an example that demonstrates exception handling:

```
function a() {
   console.log('a: calling b');
   b();
   console.log('a: done');
}
function b() {
   console.log('b: calling c');
   c();
   console.log('b: done');
}
function c() {
   console.log('c: throwing error');
   throw new Error('c error');
   console.log('c: done');
}
function d() {
   console.log('d: calling c');
   c();
   console.log('d: done');
}

try {
   a();
} catch(err) {
```

```
    console.log(err.stack);
}

try {
    d();
} catch(err) {
    console.log(err.stack);
}
```

Running this example in Firefox yields the following console output:

```
a: calling b
b: calling c
c: throwing error
c@debugger eval code:13:1
b@debugger eval code:8:4
a@debugger eval code:3:4
@debugger eval code:23:4

d: calling c
c: throwing error
c@debugger eval code:13:1
d@debugger eval code:18:4
@debugger eval code:29:4
```

The lines with the at signs in them are the stack traces, starting with the "deepest" function (`c`), and ending with no function at all (the browser itself). You can see that we have two different stack traces: one showing that we called `c` from `b`, which was called from `a`, and one that `c` was called directly from `d`.

# try...catch...finally

There are times when the code in a `try` block involves some sort of resource, such as an HTTP connection or a file. Whether or not there is an error, we want to free this resource so that it's not permanently tied up by your program. Because the `try` block can contain as many statements as you want, any one of which can result in an error, it's not a safe place to free the resource (because the error could happen before we have the chance to do so). It's also not safe to free the resource in the `catch` block, because then it won't get freed if there is no error. This is exactly the situation that demands the `finally` block, which gets called whether or not there is an error.

Because we haven't covered file handling or HTTP connections yet, we'll simply use an example with `console.log` statements to demonstrate the `finally` block:

```
try {
    console.log("this line is executed...");
    throw new Error("whoops");
    console.log("this line is not...");
} catch(err) {
    console.log("there was an error...");
```

```
} finally {
    console.log("...always executed");
    console.log("perform cleanup here");
}
```

Try this example with and without the `throw` statement; you will see that the `finally` block is executed in either case.

## Let Exceptions Be Exceptional

Now that you know what exception handling is and how to do it, you might be tempted to use it for all of your error handling—both the common errors you anticipate, and the errors that you don't. Throwing an error is, after all, extremely easy, and it's a convenient way to "give up" when you encounter a condition that you don't know how to handle. But exception handling comes at a cost. In addition to the risk of the exception never being caught (thereby crashing your program), exceptions carry a certain computational cost. Because exceptions have to "unwind" the stack trace until a `catch` block is encountered, the JavaScript interpreter has to do extra housekeeping. With ever-increasing computer speeds, this becomes less and less of a concern, but throwing exceptions in frequently used execution paths can cause a performance issue.

Remember that every time you throw an exception, you have to catch it (unless you want your program to crash). You can't get something for nothing. It's best to leave exceptions as a last line of defense, for handling the exceptional errors you can't anticipate, and to manage anticipated errors with control flow statements.

CHAPTER 12

# Iterators and Generators

ES6 introduces two very important new concepts: *iterators* and *generators*. Generators depend on iterators, so we'll start with iterators.

An iterator is roughly analogous to a bookmark: it helps you keep track of where you are. An array is an example of an *iterable* object: it contains multiple things (like pages in a book), and can give you an iterator (which is like a bookmark). Let's make this analogy concrete: imagine you have an array called `book` where each element is a string that represents a page. To fit the format of this book, we'll use Lewis Carroll's "Twinkle, Twinkle, Little Bat" from *Alice's Adventures in Wonderland* (you can imagine a children's book version with one line per page):

```
const book = [
   "Twinkle, twinkle, little bat!",
   "How I wonder what you're at!",
   "Up above the world you fly,",
   "Like a tea tray in the sky.",
   "Twinkle, twinkle, little bat!",
   "How I wonder what you're at!",
];
```

Now that we have our `book` array, we can get an iterator with its `values` method:

```
const it = book.values();
```

To continue our analogy, the iterator (commonly abbreviated as `it`) is a bookmark, but it works only for this specific book. Furthermore, we haven't put it anywhere yet; we haven't started reading. To "start reading," we call the iterator's `next` method, which returns an object with two properties: `value` (which holds the "page" you're now on) and `done`, which becomes `false` after you read the last page. Our book is only six pages long, so it's easy to demonstrate how we can read it in its entirety:

```
it.next();  // { value: "Twinkle, twinkle, little bat!", done: false }
it.next();  // { value: "How I wonder what you're at!", done: false }
it.next();  // { value: "Up above the world you fly,", done: false }
it.next();  // { value: "Like a tea tray in the sky.", done: false }
it.next();  // { value: "Twinkle, twinkle, little bat!", done: false }
it.next();  // { value: "How I wonder what  you're at!", done: false }
it.next();  // { value: undefined, done: true }
it.next();  // { value: undefined, done: true }
it.next();  // { value: undefined, done: true }
```

There are a couple of important things to note here. The first is that when `next` gives us the last page in the book, it tells us we're not done. This is where the book analogy breaks down a little bit: when you read the last page of a book, you're done, right? Iterators can be used for more than books, and knowing when you're done is not always so simple. When you *are* done, note that `value` is `undefined`, and also note that you can keep calling `next`, and it's going to keep telling you the same thing. Once an iterator is done, it's done, and it shouldn't ever go back to providing you data.[1]

While this example doesn't illustrate it directly, it should be clear to you that we can do things *between* the calls to `it.next()`. In other words, `it` will save our place for us.

If we needed to enumerate over this array, we know we can use a `for` loop or a `for...of` loop. The mechanics of the `for` loop are simple: we know the elements in an array are numeric and sequential, so we can use an index variable to access each element in the array in turn. But what of the `for...of` loop? How does it accomplish its magic without an index? As it turns out, it uses an iterator: the `for...of` loop will work with *anything* that provides an iterator. We'll soon see how to take advantage of that. First, let's see how we can emulate a `for...of` loop with a `while` loop with our newfound understanding of iterators:

```
const it = book.values();
let current = it.next();
while(!current.done) {
   console.log(current.value);
   current = it.next();
}
```

Note that iterators are distinct; that is, every time you create a new iterator, you're starting at the beginning, and it's possible to have multiple iterators that are at different places:

```
const it1 = book.values();
const it2 = book.values();
// neither iterator have started
```

1 Because objects are responsible for providing their own iteration mechanism, as we'll see shortly, it's actually possible to create a "bad iterator" that can reverse the value of `done`; that would be considered a faulty iterator. In general, you should rely on correct iterator behavior.

```
// read two pages with it1:
it1.next();  // { value: "Twinkle, twinkle, little bat!", done: false }
it1.next();  // { value: "How I wonder what you're at!", done: false }

// read one page with it2:
it2.next();  // { value: "Twinkle, twinkle, little bat!", done: false }

// read another page with it1:
it1.next();  // { value: "Up above the world you fly,", done: false }
```

In this example, the two iterators are independent, and iterating through the array on their own individual schedules.

# The Iteration Protocol

Iterators, by themselves, are not that interesting: they are plumbing that supports more interesting behavior. The *iterator protocol* enables any object to be iterable. Imagine you want to create a logging class that attaches timestamps to messages. Internally, you use an array to store the timestamped messages:

```
class Log {
   constructor() {
      this.messages = [];
   }
   add(message) {
      this.messages.push({ message, timestamp: Date.now() });
   }
}
```

So far, so good...but what if we want to then iterate over the entries in the log? We could, of course, access `log.messages`, but wouldn't it be nicer if we could treat `log` as if it were directly iterable, just like an array? The iteration protocol allows us to make this work. The iteration protocol says that if your class provides a symbol method `Symbol.iterator` that returns an object with iterator behavior (i.e., it has a `next` method that returns an object with `value` and `done` properties), it is then iterable! Let's modify our `Log` class to have a `Symbol.iterator` method:

```
class Log {
   constructor() {
      this.messages = [];
   }
   add(message) {
      this.messages.push({ message, timestamp: Date.now() });
   }
   [Symbol.iterator]() {
      return this.messages.values();
   }
}
```

Now we can iterate over an instance of `Log` just as if it were an array:

```
const log = new Log();
log.add("first day at sea");
log.add("spotted whale");
log.add("spotted another vessel");
//...

// iterate over log as if it were an array!
for(let entry of log) {
   console.log(`${entry.message} @ ${entry.timestamp}`);
}
```

In this example, we're adhering to the iterator protocol by getting an iterator from the `messages` array, but we could have also written our own iterator:

```
class Log {
   //...

   [Symbol.iterator]() {
      let i = 0;
      const messages = this.messages;
      return {
         next() {
            if(i >= messages.length)
               return { value: undefined, done: true };
            return { value: messages[i++], done: false };
         }
      }
   }
}
```

The examples we've been considering thus far involve iterating over a predetermined number of elements: the pages in a book, or the messages to date in a log. However, iterators can also be used to represent object that never run out of values.

To demonstrate, we'll consider a very simple example: the generation of Fibonacci numbers. Fibonacci numbers are not particularly hard to generate, but they do depend on what came before them. For the uninitiated, the Fibonacci sequence is the sum of the previous two numbers in the sequence. The sequence starts with 1 and 1: the next number is 1 + 1, which is 2. The next number is 1 + 2, which is 3. The fourth number is 2 + 3, which is 5, and so on. The sequence looks like this:

1, 1, 2, 3, 5, 8, 13, 21, 34, 55, 89, 144,...

The Fibonacci sequence goes on forever. And our application doesn't know how many elements will be needed, which makes this an ideal application for iterators. The only difference between this and previous examples is that this iterator will never return `true` for done:

```
class FibonacciSequence {
   [Symbol.iterator]() {
      let a = 0, b = 1;
      return {
         next() {
            let rval = { value: b, done: false };
            b += a;
            a = rval.value;
            return rval;
         }
      };
   }
}
```

If we used an instance of `FibonacciSequence` with a `for...of` loop, we'll end up with an infinite loop...we'll never run out of Fibonacci numbers! To prevent this, we'll add a `break` statement after 10 elements:

```
const fib = new FibonacciSequence();
let i = 0;
for(let n of fib) {
   console.log(n);
   if(++i > 9) break;
}
```

# Generators

Generators are functions that use an iterator to control their execution. A regular function takes arguments and returns a value, but otherwise the caller has no control of it. When you call a function, you relinquish control to the function until it returns. Not so with generators, which allow you to control the execution of the function.

Generators bring two things to the table: the first is the ability to control the execution of a function, having it execute in discrete steps. The second is the ability to communicate with the function as it executes.

A generator is like a regular function with two exceptions:

- The function can *yield* control back to the caller at any point.
- When you call a generator, it doesn't run right away. Instead, you get back an iterator. The function runs as you call the iterator's `next` method.

Generators are signified in JavaScript by the presence of an asterisk after the `function` keyword; otherwise, their syntax is identical to regular functions. If a function is a generator, you can use the `yield` keyword in addition to `return`.

Let's look at a simple example—a generator that returns all the colors of the rainbow:

```
function* rainbow() {   // the asterisk marks this as a generator
   yield 'red';
   yield 'orange';
   yield 'yellow';
   yield 'green';
   yield 'blue';
   yield 'indigo';
   yield 'violet';
}
```

Now let's see how we call this generator. Remember that when you call a generator, you get back an iterator. We'll call the function, and then step through the iterator:

```
const it = rainbow();
it.next();  // { value: "red", done: false }
it.next();  // { value: "orange", done: false }
it.next();  // { value: "yellow", done: false }
it.next();  // { value: "green", done: false }
it.next();  // { value: "blue", done: false }
it.next();  // { value: "indigo", done: false }
it.next();  // { value: "violet", done: false }
it.next();  // { value: undefined, done: true }
```

Because the `rainbow` generator returns an iterator, we can also use it in a `for...of` loop:

```
for(let color of rainbow()) {
   console.log(color):
}
```

This will log all the colors of the rainbow!

## yield Expressions and Two-Way Communication

We mentioned earlier that generators allow *two-way* communication between a generator and its caller. This happens through the `yield` expression. Remember that expressions evaluate to a value, and because `yield` is an expression, it must evaluate to something. What it evaluates to are the arguments (if any) provided by the caller every time it calls `next` on the generator's iterator. Consider a generator that can carry on a conversation:

```
function* interrogate() {
   const name = yield "What is your name?";
   const color = yield "What is your favorite color?";
   return `${name}'s favorite color is ${color}.`;
}
```

When we call this generator, we get an iterator, and no part of the generator has been run yet. When we call `next`, it attempts to run the first line. However, because that line contains a `yield` expression, the generator must yield control back to the caller. The caller must call `next` again before the first line can resolve, and `name` can receive the value that was passed in by `next`. Here's what it looks like when we run this generator through to completion:

```
const it = interrogate();
it.next();          // { value: "What is your name?", done: false }
it.next('Ethan');   // { value: "What is your favorite color?", done: false }
it.next('orange');  // { value: "Ethan's favorite color is orange.", done: true }
```

Figure 12-1 shows the sequence of events as this generator is run.

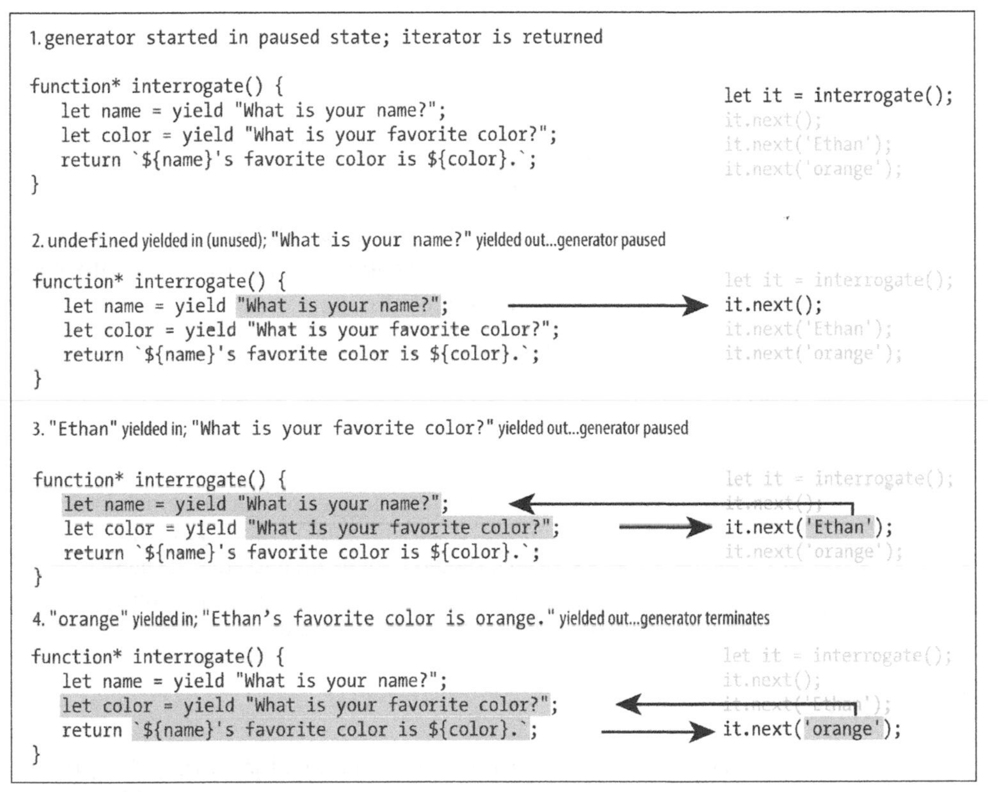


*Figure 12-1. Generator example*

This example demonstrates that generators are quite powerful, allowing the execution of functions to be controlled by the caller. Also, because the caller can pass information into the generator, the generator can even modify its own behavior based on what information is passed in.

You can't create a generator with arrow notation; you have to use `function*`.

## Generators and return

The yield statement by itself doesn't end a generator, even if it's the last statement in the generator. Calling return from anywhere in the generator will result in done being true, with the value property being whatever you returned. For example:

```
function* abc() {
    yield 'a';
    yield 'b';
    return 'c';
}

const it = count();
it.next();  // { value: 'a', done: false }
it.next();  // { value: 'b', done: false }
it.next();  // { value: 'c', done: true }
```

While this is correct behavior, keep in mind that things that use generators don't always pay attention to the value property when done is true. For example, if we use this in a for...of loop, "c" won't be printed out at all:

```
// will print out "a" and "b", but not "c"
for(let l of abc()) {
    console.log(l);
}
```

I recommend that you do not use return to provide a meaningful value in a generator. If you expect a useful value out of a generator, you should use yield; return should only be used to stop the generator early. For this reason, I generally recommend not providing a value at all when you call return from a generator.

# Conclusion

Iterators provide a standard mechanism for collections or objects that can provide multiple values. While iterators don't provide anything that wasn't possible prior to ES6, they do standardize an important and common activity.

Generators allow functions that are much more controllable and customizable: no longer is the caller limited to providing data up front, waiting for the function to return, and then receiving the result of the function. Generators essentially allow computation to be deferred, and performed only as necessary. We will see in Chapter 14 how they provide powerful patterns for managing asynchronous execution.

CHAPTER 13

# Functions and the Power of Abstract Thinking

If JavaScript were a Broadway play, functions would be the glittering starlet: they would hog the spotlight and take the last bow to thunderous applause (and some boos, no doubt: you can't please everyone). We covered the mechanics of functions in Chapter 6, but now we're going to consider the ways functions can be used, and how they can transform your approach to solving problems.

The very concept of a function is chameleon-like: it takes on different aspects when viewed in different contexts. The first—and simplest—perspective on functions we're going to consider is that of a code reuse vehicle.

## Functions as Subroutines

The idea of *subroutines* is a very old one, a practical concession to managing complexity. Without subroutines, programming would be a very repetitive affair indeed. Subroutines simply package some bit of repetitive functionality, give it a name, and allow you to execute that bit of functionality at any time simply by referring to that name.

Other names for a subroutine are *procedure*, *routine*, *subprogram*, *macro*, and the very bland and generic *callable unit*. Note that in JavaScript, we don't actually use the word *subroutine*. We just call a function a function (or a method). We're using the term *subroutine* here to emphasize this simple use of functions.

Very often, a subroutine is used to package an *algorithm*, which is simply an understood recipe for performing a given task. Let's consider the algorithm for determining whether the current date is in a leap year or not:

```
const year = new Date().getFullYear();
if(year % 4 !== 0) console.log(`${year} is NOT a leap year.`)
else if(year % 100 != 0) console.log(`${year} IS a leap year.`)
else if(year % 400 != 0) console.log(`${year} is NOT a leap year.`)
else console.log(`{$year} IS a leap year`);
```

Imagine if we had to execute this code 10 times in our program...or even worse, 100 times. Now imagine further that you wanted to change the verbiage of the message that gets printed to the console; you have to find all the instances that use this code and change four strings! This is exactly the problem that subroutines address. In JavaScript, a function can fill this need:

```
function printLeapYearStatus() {
   const year = new Date().getFullYear();
   if(year % 4 !== 0) console.log(`${year} is NOT a leap year.`)
   else if(year % 100 != 0) console.log(`${year} IS a leap year.`)
   else if(year % 400 != 0) console.log(`${year} is NOT a leap year.`)
   else console.log(`{$year} IS a leap year`);
}
```

Now we've created a *reusable* subroutine (function) called `printLeapYearStatus`. This should all be pretty familiar to us now.

Note the name we chose for the function: `printLeapYearStatus`. Why didn't we call it `getLeapYearStatus` or simply `leapYearStatus` or `leapYear`? While those names would be shorter, they miss an important detail: this function simply prints out the current leap year status. Naming functions meaningfully is part science, part art. The name is not for JavaScript: it doesn't care what name you use. The name is for other people (or you in the future). When you name functions, think carefully about what another person would understand about the function if all they could see was the name. Ideally, you want the name to communicate exactly what the function does. On the flip side, you can be *too* verbose in the naming of your functions. For example, we might have named this function `calculateCurrentLeapYearStatusAndPrintToConsole`, but the extra information in this longer name has passed the point of diminishing returns; this is where the art comes in.

## Functions as Subroutines That Return a Value

In our previous example, `printLeapYearStatus` is a subroutine in the usual sense of the word: it just bundles some functionality for convenient reuse, nothing more. This simple use of functions is one that you won't find yourself using very often—and even less so as your approach to programming problems becomes more sophisticated and abstract. Let's take the next step in abstract thinking and consider functions as subroutines that *return a value.*

Our printLeapYearStatus is nice, but as we build out our program, we quickly grow out of logging things to the console. Now we want to use HTML for output, or write to a file, or use the current leap year status in *other* calculations, and our subroutine isn't helping with that. However, we still don't want to go back to spelling out our algorithm every time we want to know whether it's currently a leap year or not.

Fortunately, it's easy enough to rewrite (and rename!) our function so that it's a subroutine that returns a value:

```
function isCurrentYearLeapYear() {
   const year = new Date().getFullYear();
   if(year % 4 !== 0) return false;
   else if(year % 100 != 0) return true;
   else if(year % 400 != 0) return false;
   else return true;
}
```

Now let's look at some examples of how we might use the return value of our new function:

```
const daysInMonth =
   [31, isCurrentYearLeapYear() ? 29 : 28, 31, 30, 31, 30,
      31, 31, 30, 31, 30, 31];
if(isCurrentYearLeapYear()) console.log('It is a leap year.');
```

Before we move on, consider what we've named this function. It's very common to name functions that return a boolean (or are designed to be used in a boolean context) with an initial is. We also included the word *current* in the function name; why? Because in this function, it's explicitly getting the *current date.* In other words, this function will return a different value if you run it on December 31, 2016, and then a day later on January 1, 2017.

## Functions as...Functions

Now that we've covered some of the more obvious ways to think about functions, it's time to think about functions as...well, functions. If you were a mathematician, you would think of a function as a *relation*: inputs go in, outputs come out. Every input is related to some output. Functions that adhere to the mathematical definition of the function are sometimes called *pure functions* by programmers. There are even languages (such as Haskell) that allow only pure functions.

How is a pure function different than the functions we've been considering? First of all, a pure function must *always return the same output for the same set of inputs.* isCurrentYearLeapYear is not a pure function because it will return something different depending on when you call it (one year it may return true, while the next year it may return `false`). Secondly, a function must not have *side effects*. That is, invoking the function must not alter the state of the program. In our discussion of functions, we haven't seen functions with side effects (we are not considering console output to be a side effect). Let's consider a simple example:

```
const colors = ['red', 'orange', 'yellow', 'green',
   'blue', 'indigo', 'violet'];
let colorIndex = -1;
function getNextRainbowColor() {
   if(++colorIndex >= colors.length) colorIndex = 0;
   return colors[colorIndex];
}
```

The function `getNextRainbowColor` will return a different color each time, cycling through the colors of the rainbow. This function is breaking both of the rules of a pure function: it has a different return value each time for the same input (it has no arguments, so its input is nothing), and it is causing a side effect (the variable `colorIndex` changes). The variable `colorIndex` is not part of the function; invoking `getNextRainbowColor` modifies it, which is a side effect.

Going back to our leap year problem for a moment, how can we take our leap year function and turn it into a pure function? Easy:

```
function isLeapYear(year) {
   if(year % 4 !== 0) return false;
   else if(year % 100 != 0) return true;
   else if(year % 400 != 0) return false;
   else return true;
}
```

This new function will always return the same output given the same input, and it causes no side effects, making this a pure function.

Our `getNextRainbowColor` function is a little bit trickier. We can eliminate the side effect by putting the external variables in a closure:

```
const getNextRainbowColor = (function() {
   const colors = ['red', 'orange', 'yellow', 'green',
      'blue', 'indigo', 'violet'];
   let colorIndex = -1;
   return function() {
      if(++colorIndex >= colors.length) colorIndex = 0;
      return colors[colorIndex];
   };
})();
```

We now have a function that has no side effects, but it still isn't a pure function because it doesn't always return the same result for the same input. To fix this problem, we have to carefully consider how we use this function. Chances are, we're calling it repeatedly—for example, in a browser to change the color of an element every half-second (we will learn more about browser code in Chapter 18):

```
setInterval(function() {
   document.querySelector('.rainbow')
      .style['background-color'] = getNextRainbowColor();
}, 500);
```

This may not look so bad, and certainly the intent is clear: some HTML element with the class `rainbow` will cycle through the colors of the rainbow. The problem is that if something else calls `getNextRainbowColor()`, it will interfere with this code! This is the point we should stop and question whether a function with side effects is a good idea. In this case, an iterator would probably be a better choice:

```
function getRainbowIterator() {
   const colors = ['red', 'orange', 'yellow', 'green',
      'blue', 'indigo', 'violet'];
   let colorIndex = -1;
   return {
      next() {
         if(++colorIndex >= colors.length) colorIndex = 0;
         return { value: colors[colorIndex], done: false };
      }
   };
}
```

Our function `getRainbowIterator` is now a pure function: it returns the same thing every time (an iterator), and it has no side effects. We have to use it differently, but it's much safer:

```
const rainbowIterator = getRainbowIterator();
setInterval(function() {
   document.querySelector('.rainbow')
      .style['background-color'] = rainbowIterator.next().value;
}, 500);
```

You may be thinking that we've just kicked the can down the road: isn't the `next()` method returning a different value every time? It is, but remember that `next()` is a *method*, not a function. It operates in the context of the object to which it belongs, so its behavior is controlled by that object. If we use `getRainbowIterator` in other parts of our program, they will produce different iterators, which will not interfere with any other iterator.

# So What?

Now that we've seen three different hats that a function can wear (subroutine, subroutine with return value, and pure function), we pause and ask ourselves "So what?" Why do these distinctions matter?

My goal in this chapter is less to explain the syntax of JavaScript than to get you to think about *why*. Why do you need functions? Thinking about a function as a subroutine offers one answer for that question: to avoid repeating yourself. Subroutines give you a way to package commonly used functionality—a pretty obvious benefit.

Avoiding repetition by packaging code is such a foundational concept that it's spawned its own acronym: DRY (don't repeat yourself). While it may be linguistically questionable, you'll find people using this acronym as an adjective to describe code. "This code here could be more DRY." If someone tells you that, they are telling you that you are unnecessarily repeating functionality.

Pure functions are a slightly harder sell—and answer the question of "why" in a more abstract fashion. One answer might be "because they make programming more like math!"—an answer that might reasonably prompt a further question: "Why is that a good thing?" A better answer might be "because pure functions make your code easier to test, easier to understand, and more portable."

Functions that return a different value under different circumstances, or have side effects, are *tied to their context*. If you have a really useful function that has side effects, for example, and you pluck it out of one program and put it into another, it may not work. Or, worse, it may work 99% of the time, but 1% of the time causes a terrible bug. Any programmer knows that intermittent bugs are the worst kind of bugs: they can go unnoticed for long periods of time, and by the time they're discovered, locating the offending code is like finding a needle in a haystack.

If you are wondering if I'm suggesting that pure functions are better, I am: *you should always prefer pure functions*. I say "prefer" because sometimes it's just plain easier to make a function with side effects. If you're a beginning programmer, you'll be tempted to do it quite often. I'm not going to tell you not to, but I am going to challenge you to stop and think if you can find a way to use a pure function instead. Over time, you'll find yourself naturally gravitating toward pure functions.

Object-oriented programming, which we covered in Chapter 9, offers a paradigm that allows you to use side effects in a controlled and sensible manner, by tightly restricting their scope.

## Functions Are Objects

In JavaScript, functions are instances of the `Function` object. From a practical perspective, this should have no bearing on how you use them; it's just a tidbit to file away. It is worth mentioning that if you're trying to identify the type of a variable `v`, `typeof v` will return `"function"` for functions. This is good and sensible, in contrast to what happens if `v` is an array: it will return `"object"`. The upshot is that you can use `typeof v` to identify functions. Note, however, that if `v` is a function, `v instanceof Object` will be true, so if you are trying to distinguish between functions and other types of objects, you'll want to test `typeof` first.

## IIFEs and Asynchronous Code

We were introduced to IIFEs (immediately invoked function expressions) in Chapter 6, and we saw that they were a way of creating a closure. Let's look at an important example (one that we will revisit in Chapter 14) of how IIFEs can help us with asynchronous code.

One of the first uses of IIFEs was to create new variables in new scopes so that asynchronous code would run correctly. Consider the classic example of a timer that starts at 5 seconds and counts down to "go!" (0 seconds). This code uses the built-in function `setTimeout`, which delays the execution of its first argument (a function) by its second argument (some number of milliseconds). For example, this will print out `hello` after 1.5 seconds:

```
setTimeout(function() { console.log("hello"); }, 1500);
```

Now that we're armed with that knowledge, here's our countdown function:

```
var i;
for(i=5; i>=0; i--) {
   setTimeout(function() {
       console.log(i===0 ? "go!" : i);
    }, (5-i)*1000);
}
```

Take note that we're using `var` instead of `let` here; we're having to step back in time to understand why IIFEs were important. If you expect this to print out `5, 4, 3, 2, 1, go!`, you will be disappointed. Instead, you will find `-1` printed out six times. What's happening here is that the function being passed to `setTimeout` is not invoked in the loop: it will be invoked at some point in the future. So the loop will run, and `i` will start at 5, and eventually reach –1...all before any of the functions are invoked. So by the time the functions are invoked, the value of `i` is `-1`.

Even though block-level scope (with `let` variables) essentially solves this problem, this is still a very important example if you're new to asynchronous programming. It can be hard to wrap your head around, but it's critical to understanding asynchronous execution (the subject of Chapter 14).

Before block-scoped variables, the way to solve this problem would have been to use another function. Using an additional function creates a new scope, and the value of `i` can be "captured" (in a closure) at each step. Consider first using a named function:

```
function loopBody(i) {
   setTimeout(function() {
      console.log(i===0 ? "go!" : i);
   }, (5-i)*1000);
}
var i;
for(i=5; i>0; i--) {
   loopBody(i);
}
```

At each step in the loop, the function `loopBody` is invoked. Recall how arguments are passed in JavaScript: by value. So at each step, it's not the variable `i` that gets passed into the function, but the *value* of `i`. So the first time, the value `5` is passed in, the second time the value `4`, and so on. It doesn't matter that we use the same variable name (`i`) in both places: we're essentially creating six different scopes and six independent variables (one for the outer scope, and five for each of the `loopBody` invocations).

Creating a named function for loops that you are only going to use once can get tedious, though. Enter IIFEs: they essentially create equivalent anonymous functions that are invoked immediately. Here's how the previous example looks with an IIFE:

```
var i;
for(i=5; i>0; i--) {
   (function(i) {
      setTimeout(function() {
         console.log(i===0 ? "go!" : i);
      }, (5-i)*1000);
   })(i);
}
```

That's a lot of parentheses! If you think about it, though, the exact same thing is being accomplished: we're creating a function that takes a single argument, and invokes it for each step in the loop (see Figure 13-1 for a visual explanation).

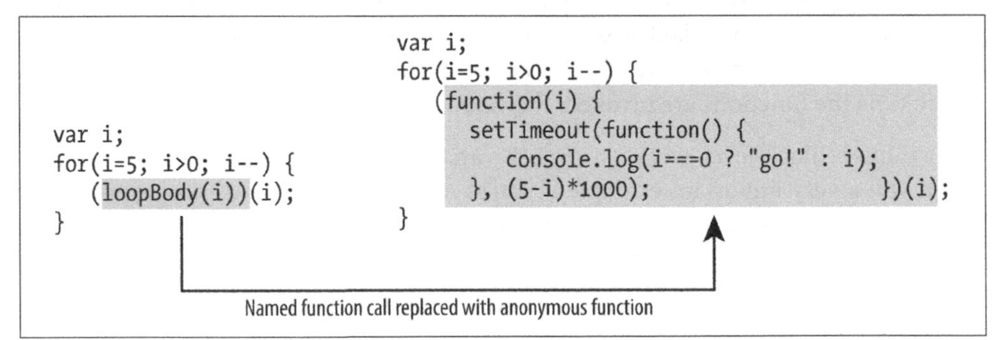


*Figure 13-1. Immediately invoked function expression*

Block-scoped variables solve this problem for us without the extra hassle of requiring a function to create a new scope for us. This example is simplified greatly with the use of block-scoped variables:

```
for(let i=5; i>0; i--) {
   setTimeout(function() {
      console.log(i===0 ? "go!" : i);
   }, (5-i)*1000);
}
```

Note that we use the `let` keyword *inside* the `for` loop arguments. If we put it outside the `for` loop, we'd have the same problem as before. Using the `let` keyword in this way signals to JavaScript that at each step of the loop, there is to be a new, independent copy of the `i` variable. So when the functions passed to `setTimeout` execute in the future, they're each receiving their value from a variable in its own scope.

# Function Variables

If you're new to programming, you might want to pour another cup of coffee and sit up straight: this section is something beginners often struggle with, but is one of the most important concepts to wrap your head around.

It's easy enough to think of numbers, strings, and even arrays as variables; it leads us to this comfortable idea that a variable is a bit of data (or a collection of data in the case of an array or object). Thinking about variables this way, however, makes it more difficult to realize the full potential of functions, because you can pass a function around just as if it were any other variable. Because functions are *active*, we don't think about them as bits of data (which we consider to be passive). And it's true, a function is active *when it's invoked*. Before it's invoked, however...it's passive just like any other variable.

Here's an analogy that might help you. If you go to the supermarket, you can think of fruit as bits of data: 2 bananas, 1 apple, and so on. You decide that you'd like to make a smoothie with your fruit, so you buy a blender as well. A blender is more like a function: it does something (namely, converts fruit into delicious smoothies). But when the blender is in your basket—not plugged in, not actively blending—it is just another item in your cart, and you can do the same things with it as you do with your fruit: move it from the cart to the conveyor belt, pay for it, put it in a shopping bag, take it home, and so on. It's only when you plug it in and put fruit into it and turn it on that it becomes something different than the fruit.

So a function can be used wherever a variable is used, but what does that mean? In particular, it means you can do the following things:

- Alias a function by creating a variable that points to it.
- Put functions in an array (possibly mixed with other types of data).

- Use functions as properties of an object (see Chapter 9).
- Pass a function into a function.
- Return a function from a function.
- Return a function from a function that itself takes a function as an argument.

Is your head spinning yet? Written out this way, it does seem incredibly abstract, and you might reasonably be wondering "Why on earth would you want to do that?" The fact is, this flexibility is incredibly powerful, and all of these things are done quite frequently.

Let's start with the most comprehensible item on that list: aliasing a function. Imagine you have a function with an incredibly long name and you want to use it multiple times within a few lines, and it's getting exhausting typing it, and it results in code that's very hard to read. Because a function is just a data type like any other, you can create a new variable with a shorter name:

```
function addThreeSquareAddFiveTakeSquareRoot(x) {
   // this is a very silly function, isn't it?
   return Math.sqrt(Math.pow(x+3, 2)+5);
}

// before
const answer = (addThreeSquareAddFiveTakeSquareRoot(5) +
   addThreeSquareAddFiveTakeSquareRoot(2)) /
   addThreeSquareAddFiveTakeSqureRoot(7);

// after
const f = addThreeSquareAddFiveTakeSquareRoot;
const answer = (f(5) + f(2)) / f(7);
```

Note that in the "after" example, *we don't use parentheses after* `addThreeSquareAddFiveTakeSquareRoot`. If we did, we would be *invoking* the function, and `f`—instead of being an alias of `addThreeSquareAddFiveTakeSquareRoot`—would contain the *result* of invoking it. Then when we tried to use it like a function (`f(5)`, for example) it would result in an error because `f` wouldn't be a function, and you can only invoke functions.

This is a completely contrived example, of course, and something you don't really see that often. Where it does come up, however, is in *namespacing*, which is common in Node development (see Chapter 20). For example:

```
const Money = require('math-money');  // require is a Node function to
                                      // import a library
const oneDollar = Money.Dollar(1);
// or, if we don't want to have to say "Money.Dollar" everywhere:
const Dollar = Money.Dollar;
const twoDollars = Dollar(2);
// note that oneDollar and twoDollars are instances of the same type
```

In this case, we aren't so much *aliasing* `Dollar` as shortening it from `Money.Dollar` to simply `Dollar`, which seems a reasonable enough thing to do.

Now that we've done the mental equivalent of stretching before exercising, let's move on to more vigorous abstract thinking.

## Functions in an Array

This is a pattern that hasn't been used very much historically, but its usage is increasing, and it is extremely useful in certain circumstances. One application is the idea of a *pipeline*—that is, a set of individual steps we want to do frequently. The advantage of using arrays is that you can modify an array at any time. Need to take a step out? Just remove it from the array. Need to add a step? Just append something to the array.

One example is graphics transformations. If you're building some kind of visualization software, there is often a "pipeline" of transformations that you apply to many points. The following shows an example of common 2D transforms:

```
const sin = Math.sin;
const cos = Math.cos;
const theta = Math.PI/4;
const zoom = 2;
const offset = [1, -3];

const pipeline = [
   function rotate(p) {
      return {
         x: p.x * cos(theta) - p.y * sin(theta),
         y: p.x * sin(theta) + p.y * cos(theta),
      };
   },
   function scale(p) {
      return { x: p.x * zoom, y: p.y * zoom };
   },
   function translate(p) {
      return { x: p.x + offset[0], y: p.y + offset[1]; };
   },
];

// pipeline is now an array of functions for a specific 2D transform
// we can now transform a point:

const p = { x: 1, y: 1 };
let p2 = p;
for(let i=0; i<pipeline.length; i++) {
   p2 = pipeline[i](p2);
}

// p2 is now p1 rotated 45 degrees (pi/4 radians) around the origin,
```

```
// moved 2 units farther from the origin, and translated 1 unit to the
// right and 3 units down
```

This example is very basic for a graphics transformation, but hopefully it gives you a glimpse into the power of storing functions in an array. Note the syntax as we apply each function in the pipeline: `pipeline[i]` accesses element `i` of the pipeline, which evaluates to a function. Then the function is invoked (parentheses). The point is passed in, and then assigned back to itself. In this way, the point is the cumulative result of executing each step in the pipeline.

Pipeline processing is not just found in graphics applications: it's also popular in audio processing and many scientific and engineering applications. In reality, any time you have a series of functions you need to execute in a specified order, a pipeline is a useful abstraction.

## Pass a Function into a Function

We've already seen some examples of passing functions to functions: we have passed functions to `setTimeout` or `forEach`. Another reason to pass a function to a function is to manage asynchronous programming, a paradigm that's exploded as asynchronous programming has become more popular. A common way to achieve asynchronous execution is to pass a function (usually called a *callback*, and often abbreviated *cb*) into another function. This function is invoked (called) when the enclosing function is done with whatever it's doing. We will be discussing callbacks extensively in Chapter 14.

Callbacks aren't the only reason you might want to pass a function into another function; it's also a great way to "inject" functionality. Let's consider a function called `sum` that simply sums all of the numbers in an array (for the sake of simplicity, we won't do any checking or error handling if the array contains elements other than numbers). This is an easy enough exercise, but what if we then need a function that returns the sum of *squares*? We could, of course, simply write a new function called `sumOfSquares`...but what happens when we need the sum of cubes? This is where the ability to pass a function can be very helpful. Consider this implementation of `sum`:

```
function sum(arr, f) {
   // if no function is supplied, use a "null function" that
   // simply returns its argument unmodified
   if(typeof f != 'function') f = x => x;

   return arr.reduce((a, x) => a += f(x), 0);
}
sum([1, 2, 3]);                       // returns 6
sum([1, 2, 3], x => x*x);             // returns 14
sum([1, 2, 3], x => Math.pow(x, 3));  // returns 36
```

By passing an arbitrary function into `sum`, we can make it do...well, anything we want. Need the sum of square roots? No problem. Need the sum of the numbers taken to the 4.233 power? Simple. Note that we want to be able to call `sum` without doing anything special...meaning there is no function. Inside the function, the parameter `f` will have the value `undefined`, and if we tried to invoke it, it would cause an error. To prevent this, we turn anything that isn't a function into the "null function," which, in essence, does nothing. That is, if you pass it 5, it returns 5, and so on. There are more efficient ways we could have handled this situation (such as invoking a different function without the overhead of invoking the null function on every element), but it's good practice to see "safe" functions created this way.

## Return a Function from a Function

Returning a function from a function is perhaps the most esoteric usage for functions, but is extremely useful. You can think of returning a function from a function like a 3D printer: it's a thing that does something (like a function) that can, in turn, make something that also does something. And the exciting part is that the function you get back can be customized—much like you can customize what you print from a 3D printer.

Let's consider our `sum` function from earlier that takes an optional function to operate on each element before summing it. Remember how we said we could create a separate function called `sumOfSquares` if we wanted to? Let's consider the situation in which we *need* such a function. Specifically, a function that takes an array *and* a function is not good enough: we explicitly need a function that takes *only* an array and returns the sum of squares. (If you are wondering when such a circumstance might arise, consider an API that allows you to provide a `sum` function, but only accepts functions that take a single argument.)

One approach would be to create a new function that simply calls our old function:

```
function sumOfSquares(arr) {
   return sum(arr, x => x*x);
}
```

While this approach is fine, and may work if all we need is the one function, what if we need to be able to repeat this pattern over and over? A solution to our problem might be creating a function that returns a specialized function:

```
function newSummer(f) {
   return arr => sum(arr, f);
}
```

This new function—`newSummer`—creates a brand new `sum` function that has only one argument, but uses a custom function. Let's see how we might use it to get different kinds of summers:

```
const sumOfSquares = newSummer(x => x*x);
const sumOfCubes = newSummer(x => Math.pow(x, 3));
sumOfSquares([1, 2, 3]);   // returns 14
sumOfCubes([1, 2, 3]);     // returns 36
```

This technique—where we have taken a function with multiple arguments and converted it to a function with a single argument—is called *currying*, after its developer, American mathematician Haskell Curry.

The applications for returning a function from a function are often deep and complicated. If you want to see more examples of this, look at middleware packages for Express or Koa (popular JavaScript web development frameworks); more often than not, middleware is a function that returns a function.

# Recursion

Another common and important way that functions are used is *recursion*. Recursion refers to a function that calls itself. This is a particularly powerful technique when the function does the same thing with progressively smaller sets of input.

Let's start with a contrived example: finding a needle in a haystack. If you were confronted with a real-life haystack and had to find a needle in it, a viable approach might be this:

1. If you can see the needle in the haystack, go to step 3.
2. Remove a piece of hay from the haystack. Go to step 1.
3. Done!

Basically you're whittling the haystack down until you find the needle; in essence, this is recursion. Let's see how we would translate this example into code:

```
function findNeedle(haystack) {
   if(haystack.length === 0) return "no haystack here!";
   if(haystack.shift() === 'needle') return "found it!"
   return findNeedle(haystack);    // haystack has one fewer element
}

findNeedle(['hay', 'hay', 'hay', 'hay', 'needle', 'hay', 'hay']);
```

The important thing to note in this recursive function is that it is handling all the possibilities: either `haystack` is empty (in which case there's nothing to look for), the needle is the first element in the array (done!), or it's not (it's somewhere in the rest of the array, so we remove the first element and repeat the function—remember that `Array.prototype.shift` removes the first element from the array in place).

It's important that a recursive function has a *stopping condition*; without it, it will keep recursing until the JavaScript interpreter decides the call stack is too deep (which will cause your program to crash). In our `findNeedle` function, we have two stopping conditions: we stop because we found the needle, or we stop because there is no haystack. Because we're reducing the size of the haystack every time, it's inevitable that we will eventually reach one of these stopping conditions.

Let's consider a more useful, time-honored example: finding the factorial of a number. The factorial of a number is the number multiplied by every number up to it and is denoted by an exclamation point after a number. So 4! would be 4 × 3 × 2 × 1 = 24. Here's how we would implement this as a recursive function:

```
function fact(n) {
   if(n === 1) return 1;
   return n * fact(n-1);
}
```

Here we have a stopping condition (`n === 1`), and every time we make the recursive call, we reduce the number `n` by one. So eventually we'll get to 1 (this function will fail if you pass it `0` or a negative number, though of course we could add some error conditions to prevent that from happening).

## Conclusion

If you have experience with other functional languages—like ML, Haskell, Clojure, or F#—this chapter was probably a cakewalk for you. If not, it probably stretched your mind a bit, and you might be reeling a little from the abstract possibility of functional programming (believe me, when I first encountered these ideas, I certainly was). You might be a little overwhelmed by the various ways you can accomplish the same thing, and wondering which way is "better." I'm afraid there's no easy answer to that question. Often it depends on the problem at hand: some problems strongly suggest a certain technique. A lot also depends on you: what techniques resonate with you? If you find the techniques presented in this chapter bewildering, I encourage you to reread it a few times. The concepts here are extremely powerful, and the only way you'll know if they're useful techniques for you is if you take some time to understand them.

CHAPTER 14

# Asynchronous Programming

We got a hint of asynchronous programming in Chapter 1 when we responded to user interaction. Recall that user interaction is naturally asynchronous: you can't control when a user clicks, touches, speaks, or types. But user input isn't the only reason for asynchronous execution: the very nature of JavaScript makes it necessary for many things.

When a JavaScript application runs, it runs *single-threaded*. That is, JavaScript only ever does one thing at a time. Most modern computers are capable of doing multiple things at once (assuming they have multiple cores), and even computers with a single core are so fast that they can simulate doing multiple things at once by doing a tiny bit of task A, then a tiny bit of task B, then a tiny bit of task C, and so on until all the tasks are done (this is called *preemptive multitasking*). From the user's perspective, tasks A, B, and C ran simultaneously, whether or not the tasks were actually running simultaneously on multiple cores.

So JavaScript's single-threaded nature might strike you as a limiting factor, but it actually frees you from having to worry about some very thorny problems that are present in multithreaded programming. This freedom comes at a cost, though: it means that to write smoothly running software, you have to think asynchronously, and not just for user input. Thinking this way can be difficult at first, especially if you're coming from a language where execution is normally synchronous.

JavaScript has had a mechanism for asynchronous execution from the earliest days of the language. However, as the popularity of JavaScript has grown—and the sophistication of the software being written for it—new constructs to manage asynchronous programming have been added to the language. As a matter of fact, we can think of JavaScript as having three distinct eras of asynchronous support: the callback era, the promise era, and the generator era. If it were a simple matter of generators being better than everything that came before them, we would explain how generators work and leave the rest in the past. It's not that simple, though. Generators by themselves do not provide any sort of asynchronous support: they rely on either promises or a special type of callback to provide asynchronous behavior. Likewise, as useful as promises are, they rely on callbacks (and callbacks by themselves are still useful for things like events).

Aside from user input, the three primary things you'll be using asynchronous techniques for are:

- Network requests (Ajax calls, for instance)
- Filesystem operations (reading/writing files, etc.)
- Intentionally time-delayed functionality (an alarm, for example)

## The Analogy

The analogy I like to use for both callbacks and promises is getting a table at a busy restaurant when you don't have a reservation. So you don't have to wait in line, one restaurant will take your mobile phone number and call you when your table is ready. This is like a callback: you've provided the host with something that allows them to let you know when your table is ready. The restaurant is busy doing things, and you can busy yourself with other things; nobody's waiting on anyone else. Another restaurant might give you a pager that will buzz when your table is ready. This is more like a promise: something the host gives to you that will let you know when your table is ready.

As we move through callbacks and promises, keep these analogies in mind, especially if you are new to asynchronous programming.

## Callbacks

Callbacks are the oldest asynchronous mechanism in JavaScript, and we've already seen them used to handle user input and timeouts. A callback is simply a function that you write that will be invoked at some point in the future. There's nothing special about the function itself: it's just a regular JavaScript function. Typically, you provide these callback functions to other functions, or set them as properties on objects (or, rarely, provide them in an array). Callbacks are very often (but not always) anonymous functions.

Let's start with a simple example, using `setTimeout`, a built-in function that delays execution some number of milliseconds:

```
console.log("Before timeout: " + new Date());
function f() {
   console.log("After timeout: " + new Date());
```

```
}
setTimeout(f, 60*1000); // one minute
console.log("I happen after setTimeout!");
console.log("Me too!");
```

If you run this at the console—unless you are a very slow typist indeed—you should see something like this:

```
Before timeout: Sun Aug 02 2015 17:11:32 GMT-0700 (Pacific Daylight Time)
I happen after setTimeout!
Me too!
After timeout: Sun Aug 02 2015 17:12:32 GMT-0700 (Pacific Daylight Time)
```

What beginners struggle with is the disconnect between the linear nature of the code we *write* and the actual *execution* of that code. There is a part of us that wants—that expects—a computer to do things in the exact order in which we write them. In other words, we want to see this:

```
Before timeout: Sun Aug 02 2015 17:11:32 GMT-0700 (Pacific Daylight Time)
After timeout: Sun Aug 02 2015 17:12:32 GMT-0700 (Pacific Daylight Time)
I happen after setTimeout!
Me too!
```

We may want to see that...but it wouldn't be asynchronous. The whole point of asynchronous execution is that it doesn't *block* anything. Because JavaScript is single-threaded, if we told it to wait for 60 seconds before doing some code, and we did that synchronously, nothing would work. Your program would freeze up: it wouldn't accept user input, it wouldn't update the screen, and so on. We've all had this experience, and it's not desirable. Asynchronous techniques help prevent this kind of lock-up.

In this example, for clarity, we used a named function to pass to `setTimeout`. Unless there were some compelling reason to have a named function, we would normally just use an anonymous function:

```
setTimeout(function() {
   console.log("After timeout: " + new Date());
}, 60*1000);
```

`setTimeout` is a little bit problematic because the numeric timeout parameter is the last argument; with anonymous functions, especially if they're long, it can get lost or look like it's part of the function. This is common enough, however, that you'll have to get used to seeing `setTimeout` (and its companion, `setInterval`) used with anonymous functions. Just remember that the last line contains the delay parameter.

## setInterval and clearInterval

In addition to `setTimeout`, which runs its function once and stops, there's `setInterval`, which runs the callback at the specified interval forever, or until you call `clearInterval`. Here's an example that runs every 5 seconds until the minute rolls over, or 10 times, whichever comes first:

```
const start = new Date();
let i=0;
const intervalId = setInterval(function() {
   let now = new Date();
   if(now.getMinutes() !== start.getMinutes() || ++i>10)
      return clearInterval(intervalId);
   console.log(`${i}: ${now}`);
}, 5*1000);
```

We see here that `setInterval` returns an ID that we can use to cancel (stop) it later. There's a corresponding `clearTimeout` that works the same way and allows you to stop a timeout before it runs.

`setTimeout`, `setInterval`, and `clearInterval` are all defined on the global object (`window` in a browser, and `global` in Node).

## Scope and Asynchronous Execution

A common source of confusion—and errors—with asynchronous execution is how scope and closures affect asynchronous execution. Every time you invoke a function, you create a closure: all of the variables that are created inside the function (including the arguments) exist as long as something can access them.

We've seen this example before, but it bears repeating for the important lesson we can learn from it. Consider the example of a function called `countdown`. The intended purpose is to create a 5-second countdown:

```
function countdown() {
   let i;                     // note we declare let outside of the for loop
   console.log("Countdown:");
   for(i=5; i>=0; i--) {
      setTimeout(function() {
         console.log(i===0 ? "GO!" : i);
      }, (5-i)*1000);
   }
}
countdown();
```

Go ahead and work through this example in your head first. You probably remember from the last time you saw this that something's wrong. It looks like what's expected is a countdown from 5. What you get instead is `-1` six times and no `"GO!"`. The first time we saw this, we were using `var`; this time we're using `let`, but it's declared outside of the `for` loop, so we have the same problem: the `for` loop executes completely, leaving i with the value -1, and only *then* do the callbacks start executing. The problem is, when they execute, i already has the value -1.

The important lesson here is understanding the way scope and asynchronous execution relate to each other. When we invoke countdown, we're creating a closure that contains the variable i. All of the (anonymous) callbacks that we create in the for loop all have access to i—the same i.

The tidy thing about this example is that inside the for loop, we see i used in two different ways. When we use it to calculate the timeout ((5-i)*1000), it works as expected: the first timeout is 0, the second timeout is 1000, the third timeout is 2000, and so on. That's because that calculation is synchronous. As a matter of fact, the call to setTimeout is also synchronous (which requires the calculation to happen so that setTimeout knows when to invoke the callback). The asynchronous part is the function that's passed to setTimeout, and that's where the problem occurs.

Recall that we can solve this problem with an immediately invoked function expression (IIFE), or more simply by just moving the declaration of i into the for loop declaration:

```
function countdown() {
   console.log("Countdown:");
   for(let i=5; i>=0; i--) {     // i is now block-scoped
      setTimeout(function() {
         console.log(i===0 ? "GO!" : i);
      }, (5-i)*1000);
   }
}
countdown();
```

The takeaway here is that you have to be mindful of the scope your callbacks are declared in: they will have access to everything in that scope (closure). And because of that, the value may be different when the callback actually executes. This principle applies to *all* asynchronous techniques, not just callbacks.

## Error-First Callbacks

At some point during the ascendancy of Node, a convention called *error-first callbacks* established itself. Because callbacks make exception handling difficult (which we'll see soon), there needed to be a standard way to communicate a failure to the callback. The convention that emerged was to use the first argument to a callback to receive an error object. If that error is null or undefined, there was no error.

Whenever you're dealing with an error-first callback, the first thing you should do is check the error argument and take appropriate action. Consider reading the contents of a file in Node, which adheres to the error-first callback convention:

```
const fs = require('fs');

const fname = 'may_or_may_not_exist.txt';
fs.readFile(fname, function(err, data) {
   if(err) return console.error(`error reading file ${fname}: ${err.message}`);
   console.log(`${fname} contents: ${data}`);
});
```

The first thing we do in the callback is see if `err` is truthy. If it is, there was an issue reading the file, and we report that to the console and *immediately return* (`console.error` doesn't evaluate to a meaningful value, but we're not using the return value anyway, so we just combine it into one statement). This is probably the most often overlooked mistake with error-first callbacks: the programmer will remember to check it, and perhaps log the error, but not return. If the function is allowed to continue, it may rely on the callback having been successful, which it wasn't. (It is possible, of course, that the callback doesn't completely rely on success, in which case it may be acceptable to note the error and proceed anyway.)

Error-first callbacks are the de facto standard in Node development (when promises aren't being used), and if you're writing an interface that takes a callback, I strongly advise you to adhere to the error-first convention.

## Callback Hell

While callbacks allow you to manage asynchronous execution, they have a practical drawback: they're difficult to manage when you need to wait on multiple things before proceeding. Imagine the scenario where you're writing a Node app that needs to get the contents of three different files, then wait 60 seconds before combining the contents of those files and writing to a fourth file:

```
const fs = require('fs');

fs.readFile('a.txt', function(err, dataA) {
   if(err) console.error(err);
   fs.readFile('b.txt', function(err, dataB) {
      if(err) console.error(err);
      fs.readFile('c.txt', function(err, dataC) {
         if(err) console.error(err);
         setTimeout(function() {
            fs.writeFile('d.txt', dataA+dataB+dataC, function(err) {
               if(err) console.error(err);
            });
         }, 60*1000);
      });
   });
});
```

This is what programmers refer to as "callback hell," and it's typified by a triangle-shaped block of code with curly braces nested to the sky. Worse still is the problem of error handling. In this example, all we're doing is logging the errors, but if we tried throwing an exception, we'd be in for another rude surprise. Consider the following simpler example:

```
const fs = require('fs');
function readSketchyFile() {
   try {
      fs.readFile('does_not_exist.txt', function(err, data) {
         if(err) throw err;
      });
   } catch(err) {
      console.log('warning: minor issue occurred, program continuing');
   }
}
readSketchyFile();
```

Glancing over this, it seems reasonable enough, and hooray for us for being defensive programmers and using exception handling. Except it won't work. Go ahead and try it: the program will crash, even though we took some care to make sure this semi-expected error didn't cause problems. That's because `try...catch` blocks only work within the same function. The `try...catch` block is in `readSketchyFile`, but the error is thrown inside the anonymous function that `fs.readFile` invokes as a callback.

Additionally, there's nothing to prevent your callback from accidentally getting called twice—or never getting called at all. If you're relying on it getting called once and exactly once, the language itself offers no protection against that expectation being violated.

These are not insurmountable problems, but with the prevalence of asynchronous code, it makes writing bug-free, maintainable code very difficult, which is where promises come in.

# Promises

Promises attempt to address some of the shortcomings of callbacks. Using promises —while sometimes a hassle—generally results in safer, easier-to-maintain code.

Promises don't eliminate callbacks; as a matter of fact, you still have to use callbacks with promises. What promises do is ensure that callbacks are always handled in the same predictable manner, eliminating some of the nasty surprises and hard-to-find bugs you can get with callbacks alone.

The basic idea of a promise is simple: when you call a promise-based asynchronous function, it returns a `Promise` instance. Only two things can happen to that promise: it can be *fulfilled* (success) or *rejected* (failure). You are guaranteed that *only* one of those things will happen (it won't be fulfilled and then later rejected), and the result will happen only *once* (if it's fulfilled, it'll only be fulfilled once; if it's rejected, it'll only be rejected once). Once a promise has either been fulfilled or rejected, it's considered to be *settled*.

Another convenient advantage of promises over callbacks is that, because they're just objects, they can be passed around. If you want to kick off an asynchronous process, but would prefer someone else handle the results, you can just pass the promise to them (this would be analogous to giving the reservation pager to a friend of yours—ostensibly the restaurant won't mind who takes the reservation as long as the party size is the same).

## Creating Promises

Creating a promise is a straightforward affair: you create a new `Promise` instance with a function that has `resolve` (fulfill) and `reject` callbacks (I did warn you that promises don't save us from callbacks). Let's take our `countdown` function, parameterize it (so we're not stuck with only a 5-second countdown), and have it return a promise when the countdown is up:

```
function countdown(seconds) {
   return new Promise(function(resolve, reject) {
      for(let i=seconds; i>=0; i--) {
         setTimeout(function() {
            if(i>0) console.log(i + '...');
            else resolve(console.log("GO!"));
         }, (seconds-i)*1000);
      }
   });
}
```

This isn't a very flexible function right now. We might not want to use the same verbiage—we may not even want to use the console at all. This wouldn't do us very much good on a web page where we wanted to update a DOM element with our countdown. But it's a start...and it shows how to create a promise. Note that `resolve` (like `reject`) is a function. You might be thinking "Ah ha! I could call `resolve` multiple times, and break the er...promise of promises." You could indeed call `resolve` or `reject` multiple times or mix them up...but only the first call will count. The promise will make sure that whoever is using your promise will only get a fulfillment or a rejection (currently, our function doesn't have a rejection pathway).

## Using Promises

Let's see how we can use our `countdown` function. We could just call it and ignore the promise altogether: `countdown(5)`. We'll still get our countdown, and we didn't have to fuss with the promise at all. But what if we want to take advantage of the promise? Here's how we use the promise that's returned:

```
countdown(5).then(
   function() {
      console.log("countdown completed successfully");
   },
   function(err) {
      console.log("countdown experienced an error: " + err.message);
   }
);
```

In this example, we didn't bother assigning the returned promise to a variable; we just called its `then` handler directly. That handler takes two callbacks: the first one is the fulfilled callback, and the second is the error callback. At most, only one of these functions will get called. Promises also support a `catch` handler so you can split up the two handlers (we'll also store the promise in a variable to demonstrate that):

```
const p = countdown(5);
p.then(function() {
      console.log("countdown completed successfully");
});
p.catch(function(err) {
      console.log("countdown experienced an error: " + err.message);
});
```

Let's modify our `countdown` function to have an error condition. Imagine we're superstitious, and we'll have an error if we have to count the number 13.

```
function countdown(seconds) {
   return new Promise(function(resolve, reject) {
      for(let i=seconds; i>=0; i--) {
         setTimeout(function() {
            if(i===13) return reject(new Error("DEFINITELY NOT COUNTING THAT"));
            if(i>0) console.log(i + '...');
            else resolve(console.log("GO!"));
         }, (seconds-i)*1000);
      }
   });
}
```

Go ahead and play around with this. You'll notice some interesting behavior. Obviously, you can count down from any number less than 13, and it will behave normally. Count down from 13 or higher, and it will fail when it gets to 13. However... the console logs still happen. Calling `reject` (or `resolve`) doesn't stop your function; it just manages the state of the promise.

Clearly our `countdown` function needs some improvements. Normally, you wouldn't want a function to keep working after it had settled (successfully or otherwise), and ours does. We've also already mentioned that the console logs aren't very flexible. They don't really give us the control we'd like.

Promises give us an extremely well-defined and safe mechanism for asynchronous tasks that either fulfill or reject, but they do not (currently) provide any way to report *progress*. That is, a promise is either fulfilled or rejected, never "50% done." Some promise libraries[1] add the very useful ability to report on progress, and it is possible that functionality will arrive in JavaScript promises in the future, but for now, we must make do without it. Which segues nicely into....

## Events

Events are another old idea that's gained traction in JavaScript. The concept of events is simple: an event emitter broadcasts events, and anyone who wishes to listen (or "subscribe") to those events may do so. How do you subscribe to an event? A callback, of course. Creating your own event system is quite easy, but Node provides built-in support for it. If you're working in a browser, jQuery also provides an event mechanism (*http://api.jquery.com/category/events/*). To improve `countdown`, we'll use Node's `EventEmitter`. While it's possible to use `EventEmitter` with a function like `countdown`, it's designed to be used with a class. So we'll make our `countdown` function into a `Countdown` class instead:

```
const EventEmitter = require('events').EventEmitter;

class Countdown extends EventEmitter {
   constructor(seconds, superstitious) {
      super();
      this.seconds = seconds;
      this.superstitious = !!superstitious;
   }
   go() {
      const countdown = this;
      return new Promise(function(resolve, reject) {
         for(let i=countdown.seconds; i>=0; i--) {
            setTimeout(function() {
               if(countdown.superstitious && i===13)
                  return reject(new Error("DEFINITELY NOT COUNTING THAT"));
               countdown.emit('tick', i);
               if(i===0) resolve();
            }, (countdown.seconds-i)*1000);
         }
      });
   }
}
```

The `Countdown` class extends `EventEmitter`, which enables it to emit events. The `go` method is what actually starts the countdown and returns a promise. Note that inside the `go` method, the first thing we do is assign `this` to `countdown`. That's because we need to use the value of `this` to get the length of the countdown, and whether or not the countdown is superstitious *inside the callbacks*. Remember that `this` is a special

1 Such as Q (*https://github.com/kriskowal/q*).

variable, and it won't have the same value inside a callback. So we have to save the current value of `this` so we can use it inside the promises.

The magic happens when we call `countdown.emit('tick', i)`. Anyone who wants to listen for the `tick` event (we could have called it anything we wanted; "tick" seemed as good as anything) can do so. Let's see how we would use this new, improved countdown:

```
const c = new Countdown(5);

c.on('tick', function(i) {
   if(i>0) console.log(i + '...');
});

c.go()
   .then(function() {
      console.log('GO!');
   })
   .catch(function(err) {
      console.error(err.message);
   })
```

The `on` method of `EventEmitter` is what allows you to listen for an event. In this example, we provide a callback for every `tick` event. If that `tick` isn't `0`, we print it out. Then we call `go`, which starts the countdown. When the countdown is finished, we log `GO!`. We could have, of course, put the `GO!` inside the `tick` event listener, but doing it this way underscores the difference between events and promises.

What we're left with is definitely more verbose than our original `countdown` function, but we've gained a lot of functionality. We now have complete control over how we report the ticks in the countdown, and we have a promise that's fulfilled when the countdown is finished.

We still have one task left—we haven't addressed the problem of a superstitious `Countdown` instance continuing to count down past 13, even though it's rejected the promise:

```
const c = new Countdown(15, true)
   .on('tick', function(i) {                 // note we can chain the call to 'on'
      if(i>0) console.log(i + '...');
   });

c.go()
   .then(function() {
      console.log('GO!');
   })
   .catch(function(err) {
      console.error(err.message);
   })
```

We still get all the ticks, all the way down to 0 (even though we don't print it). Fixing this problem is a little involved because we have already created all the timeouts (of course, we could just "cheat" and immediately fail if a superstitious timer is created for 13 seconds or longer, but that would miss the point of the exercise). To solve this problem, once we discover we can't continue, we'll have to clear all of the pending timeouts:

```
const EventEmitter = require('events').EventEmitter;

class Countdown extends EventEmitter {
   constructor(seconds, superstitious) {
      super();
      this.seconds = seconds;
      this.superstitious = !!superstitious;
   }
   go() {
      const countdown = this;
      const timeoutIds = [];
      return new Promise(function(resolve, reject) {
         for(let i=countdown.seconds; i>=0; i--) {
            timeoutIds.push(setTimeout(function() {
               if(countdown.superstitious && i===13) {
                  // clear all pending timeouts
                  timeoutIds.forEach(clearTimeout);
                  return reject(new Error("DEFINITELY NOT COUNTING THAT"));
               }
               countdown.emit('tick', i);
               if(i===0) resolve();
            }, (countdown.seconds-i)*1000));
         }
      });
   }
}
```

## Promise Chaining

One of the advantages of promises is that they can be *chained*; that is, when one promise is fulfilled, you can have it immediately invoke another function that returns a promise...and so on. Let's create a function called `launch` that we can chain to a countdown:

```
function launch() {
   return new Promise(function(resolve, reject) {
      console.log("Lift off!");
      setTimeout(function() {
         resolve("In orbit!");
      }, 2*1000);     // a very fast rocket indeed
   });
}
```

It's easy to chain this function to a countdown:

```
const c = new Countdown(5)
   .on('tick', i => console.log(i + '...'));

c.go()
   .then(launch)
   .then(function(msg) {
      console.log(msg);
   })
   .catch(function(err) {
      console.error("Houston, we have a problem....");
   })
```

One of the advantages of promise chains is that you don't have to catch errors at every step; if there's an error anywhere in the chain, the chain will stop and fall through to the `catch` handler. Go ahead and change the countdown to a 15-second superstitious countdown; you'll find that `launch` is never called.

## Preventing Unsettled Promises

Promises can simplify your asynchronous code and protect you against the problem of callbacks being called more than once, but they don't protect you from the problem of promises that never settle (that is, you forget to call either `resolve` or `reject`). This kind of mistake can be hard to track down because there's no error…in a complex system, an unsettled promise may simply get lost.

One way to prevent that is to specify a timeout for promises; if the promise hasn't settled in some reasonable amount of time, automatically reject it. Obviously, it's up to you to know what "reasonable amount of time" is. If you have a complex algorithm that you expect to take 10 minutes to execute, don't set a 1-second timeout.

Let's insert an artificial failure into our `launch` function. Let's say our rocket is *very* experimental indeed, and fails approximately half the time:

```
function launch() {
   return new Promise(function(resolve, reject) {
      if(Math.random() < 0.5) return;    // rocket failure
      console.log("Lift off!");
      setTimeout(function() {
         resolve("In orbit!");
      }, 2*1000);    // a very fast rocket indeed
   });
}
```

In this example, the way we're failing is not very responsible: we're not calling `reject`, and we're not even logging anything to the console. We just silently fail half the time. If you run this a few times, you'll see that sometimes it works, and sometimes it doesn't…with no error message. Clearly undesirable.

We can write a function that attaches a timeout to a promise:

```
function addTimeout(fn, timeout) {
   if(timeout === undefined) timeout = 1000; // default timeout
   return function(...args) {
         return new Promise(function(resolve, reject) {
            const tid = setTimeout(reject, timeout,
               new Error("promise timed out"));
            fn(...args)
               .then(function(...args) {
                  clearTimeout(tid);
                  resolve(...args);
               })
               .catch(function(...args) {
                  clearTimeout(tid);
                  reject(...args);
               });
         });
   }
}
```

If you're saying "Whoa...a function that returns a function that returns a promise that calls a function that returns a promise...my head is spinning!", I can't blame you: to add a timeout to a promise-returning function is not trivial, and requires all of the preceding contortions. Completely understanding this function is left as an advanced reader's exercise. Using this function, however, is quite easy: we can add a timeout to any function that returns a promise. Let's say our very slowest rocket attains orbit in 10 seconds (isn't future rocket technology great?), so we set a timeout of 11 seconds:

```
c.go()
   .then(addTimeout(launch, 4*1000))
   .then(function(msg) {
      console.log(msg);
   })
   .catch(function(err) {
      console.error("Houston, we have a problem: " + err.message);
   });
```

Now our promise chain will always settle, even when the `launch` function behaves badly.

## Generators

As already discussed in Chapter 12, generators allow two-way communication between a function and its caller. Generators are synchronous in nature, but when combined with promises, they offer a powerful technique for managing async code in JavaScript.

Let's revisit the central difficulty with async code: it's harder to write than synchronous code. When we tackle a problem, our minds want to approach it in a synchronous fashion: step 1, step 2, step 3, and so on. However, that can have performance consequences, which is why async exists. Wouldn't it be nice if you could have the performance benefits of async without the additional conceptual difficulty? That's where generators can help us.

Consider the "callback hell" example we used previously: reading three files, delaying for one minute, then writing the contents of the first three files out to a fourth file. How our human minds would *like* to write this is something like this pseudocode:

```
dataA = read contents of 'a.txt'
dataB = read contents of 'b.txt'
dataC = read contents of 'c.txt'
wait 60 seconds
write dataA + dataB + dataC to 'd.txt'
```

Generators enable us to write code that looks very much like this...but the functionality doesn't come out of the box: we'll have to do a little work first.

The first thing we need is a way to turn Node's error-first callbacks into promises. We'll encapsulate that into a function called `nfcall` (Node function call):

```
function nfcall(f, ...args) {
   return new Promise(function(resolve, reject) {
      f.call(null, ...args, function(err, ...args) {
         if(err) return reject(err);
         resolve(args.length<2 ? args[0] : args);
      });
   });
}
```

This function is named after (and based on) the `nfcall` method in the Q promise library (*https://github.com/kriskowal/q*). If you need this functionality, you should probably use Q. It includes not only this method, but many more helpful promise-related methods as well. I present an implementation of `nfcall` here to demonstrate that there is no "magic."

Now we can convert any Node-style method that takes a callback to a promise. We'll also need `setTimeout`, which takes a callback...but because it predates Node, it wasn't hip to the error-first convention. So we'll create `ptimeout` (promise timeout):

```
function ptimeout(delay) {
   return new Promise(function(resolve, reject) {
      setTimeout(resolve, delay);
   });
}
```

The next thing we'll need is a *generator runner*. Recall that generators are not inherently asynchronous. But because generators allow the function to communicate to the caller, we can create a function that will manage that communication—and know how to handle asynchronous calls. We'll create a function called grun (generator run):

```
function grun(g) {
   const it = g();
   (function iterate(val) {
      const x = it.next(val);
      if(!x.done) {
         if(x.value instanceof Promise) {
            x.value.then(iterate).catch(err => it.throw(err));
         } else {
            setTimeout(iterate, 0, x.value);
         }
      }
   })();
}
```

grun is based heavily on runGenerator, presented in Kyle Simpson's excellent series of articles on generators (*http://davidwalsh.name/es6-generators*). I highly recommend that you read those articles as a supplement to this text.

This is a very modest recursive generator runner. You pass it a generator function, and it runs it. As you learned in Chapter 6, generators that call yield will pause until next is called on their iterator. This function does so recursively. If the iterator returns a promise, it waits for the promise to be fulfilled before resuming the iterator. On the other hand, if the iterator returns a simple value, it immediately resumes the iteration. You may be wondering why we call setTimeout instead of just calling iterate directly; the reason is that we gain a little efficiency by avoiding synchronous recursion (asynchronous recursion allows the JavaScript engine to free resources more quickly).

You may be thinking "This is a lot of fuss!" and "This is supposed to *simplify* my life?", but the hard part is over. nfcall allows us to adopt the past (Node error-first callback functions) to the present (promises), and grun allows us access to the future today (expected in ES7 is the await keyword, which will essentially function as grun, with an even more natural syntax). So now that we've got the hard part out of the way, let's see how all of this makes our life easier.

Remember our "wouldn't it be nice" pseudocode from earlier in this chapter? Now we can realize that:

```
function* theFutureIsNow() {
   const dataA = yield nfcall(fs.readFile, 'a.txt');
   const dataB = yield nfcall(fs.readFile, 'b.txt');
   const dataC = yield nfcall(fs.readFile, 'c.txt');
   yield ptimeout(60*1000);
```

```
    yield nfcall(fs.writeFile, 'd.txt', dataA+dataB+dataC);
}
```

It looks a lot better than callback hell, doesn't it? It's also neater than promises alone. It flows the way we think. Running it is simple:

```
grun(theFutureIsNow);
```

## One Step Forward and Two Steps Back?

You might (quite reasonably) be thinking that we've gone to *so much trouble* to understand asynchronous execution, then make it easier...and now we're right back where we started, except with the extra complication of generators and converting things to promises and `grun`. And there is some truth in this: in our `theFutureIsNow` function, we have somewhat thrown the baby out with the bathwater. It's easier to write, easier to read, and we're reaping *some* of the benefits of asynchronous execution, but not all of them. The sharp question here is: "Would it be more efficient to read the three files in parallel?" The answer to that question depends a lot on the problem, the implementation of your JavaScript engine, your operating system, and your filesystem. But let's put aside those complexities for a moment, and recognize that *it doesn't matter* what order we read the three files in, and it's conceivable that efficiency would be gained from allowing those file read operations to happen in parallel. And this is where generator runners can lull us into a false sense of complacency: we wrote the function this way because it seemed easy and straightforward.

The problem (assuming there is a problem) is easy to solve. `Promise` provides a method called `all`, which resolves when all the promises in an array resolve...and will execute the asynchronous code in parallel if possible. All we have to do is modify our function to use `Promise.all`:

```
function* theFutureIsNow() {
    const data = yield Promise.all([
        nfcall(fs.readFile, 'a.txt'),
        nfcall(fs.readFile, 'b.txt'),
        nfcall(fs.readFile, 'c.txt'),
    ]);
    yield ptimeout(60*1000);
    yield nfcall(fs.writeFile, 'd.txt', data[0]+data[1]+data[2]);
}
```

The promise returned by `Promise.all` provides an array containing the fulfillment value of each promise *in the order they appear in the array*. Even though it's possible for *c.txt* to be read before *a.txt*, `data[0]` will still hold the contents of *a.txt*, and `data[1]` will still hold the contents of *c.txt*.

Your takeaway from this section should not be `Promise.all` (though that's a handy tool to know about); your takeaway should be to *consider what parts of your program can be run in parallel, and what parts can't*. In this example, it's even possible that the timeout could be run in parallel to the file reads: it all depends on the problem you're trying to solve. If what's important is that the three files are read and *then* 60 seconds passes and *then* the concatenated result is written to another file, we already have what we want. On the other hand, what we may want is for the three files to be read, and *in no sooner than 60 seconds*, the results to be written to a fourth file—in which case, we would want to move the timeout into the `Promise.all`.

## Don't Write Your Own Generator Runner

While it's a good exercise to write our own generator runner, as we have done with `grun`, there are many nuances and improvements we could make on it. It's better not to reinvent the wheel. The `co` generator runner (*https://github.com/tj/co*) is full-featured and robust. If you are building websites, you may want to look into Koa (*http://koajs.com/*), which is designed to work with `co`, allowing you to write web handlers using `yield`, as we have in `theFutureIsNow`.

## Exception Handling in Generator Runners

Another important benefit of generator runners is that they enable exception handling with `try/catch`. Remember that exception handling is problematic with callbacks and promises; throwing an exception inside a callback cannot be caught from outside the callback. Generator runners, because they enable synchronous semantics while still preserving asynchronous execution, have a side benefit of working with `try/catch`. Let's add a couple of exception handlers to our `theFutureIsNow` function:

```
function* theFutureIsNow() {
    let data;
    try {
        data = yield Promise.all([
          nfcall(fs.readFile, 'a.txt'),
          nfcall(fs.readFile, 'b.txt'),
          nfcall(fs.readFile, 'c.txt'),
        ]);
    } catch(err) {
        console.error("Unable to read one or more input files: " + err.message);
        throw err;
    }
    yield ptimeout(60*1000);
    try {
        yield nfcall(fs.writeFile, 'd.txt', data[0]+data[1]+data[2]);
    } catch(err) {
        console.error("Unable to write output file: " + err.message);
        throw err;
    }
}
```

I'm not claiming that `try...catch` exception handling is inherently superior to `catch` handlers on promises, or error-first callbacks, but it is a well-understood mechanism for exception handling, and if you prefer synchronous semantics, then you will want to be able to use it for exception handling.

## Conclusion

Fully understanding the complexities involved in asynchronous programming—and the various mechanisms that have evolved for managing it—is critical to understanding modern JavaScript development. We've learned:

- Asynchronous execution in JavaScript is managed with callbacks.
- Promises do not replace callbacks; indeed, promises require `then` and `catch` callbacks.
- Promises eliminate the problem of a callback getting called multiple times.
- If you need a callback to be called multiple times, consider using events (which can be combined with a promise).
- A promise cannot guarantee that it will settle; however, you can wrap it in a timeout to protect against this.
- Promises can be chained, enabling easy composition.
- Promises can be combined with generator runners to enable synchronous semantics without losing the advantages of asynchronous execution.
- When writing generator functions with synchronous semantics, you should be careful to understand what parts of your algorithm can run in parallel, and use `Promise.all` to run those parts.
- You shouldn't write your own generator runner; use `co` (*https://github.com/tj/co*) or Koa (*http://koajs.com/*).
- You shouldn't write your own code to convert Node-style callbacks to promises; use Q (*https://github.com/kriskowal/q*).
- Exception handling works with synchronous semantics, as enabled by generator runners.

If your only programming experience is with languages that have synchronous semantics, learning synchronous programming the JavaScript way can be daunting; it certainly was for me. However, it's an essential skill in modern JavaScript projects.

CHAPTER 15

# Date and Time

Most real-world applications involve working with date and time data. Unfortunately, JavaScript's `Date` object (which also stores time data) is not one of the language's best-designed features. Because of the limited utility of this built-in object, I will be introducing *Moment.js*, which extends the functionality of the `Date` object to cover commonly needed functionality.

It's an interesting bit of history that JavaScript's `Date` object was originally implemented by Netscape programmer Ken Smith—who essentially ported Java's `java.util.Date` implementation into JavaScript. So it's not *entirely* true that JavaScript has nothing to do with Java: if anyone ever asks you what they have to do with each other, you can say, "Well, aside from the `Date` object and a common syntactic ancestor, very little."

Because it gets tedious to keep repeating "date and time," I will use "date" to implicitly mean "date and time." A date without a time is implicitly 12:00 A.M. on that day.

## Dates, Time Zones, Timestamps, and the Unix Epoch

Let's face it: our modern Gregorian calendar is a fussy, overcomplicated thing, with 1-based numbering, odd divisions of time, and leap years. Time zones add even more complexity. However, it's (mostly) universal, and we have to live with it.

We'll start with something simple: the second. Unlike the complicated division of time in the Gregorian calendar, seconds are easy. Dates and times—as represented by seconds—are a single number, neatly ordered on a number line. Representing dates and time in seconds is therefore ideal for computation. However, it doesn't work so well for human communication: "Hey, Byron, want to have lunch at 1437595200?" (1437595200 is Wednesday, July 22, 2015, at 1 P.M. Pacific Standard Time). If dates are represented by seconds, what date corresponds to 0? It isn't, as it turns out, the birth of Christ, but an arbitrary date: January 1, 1970, 00:00:00 UTC.

As you're probably aware, the world is divided into *time zones* (TZs) so that, no matter where you are in the morning, 7 A.M. is morning and 7 P.M. is evening. Time zones can get complicated fast, especially as you start to consider daylight saving time. I won't attempt to explain all the nuances of the Gregorian calendar or time zones in this book—Wikipedia does an excellent job of that. However, it's important to cover some of the basics to help us understand the JavaScript `Date` object (and what Moment.js brings to the table).

All time zones are defined as offsets from *Coordinated Universal Time* (abbreviated UTC—refer to Wikipedia for the complicated and somewhat hilarious reasons). UTC is sometimes (and not entirely correctly) referred to as Greenwich Mean Time (GMT). For example, I'm currently in Oregon, which is in the Pacific time zone. Pacific time is either eight or seven hours behind UTC. Wait, eight *or* seven? Which is it? Depends on the time of year. In the summer, it's daylight saving time, and the offset is seven. The rest of the year, it's standard time, and the offset is eight. What's important here is not memorizing time zones, but understanding how the offsets are represented. If I open up a JavaScript terminal, and type `new Date()`, I see the following:

```
Sat Jul 18 2015 11:07:06 GMT-0700 (Pacific Daylight Time)
```

Note that in this very verbose format, the time zone is specified both as an offset from UTC (`GMT-0700`) and by its name (`Pacific Daylight Time`).

In JavaScript, all `Date` instances are stored as a single number: the number of milliseconds (not seconds) since the Unix Epoch. JavaScript normally converts that number to a human-readable Gregorian date whenever you request it (as just shown). If you want to see the numeric representation, simply use the `valueOf()` method:

```
const d = new Date();
console.log(d);             // formatted Gregorian date with TZ
console.log(d.valueOf());   // milliseconds since Unix Epoch
```

# Constructing Date Objects

The `Date` object can be constructed in four ways. Without any arguments (as we've seen already), it simply returns a `Date` object representing the current date. We can also provide a string that JavaScript will attempt to parse, or we can specify a specific (local) date down to the millisecond. Here are examples:

```
// all of the below are interpreted with respect to local time
new Date();                              // current date

// note that months are zero-based in JavaScript: 0=Jan, 1=Feb, etc.
```

```
new Date(2015, 0);                     // 12:00 A.M., Jan 1, 2015
new Date(2015, 1);                     // 12:00 A.M., Feb 1, 2015
new Date(2015, 1, 14);                 // 12:00 A.M., Feb 14, 2015
new Date(2015, 1, 14, 13);             // 3:00 P.M., Feb 14, 2015
new Date(2015, 1, 14, 13, 30);         // 3:30 P.M., Feb 14, 2015
new Date(2015, 1, 14, 13, 30, 5);      // 3:30:05 P.M., Feb 14, 2015
new Date(2015, 1, 14, 13, 30, 5, 500); // 3:30:05.5 P.M., Feb 14, 2015

// creates dates from Unix Epoch timestamps
new Date(0);                           // 12:00 A.M., Jan 1, 1970 UTC
new Date(1000);                        // 12:00:01 A.M., Jan 1, 1970 UTC
new Date(1463443200000);               // 5:00 P.M., May 16, 2016 UTC

// use negative dates to get dates prior to the Unix Epoch
new Date(-365*24*60*60*1000);          // 12:00 A.M., Jan 1, 1969 UTC

// parsing date strings (defaults to local time)
new Date('June 14, 1903');             // 12:00 A.M., Jun 14, 1903 local time
new Date('June 14, 1903 GMT-0000');    // 12:00 A.M., Jun 14, 1903 UTC
```

If you're trying these examples out, one thing you'll notice is that the results you get are always in local time. Unless you are on UTC (hello, Timbuktu, Madrid, and Greenwich!), the results listed in UTC will be different than shown in this example. This brings us to one of the main frustrations of the JavaScript `Date` object: there's no way to specify what time zone it should be in. It will always store objects internally as UTC, and format them according to local time (which is defined by your operating system). Given JavaScript's origin as a browser-based scripting language, this has traditionally been the "right thing to do." If you're working with dates, you probably want to display dates in the user's time zone. However, with the global nature of the Internet—and with Node bringing JavaScript to the server—more robust handling of time zones would be useful.

# Moment.js

While this book is about the JavaScript language itself—not libraries—date manipulation is such an important and common problem that I have decided to introduce a prominent and robust date library, *Moment.js*.

Moment.js comes in two flavors: with or without time zone support. Because the time zone version is significantly larger (it has information about all the world's time zones), you have the option of using Moment.js without time zone support. For simplicity, the following instructions all reference the time zone–enabled version. If you want to use the smaller version, visit *http://momentjs.com* for information about your options.

If you're doing a web-based project, you can reference Moment.js from a CDN, such as cdnjs:

```
<script src="//cdnjs.cloudflare.com/ajax/libs/moment-timezone/0.4.0/ ↩
moment-timezone.min.js"></script>
```

If you're working with Node, you can install Moment.js with `npm install --save moment-timezone` and then reference it from your script with `require`:

```
const moment = require('moment-timezone');
```

Moment.js is large and robust, and chances are, if you need to manipulate dates, it has exactly the functionality you need. Consult its excellent documentation (*http://momentjs.com/*) for more information.

# A Practical Approach to Dates in JavaScript

Now that we have the basics out of the way, and you have Moment.js available, we're going to take a slightly different approach to covering this information. An exhaustive coverage of the methods available on the `Date` object would be dry and not very useful to most people. Furthermore, if you need that reference, MDN's coverage of the `Date` object (*https://developer.mozilla.org/en-US/docs/Web/JavaScript/Reference/Global_Objects/Date*) is exhaustive and well-written.

Instead, this book will take a more cookbook-based approach and cover the common date processing needs that people have, and use `Date` and Moment.js where appropriate.

# Constructing Dates

We've already covered the construction options available to you with JavaScript's `Date` object, which are, for the most part, adequate. Whenever you construct a date without an explicit time zone, you have to think about what time zone is being used, which is going to be dependent on *where* the date is being constructed. This has tripped up many a beginner in the past: they use the same date code on a server in Arlington, Virginia, as they use in a user's browser connecting from Los Angeles, California, and they are surprised when the dates are off by three hours.

## Constructing Dates on the Server

If you're constructing dates on the server, I recommend always either using UTC or explicitly specifying the time zone. With today's cloud-based approach to application development, the same code base could be running on servers all over the world. If you're constructing local dates, you're asking for trouble. If you are able to use UTC dates, you can construct them with the `Date` object's `UTC` method:

```
const d = new Date(Date.UTC(2016, 4, 27));  // May 27, 2016 UTC
```

Date.UTC takes all the same variations of arguments as the Date constructor, but instead of returning a new Date instance, it returns the numeric value of the date. That number can then be passed into the Date constructor to create a date instance.

If you need to construct dates on the server that are in a specific time zone (and don't want to do the time zone conversion by hand), you can use moment.tz to construct Date instances using a specific time zone:

```
// passing an array to Moment.js uses the same parameters as JavaScript's Date
// constructor, including zero-based moths (0=Jan, 1=Feb, etc.).  toDate()
// converts back to a JavaScript Date object.
const d = moment.tz([2016, 3, 27, 9, 19], 'America/Los_Angeles').toDate();
```

## Constructing Dates in the Browser

Generally, JavaScript's default behavior is appropriate in the browser. The browser knows from the operating system what time zone it's in, and users generally like to work in local time. If you're building an app that needs to handle dates in other time zones, then you'll want to use Moment.js to handle the conversion and display of dates in other time zones.

# Transmitting Dates

Where things get interesting is transmitting dates—either the server sending dates to the browser or vice versa. The server and browser could be in different time zones, and users want to see dates in their local time zone. Fortunately, because JavaScript Date instances store the date as a numeric offset from the UTC, Unix Epoch, it's generally safe to pass Date objects back and forth.

We've been talking about "transmitting" very vaguely, though: what exactly do we mean? The surest way to ensure that dates are transmitted safely in JavaScript is using *JavaScript Object Notation* (JSON). The JSON specification doesn't actually specify a data type for dates, which is unfortunate, because it prevents symmetric parsing of JSON:

```
const before = { d: new Date() };
before.d instanceof date            // true
const json = JSON.stringify(before);
const after = JSON.parse(json);
after.d instdanceof date            // false
typeof after.d                      // "string"
```

So the bad news is that JSON can't seamlessly and symmetrically handle dates in JavaScript. The good news is that the string serialization that JavaScript uses is always consistent, so you can "recover" a date:

```
after.d = new Date(after.d);
after.d instanceof date          // true
```

No matter what time zone was originally used to create the date, when it is encoded as JSON, it will be in UTC, and when the JSON-encoded string is passed to the `Date` constructor, the date will be displayed in the local time zone.

The other safe way to pass dates between client and server is to simply use the numeric value of the date:

```
const before = { d: new Date().valueOf() };
typeof before.d                      // "number"
const json = JSON.stringify(before);
const after = JSON.parse(json);
typeof after.d                       // "number"
const d = new Date(after.d);
```

While JavaScript is happily consistent when JSON-encoding dates as strings, the JSON libraries provided by other languages and platforms are *not*. The .NET JSON serializers in particular wrap JSON-encoded date objects in their own proprietary format. So if you're interfacing with JSON from another system, take care to understand how it serializes dates. If you have control over the source code, this is an instance where it may be safer to transmit numeric dates as offsets from the Unix Epoch. Even here you must be careful, however: often date libraries will give the numeric value in seconds, not milliseconds.

# Displaying Dates

Formatting dates for display is often one of the most frustrating problems for beginners. JavaScript's built-in `Date` object includes only a handful of prepackaged date formats, and if they don't meet your needs, it can be painful to do the formatting yourself. Fortunately, Moment.js excels in this area, and if you are particular about how dates are displayed, then I recommend you use it.

To format a date with Moment.js, use its `format` method. This method takes a string with metacharacters that are replaced with the appropriate component of the date. For example, the string `"YYYY"` will be replaced with the four-digit year. Here are some examples of date formatting with the `Date` object's built-in methods, and the more robust Moment.js methods:

```
const d = new Date(Date.UTC(1930, 4, 10));

// these show output for someone in Los Angeles

d.toLocaleDateString()       // "5/9/1930"
d.toLocaleFormat()           // "5/9/1930 4:00:00 PM"
```

```
d.toLocaleTimeString()      // "4:00:00 PM"
d.toTimeString()            // "17:00:00 GMT-0700 (Pacific Daylight Time)"
d.toUTCString()             // "Sat, 10 May 1930, 00:00:00 GMT"

moment(d).format("YYYY-MM-DD");                // "1930-05-09"
moment(d).format("YYYY-MM-DD HH:mm");          // "1930-05-09 17:00
moment(d).format("YYYY-MM-DD HH:mm Z");        // "1930-05-09 17:00 -07:00
moment(d).format("YYYY-MM-DD HH:mm [UTC]Z"); // "1930-05-09 17:00 UTC-07:00

moment(d).format("dddd, MMMM [the] Do, YYYY");  // "Friday, May the 9th, 1930"

moment(d).format("h:mm a");                    // "5:00 pm"
```

This example shows how inconsistent and inflexible the built-in date formatting options are. In JavaScript's favor, these built-in formatting options do attempt to provide formatting that's appropriate for the user's locale. If you need to support date formatting in multiple locales, this is an inexpensive but inflexible way to do it.

This is not designed to be an exhaustive reference to the formatting options available in Moment.js; see the online documentation for that. What it is designed to communicate is that if you have date formatting needs, Moment.js can almost certainly meet them. Like many such date formatting metalanguages, there are some common conventions. More letters means more verbose; that is, "M" gets you 1, 2, 3,...; "MM" gets you 01, 02, 03,...; "MMM" gets you Jan, Feb, Mar,...; and "MMMM" gets you January, February, March,.... A lowercase "o" will give you an ordinal: "Do" will give you 1st, 2nd, 3rd, and so on. If you want to include letters that you don't want interpreted as metacharacters, surround them with square brackets: "[M]M" will give you M1, M2, and so on.

One frustration that Moment.js doesn't completely solve is the use of time zone abbreviations, such as EST and PST. Moment.js has deprecated the z formatting character due to lack of consistent international standards. See the Moment.js documentation for a detailed discussion of the issues with time zone abbreviations.

## Date Components

If you need to access individual components of a Date instance, there are methods for that:

```
const d = new Date(Date.UTC(1815, 9, 10));

// these are the results someone would see in Los Angeles
d.getFullYear()      // 1815
d.getMonth()         // 9 - October
d.getDate()          // 9
d.getDay()           // 1 - Monday
```

```
d.getHours()         // 17
d.getMinutes()       // 0
d.getSeconds()       // 0
d.getMilliseconds()  // 0

// there are allso UTC equivalents to the above:
d.getUTCFullYear()   // 1815
d.getUTCMonth()      // 9 - October
d.getUTCDate()       // 10
// ...etc.
```

If you're using Moment.js, you'll find little need to work with individual components, but it's good to know that they're there.

# Comparing Dates

For simple date comparisons—does date A come after date B or vice versa?—you can use JavaScript's built-in comparison operators. Remember that `Date` instances store the date as a number, so the comparison operators simply work on the numbers:

```
const d1 = new Date(1996, 2, 1);
const d2 = new Date(2009, 4, 27);

d1 > d2      // false
d1 < d2      // true
```

# Date Arithmetic

Because dates are just numbers, you can subtract dates to get the number of milliseconds between them:

```
const msDiff = d2 - d1;                     // 417740400000 ms
const daysDiff = msDiff/1000/60/60/24;      // 4834.96 days
```

This property also makes it easy to sort dates using `Array.prototype.sort`:

```
const dates = [];
// create some random dates
const min = new Date(2017, 0, 1).valueOf();
const delta = new Date(2020, 0, 1).valueOf() - min;
for(let i=0; i<10; i++)
   dates.push(new Date(min + delta*Math.random()));
// dates are random and (probably) jumbled
// we can sort them (descending):
dates.sort((a, b) => b - a);
// or ascending:
dates.sort((a, b) => a - b);
```

Moment.js brings many powerful methods for doing common date arithmetic, allowing you to add or subtract arbitrary units of time:

```
const m = moment();          // now
m.add(3, 'days');            // m is now three days in the future
m.subtract(2, 'years');      // m is now two years minus three days in the past

m = moment();                // reset
m.startOf('year');           // m is now Jan 1 of this year
m.endOf('month');            // m is now Jan 31 of this year
```

Moment.js also allows you to chain methods:

```
const m = moment()
   .add(10, 'hours')
   .subtract(3, 'days')
   .endOf('month');

// m is the end of the month you would be in if you
// traveled 10 hours into the future then 3 days back
```

## User-Friendly Relative Dates

Very often, it's nice to be able to present date information in a relative fashion: "three days ago" as opposed to a date. Moment.js makes this easy:

```
moment().subtract(10, 'seconds').fromNow();     // a few seconds ago
moment().subtract(44, 'seconds').fromNow();     // a few seconds ago
moment().subtract(45, 'seconds').fromNow();     // a minute ago
moment().subtract(5, 'minutes').fromNOw();      // 5 minutes ago
moment().subtract(44, 'minutes').fromNOw();     // 44 minutes ago
moment().subtract(45, 'minutes').fromNOw();     // an hour ago
moment().subtract(5, 'hours').fromNOw();        // 4 hours ago
moment().subtract(21, 'hours').fromNOw();       // 21 hours ago
moment().subtract(22, 'hours').fromNOw();       // a day ago
moment().subtract(344, 'days').fromNOw();       // 344 days ago
moment().subtract(345, 'days').fromNOw();       // a year ago
```

As you can see, Moment.js has chosen some arbitrary (but reasonable) breakpoints for when to switch to displaying a different unit. It's a handy way to get user-friendly relative dates.

## Conclusion

If you take away three things from this chapter, they should be the following:

- Internally, dates are represented as the number of milliseconds from the Unix Epoch (Jan 1, 1970 UTC).
- Be aware of the time zone when you're constructing dates.
- If you want sophisticated date formatting, consider Moment.js.

In most real-world applications, it's hard to get away from date processing and manipulation. Hopefully this chapter has given you a foundation in the important concepts. The Mozilla Developer Network and Moment.js documentation serve as a thorough and detailed reference.

CHAPTER 16

# Math

This chapter describes JavaScript's built-in `Math` object, which contains math functions commonly encountered in application development (if you are doing sophisticated numeric analysis, you may have to find third-party libraries).

Before we delve into the library, let's remind ourselves how JavaScript handles numbers. In particular, there's no dedicated integer class; all numbers are IEEE 754 64-bit floating-point numbers. For most functions in the math library, this simplifies things: a number is a number. While no computer will ever be able to fully represent an arbitrary real number, for practical purposes, you can think of JavaScript numbers as real numbers. Note that there's no built-in support for complex numbers in JavaScript. If you need complex numbers, bignums, or more sophisticated structures or algorithms, I recommend starting with Math.js (*http://mathjs.org/*).

Outside of some basics, this chapter is not designed to teach you math; that's a book (or 2 or 10) of its own.

Throughout the code comments in this chapter, I will use a tilde (~) prefix to indicate that a given value is approximate. I will also refer to properties of the `Math` object as *functions*, not *methods*. While they are technically static methods, the distinction is academic here, as the `Math` object provides namespacing, not context.

## Formatting Numbers

A common need is to format numbers; that is, instead of displaying 2.0093, you want to display 2.1. Or instead of displaying 1949032, you want to display 1,949,032.[1]

1 In some cultures, periods are used as thousands separators, and commas are used as the decimal separator, opposite from what you may be used to.

JavaScript's built-in support for formatting numbers is limited, but includes support for a fixed number of decimal digits, fixed precision, and exponential notation. Furthermore, there is support for displaying numbers in other bases, such as binary, octal, and hexadecimal.

By necessity, all of JavaScript's number formatting methods return a string, not a number; only a string can preserve the desired formatting (it is easy to convert back to a number if necessary, however). The upshot of this is that you should only format numbers immediately before displaying them; while you are storing them or using them in calculations, they should remain unformatted number types.

## Fixed Decimals

If you want a fixed number of digits past the decimal point, you can use `Number.prototype.toFixed`:

```
const x = 19.51;
x.toFixed(3);      // "19.510"
x.toFixed(2);      // "19.51"
x.toFixed(1);      // "19.5"
x.toFixed(0);      // "20"
```

Note that this is not truncation: the output is rounded to the number of specified decimal digits.

## Exponential Notation

If you wish to display numbers in exponential notation, use `Number.prototype.toExponential`:

```
const x = 3800.5;
x.toExponential(4);  // "3.8005e+4";
x.toExponential(3);  // "3.801e+4";
x.toExponential(2);  // "3.80e+4";
x.toExponential(1);  // "3.8e+4";
x.toExponential(0);  // "4e+4";
```

Like `Number.prototype.toFixed`, output is rounded, not truncated. The specified precision is the number of digits past the decimal.

## Fixed Precision

If what you care about is a fixed number of digits (regardless of where the decimal place falls), you can use `Number.prototype.toPrecision`:

```
let x = 1000;
x.toPrecision(5);     // "1000.0"
x.toPrecision(4);     // "1000"
x.toPrecision(3);     // "1.00e+3"
```

```
x.toPrecision(2);      // "1.0e+3"
x.toPrecision(1);      // "1e+3"
x = 15.335;
x.toPrecision(6);      // "15.3350"
x.toPrecision(5);      // "15.335"
x.toPrecision(4);      // "15.34"
x.toPrecision(3);      // "15.3"
x.toPrecision(2);      // "15"
x.toPrecision(1);      // "2e+1"
```

Output is rounded, and will always have the specified number of digits of precision. If necessary, output will be in exponential notation.

## Different Bases

If you want to display numbers in a different base (such as binary, octal, or hexadecimal), `Number.prototype.toString` takes an argument specifying the base (in the range 2 to 36):

```
const x = 12;
x.toString();         // "12"   (base 10)
x.toString(10);       // "12"   (base 10)
x.toString(16);       // "c"    (hexadecimal)
x.toString(8);        // "14"    (octal)
x.toString(2);        // "1100" (binary)
```

## Advanced Number Formatting

If you're displaying a lot of numbers in your application, your needs may quickly surpass what the built-in JavaScript methods provide. Common needs are:

- Thousands separators
- Displaying negative numbers differently (for example, with parentheses)
- Engineering notation (similar to exponential notation)
- SI prefixes (milli-, micro-, kilo-, mega-, etc.)

Providing this functionality can be educational if you're looking for a reader's exercise. If you're not, I recommend the Numeral.js library (*http://numeraljs.com/*), which provides all of this functionality and more.

# Constants

The usual important constants are available as properties of the `Math` object:

```
// fundamental constants
Math.E    // the root of the natural logarithm: ~2.718
Math.PI   // the ratio of a circle's circumference to its diameter: ~3.142
```

```
// logarithmic convenience constants -- these can be accessed through library
// calls, but they're commonly used enough to warrant convenience constants
Math.LN2       // the natural logarithm of 2: ~0.693
Math.LN10      // the natural logarithm of 10: ~2.303
Math.LOG2E     // the base 2 logarithm of Math.E: ~1.433
Math.LOG10E    // the base 10 logarithm of Math.E: 0.434

// algebraic convenience constants
Math.SQRT1_2   // the square root of 1/2: ~0.707
Math.SQRT2     // the square root of 2: ~1.414
```

# Algebraic Functions

## Exponentiation

The basic exponentiation function is `Math.pow`, and there are convenience functions for square root, cube root, and powers of *e*, as shown in Table 16-1.

*Table 16-1. Exponentiation functions*

| Function | Description | Examples |
| --- | --- | --- |
| `Math.pow(x, y)` | $x^y$ | `Math.pow(2, 3)       // 8`<br>`Math.pow(1.7, 2.3)   // ~3.39` |
| `Math.sqrt(x)` | $\sqrt{x}$<br>Equivalent to `Math.pow(x, 0.5)` | `Math.sqrt(16)        // 4`<br>`Math.sqrt(15.5)      // ~3.94` |
| `Math.cbrt(x)` | Cube root of *x*<br>Equivalent to `Math.pow(x, 1/3)` | `Math.cbrt(27)        // 3`<br>`Math.cbrt(22)        // ~2.8` |
| `Math.exp(x)` | $e^x$ Equivalent to `Math.pow(Math.E, x)` | `Math.exp(1)          // ~2.718`<br>`Math.exp(5.5)        // ~244.7` |
| `Math.expm1(x)` | $e^x - 1$ Equivalent to `Math.exp(x) - 1` | `Math.expm1(1)        // ~1.718`<br>`Math.expm1(5.5)      // ~243.7` |
| `Math.hypot(x1, x2,...)` | Square root of sum of arguments: $\sqrt{x1^2 + x2^2 + \ldots}$ | `Math.hypot(3, 4)     // 5`<br>`Math.hypot(2, 3, 4)  // ~5.36` |

## Logarithmic Functions

The basic natural logarithm function is `Math.log`. In some languages, "log" refers to "log base 10" and "ln" refers to "natural logarithm," so keep in mind that in JavaScript, "log" means "natural logarithm." ES6 introduced `Math.log10` for convenience.

*Table 16-2. Logarithmic functions*

| Function | Description | Examples | |
|---|---|---|---|
| `Math.log(x)` | Natural logarithm of *x* | `Math.log(Math.E)`<br>`Math.log(17.5)` | `// 1`<br>`// ~2.86` |
| `Math.log10(x)` | Base 10 logarithm of *x*<br>Equivalent to `Math.log(x)/Math.log(10)` | `Math.log10(10)`<br>`Math.log10(16.7)` | `// 1`<br>`// ~1.22` |
| `Math.log2(x)` | Base 2 logarithm of *x*<br>Equivalent to `Math.log(x)/Math.log(2)` | `Math.log2(2)`<br>`Math.log2(5)` | `// 1`<br>`// ~2.32` |
| `Math.log1p(x)` | Natural logarithm of 1 + *x*<br>Equivalent to `Math.log(1 + x)` | `Math.log1p(Math.E - 1)`<br>`Math.log1p(17.5)` | `// 1`<br>`// ~2.92` |

## Miscellaneous

Table 16-3 lists miscellaneous numeric functions that allow you to perform common operations such as finding the absolute value, ceiling, floor, or sign of a number, as well as finding the minimum or maximum number in a list.

*Table 16-3. Number miscellaneous algebraic functions*

| Function | Description | Examples | |
|---|---|---|---|
| `Math.abs(x)` | Absolute value of x | `Math.abs(-5.5)`<br>`Math.abs(5.5)` | `// 5.5`<br>`// 5.5` |
| `Math.sign(x)` | The sign of *x*: if *x* is negative, −1; if *x* is positive, 1; and if *x* is 0, 0 | `Math.sign(-10.5)`<br>`Math.sign(6.77)` | `// -1`<br>`// 1` |
| `Math.ceil(x)` | The ceiling of *x*: the smallest integer greater than or equal to *x* | `Math.ceil(2.2)`<br>`Math.ceil(-3.8)` | `// 3`<br>`// -3` |
| `Math.floor(x)` | The floor of *x*: the largest integer less than or equal to *x* | `Math.floor(2.8)`<br>`Math.floor(-3.2)` | `// 2`<br>`// -4` |

| Function | Description | Examples |
| --- | --- | --- |
| `Math.trunc(x)` | The integral part of *x* (all fractional digits removed) | `Math.trunc(7.7)  // 7`<br>`Math.trunc(-5.8)  // -5` |
| `Math.round(x)` | *x* rounded to the nearest integer | `Math.round(7.2)  // 7`<br>`Math.round(7.7)  // 8`<br>`Math.round(-7.7)  // -8`<br>`Math.round(-7.2)  // -7` |
| `Math.min(x1, x2,...)` | Returns the minimum argument | `Math.min(1, 2)  // 1`<br>`Math.min(3, 0.5, 0.66)  // 0.5`<br>`Math.min(3, 0.5, -0.66)  // -0.66` |
| `Math.max(x1, x2,...)` | Returns the maximum argument | `Math.max(1, 2)  // 2`<br>`Math.max(3, 0.5, 0.66)  // 3`<br>`Math.max(-3, 0.5, -0.66)  // 0.5` |

## Pseudorandom Number Generation

Pseudorandom number generation is provided by `Math.random`, which returns a pseudorandom number greater than or equal to 0 and less than 1. You may recall from algebra that number ranges are often denoted with square brackets (inclusive) and parentheses (exclusive). In this notation, `Math.random` returns numbers in the range [0, 1).

`Math.random` does not provide any convenience methods for providing pseudorandom numbers in different ranges. Table 16-4 shows some general formulas for getting other ranges. In this table, `x` and `y` denote real numbers and `m` and `n` denote integers.

*Table 16-4. Number pseudorandom number generation*

| Range | Example |
| --- | --- |
| [0, 1) | `Math.random()` |
| [x, y) | `x + (y-x)*Math.random()` |
| Integer in [m, n) | `m + Math.floor((n-m)*Math.random())` |
| Integer in [m, n] | `m + Math.floor((n-m+1)*Math.random())` |

A common complaint about JavaScript's pseudorandom number generator is that it can't be *seeded*, which is important to testing some algorithms involving pseudorandom numbers. If you need seeded pseudorandom numbers, see David Bau's seedrandom.js package (*https://github.com/davidbau/seedrandom*).

It is common (but incorrect) for pseudorandom number generators (PRNGs) to simply be called "random number generators." PRNGs produce numbers that for most practical applications appear to be random, but true random number generation is a very difficult problem.

## Trigonometric Functions

There are no surprises here. Sine, cosine, tangent, and their inverses are all available, as shown in Table 16-5. All trigonometric functions in the `Math` library operate on radians, not degrees.

*Table 16-5. Number trigonometric functions*

| Function | Description | Examples |
| --- | --- | --- |
| `Math.sin(x)` | Sine of *x* radians | `Math.sin(Math.PI/2)    // 1`<br>`Math.sin(Math.PI/4)    // ~0.707` |
| `Math.cos(x)` | Cosine of *x* radians | `Math.cos(Math.PI)    // -1`<br>`Math.cos(Math.PI/4)    // ~0.707` |
| `Math.tan(x)` | Tangent of *x* radians | `Math.tan(Math.PI/4)    // ~1`<br>`Math.tan(0)    // 0` |
| `Math.asin(x)` | Inverse sine (arcsin) of *x* (result in radians) | `Math.asin(0)    // 0`<br>`Math.asin(Math.SQRT1_2)    // ~0.785` |
| `Math.acos(x)` | Inverse cosine (arccos) of *x* (result in radians) | `Math.acos(0)    // ~1.57+`<br>`Math.acos(Math.SQRT1_2)    // ~0.785+` |
| `Math.atan(x)` | Inverse tangent (arctan) of *x* (result in radians) | `Math.atan(0)    // 0`<br>`Math.atan(Math.SQRT1_2)    // ~0.615` |
| `Math.atan2(y, x0)` | Counterclockwise angle (in radians) from the x-axis to the point (x, y) | `Math.atan2(0, 1)    // 0`<br>`Math.atan2(1, 1)    // ~0.785` |

If you're dealing with degrees, you'll need to convert them to radians. The calculation is easy: divide by 180 and multiply by π. It's easy to write helper functions:

```
function deg2rad(d) { return d/180*Math.PI; }
function rad2deg(r) { return r/Math.PI*180; }
```

## Hyperbolic Functions

Like the trigonometric functions, the hyperbolic functions are standard, as you can see in Table 16-6.

*Table 16-6. Number hyperbolic functions*

| Function | Description | Examples |
|---|---|---|
| `Math.sinh(x)` | Hyperbolic sine of *x* | `Math.sinh(0) // 0`<br>`Math.sinh(1) // ~1.18` |
| `Math.cosh(x)` | Hyperbolic cosine of *x* | `Math.cosh(0) // 1`<br>`Math.cosh(1) // ~1.54` |
| `Math.tanh(x)` | Hyperbolic tangent of *x* | `Math.tanh(0) // 0`<br>`Math.tanh(1) // ~0.762` |
| `Math.asinh(x)` | Inverse hyperbolic sine (arcsinh) of *x* | `Math.asinh(0) // 0`<br>`Math.asinh(1) // ~0.881` |
| `Math.acosh(x)` | Inverse hyperbolic cosine (arccosh) of *x* | `Math.acosh(0) // NaN`<br>`Math.acosh(1) // 0` |
| `Math.atanh(x)` | Inverse hyperbolic tangent (arctanh) of *x* | `Math.atanh(0) // 0`<br>`Math.atanh(0) // ~0.615` |

# CHAPTER 17
# Regular Expressions

Regular expressions provide sophisticated string matching functionality. If you want to match things that "look like" an email address or a URL or a phone number, regular expressions are your friends. A natural complement to string matching is string replacement, and regular expressions support that as well—for example, if you want to match things that look like email addresses and replace them with a hyperlink for that email address.

Many introductions to regular expressions use esoteric examples such as "match *aaaba* and *abaaba* but not *abba*," which has the advantage of breaking the complexity of regular expressions into neat chunks of functionality, but has the disadvantage of seeming very pointless (when do you ever need to match *aaaba*?). I am going to try to introduce the features of regular expressions using practical examples from the get-go.

Regular expressions are often abbreviated "regex" or "regexp"; in this book, we'll use the former for brevity.

## Substring Matching and Replacing

The essential job of a regex is to match a substring within a string, and optionally replace it. Regexes allow you to do this with incredible power and flexibility, so before we dive into it, let's briefly cover the non-regex search and replace functionality of `String.prototype`, which is suitable for very modest search and replacement needs.

If all you need to do is determine if a specific substring exists in a bigger string, the following `String.prototype` methods will suffice:

```
const input = "As I was going to Saint Ives";
input.startsWith("As")         // true
input.endsWith("Ives")         // true
input.startsWith("going", 9)  // true -- start at index 9
input.endsWith("going", 14)   // true -- treat index 14 as the end of the string
input.includes("going")        // true
input.includes("going", 10)   // false -- starting at index 10
input.indexOf("going")         // 9
input.indexOf("going", 10)    // -1
input.indexOf("nope")          // -1
```

Note that all of these methods are case sensitive. So `input.startsWith("as")` would be false. If you want to do a case-insensitive comparison, you can simply convert the input to lowercase:

```
input.toLowerCase().startsWith("as")         // true
```

Note that this doesn't modify the original string; `String.prototype.toLowerCase` returns a new string and doesn't modify the original string (remember that strings in JavaScript are immutable).

If we want to go a step further and find a substring and `replace` it, we can use `String.prototype.replace`:

```
const input = "As I was going to Saint Ives";
const output = input.replace("going", "walking");
```

Again, the original string (`input`) is not modified by this replacement; `output` now contains the new string with "going" replaced with "walking" (we could have assigned back to `input`, of course, if we really wanted `input` to change).

# Constructing Regular Expressions

Before we get into the complexities of the regex metalanguage, let's talk about how they're actually constructed and used in JavaScript. For these examples, we'll be searching for a specific string, just as before—an overkill for regexes, but an easy way to understand how they're used.

Regexes in JavaScript are represented by the class `RegExp`. While you can construct a regex with the `RegExp` constructor, regexes are important enough to merit their own literal syntax. Regex literals are set off with forward slashes:

```
const re1 = /going/;              // regex that can search for the word "going"
const re2 = new RegExp("going");  // equivalent object constructor
```

There is a specific reason to use the `RegExp` constructor that we'll cover later in this chapter, but except for that special case, you should prefer the more convenient literal syntax.

## Searching with Regular Expressions

Once we have a regex, we have multiple options for using it to search in a string.

To understand the options for replacement, we're going to get a little preview of the regex metalanguage—using a static string here would be very boring. We'll use the regex `/\w{3,}/ig`, which will match all words three letters or longer (case insensitive). Don't worry about understanding this right now; that will come later in this chapter. Now we can consider the search methods available to us:

```
const input = "As I was going to Saint Ives";
const re = /\w{3,}/ig;

// starting with the string (input)
input.match(re);      // ["was", "going", "Saint", "Ives"]
input.search(re);     // 5 (the first three-letter word starts at index 5)

// starting with the regex (re)
re.test(input);       // true (input contains at least one three-letter word)
re.exec(input);       // ["was"] (first match)
re.exec(input);       // ["going"] (exec "remembers" where it is)
re.exec(input);       // ["Saint"]
re.exec(input);       // ["Ives"]
re.exec(input);       // null -- no more matches

// note that any of these methods can be used directly with a regex literal
input.match(/\w{3,}/ig);
input.search(/\w{3,}/ig);
/\w{3,}/ig.test(input);
/\w{3,}/ig.exec(input);
// ...
```

Of these methods, `RegExp.prototype.exec` provides the most information, but you'll find that it's the one you use the least often in practice. I find myself using `String.prototype.match` and `RegExp.prototype.test` the most often.

## Replacing with Regular Expressions

The same `String.prototype.replace` method we saw before for simple string replacement also accepts a regex, but it can do a lot more. We'll start with a simple example—replacing all four-letter words:

```
const input = "As I was going to Saint Ives";
const output = input.replace(/\w{4,}/ig, '****');  // "As I was ****
                                                    // to **** ****"
```

We'll learn about much more sophisticated replacement methods later in this chapter.

## Input Consumption

A naïve way to think about regexes is "a way to find a substring within a larger string" (often called, colorfully, "needle in a haystack"). While this naïve conception is often all you need, it will limit your ability to understand the true nature of regexes and leverage them for more powerful tasks.

The sophisticated way to think about a regex is a *pattern for consuming input strings*. The matches (what you're looking for) become a byproduct of this thinking.

A good way to conceptualize the way regexes work is to think of a common children's word game: a grid of letters in which you are supposed to find words. We'll ignore diagonal and vertical matches; as a matter of fact, let's think only of the first line of this word game:

X J A N L I O N A T U R E J X E E L N P

Humans are very good at this game. We can look at this, and pretty quickly pick out LION, NATURE, and EEL (and ION while we're at it). Computers—and regexes—are not as clever. Let's look at this word game as a regex would; not only will we see how regexes work, but we will also see some of the limitations that we need to be aware of.

To simplify things, let's tell the regex that we're looking for LION, ION, NATURE, and EEL; in other words, we'll give it the answers and see if it can verify them.

The regex starts at the first character, X. It notes that none of the words it's looking for start with the letter X, so it says "no match." Instead of just giving up, though, it moves on to the next character, J. It finds the same situation with J, and then moves on to A. As we move along, we consider the letters the regex engine is moving past as being *consumed*. Things don't get interesting until we hit the L. The regex engine then says, "Ah, this could be LION!" Because this could be a potential match, it *doesn't consume the L*; this is an important point to understand. The regex goes along, matching the I, then the O, then the N. Now it recognizes a match; success! Now that it has recognized a match it can then consume the whole word, so L, I, O, and N are now consumed. Here's where things get interesting. LION and NATURE overlap. As humans, we are untroubled by this. But the regex is very serious about not looking at things it's already consumed. So it doesn't "go back" to try to find matches in things it's already consumed. So the regex won't find NATURE because the N has already been consumed; all it will find is ATURE, which is not one of the words it is looking for. It will, however, eventually find EEL.

Now let's go back to the example and change the O in LION to an X. What will happen then? When the regex gets to the L, it will again recognize a potential match (LION), and therefore not consume the L. It will move on to the I without consuming it. Then it will get to the X; at this point, it realizes that there's no match: it's not looking for any word that starts with LIX. What happens next is that the regex goes back to where it thought it had a match (the L), consumes that L, and moves on, just as normal. In this instance, it *will* match NATURE, because the N hadn't been consumed as part of LION.

A partial example of this process is shown in Figure 17-1.

X J A N L I O N A T U R E J X E E L N P
↑ Possible match? No...consume X

X J A N L I O N A T U R E J X E E L N P
↑ Possible match? No...consume J

X J A N L I O N A T U R E J X E E L N P
↑ Possible match? No...consume A

X J A N L I O N A T U R E J X E E L N P
↑ Possible match? No...consume N

X J A N L I O N A T U R E J X E E L N P
↑ Possible match? **Yes!** Do NOT consume L

X J A N L I O N A T U R E J X E E L N P
↑ Possible match? **Yes!** Do NOT consume I

X J A N L I O N A T U R E J X E E L N P
↑ Possible match? **Yes!** Do NOT consume O

X J A N L I O N A T U R E J X E E L N P
↑ **Confirmed match!** Consume entire match (LION)

X J A N L I O N A T U R E J X E E L N P
↑ Possible match? No...consume A

*...continues until entire input is consumed*

*Figure 17-1. Regex example*

Before we move on to discussing the specifics of the regex metalanguage, let's consider abstractly the algorithm a regex employs when "consuming" a string:

- Strings are consumed from left to right.
- Once a character has been consumed, it is never revisited.
- If there is no match, the regex advances one character at a time attempting to find a match.

- If there is a match, the regex consumes all the characters in the match at once; matching continues with the next character (if the regex is global, which we'll talk about later).

This is the general algorithm, and it probably won't surprise you that the details are much more complicated. In particular, the algorithm can be aborted early if the regex can determine that there won't be a match.

As we move through the specifics of the regex metalanguage, try to keep this algorithm in mind; imagine your strings being consumed from left to right, one character at a time, until there are matches, at which point whole matches are consumed at once.

## Alternation

Imagine you have an HTML page stored in a string, and you want to find all tags that can reference an external resource (`<a>`, `<area>`, `<link>`, `<script>`, `<source>`, and sometimes, `<meta>`). Furthermore, some of the tags may be mixed case (`<Area>`, `<LINKS>`, etc.). Regular expression *alternations* can be used to solve this problem:

```
const html = 'HTML with <a href="/one">one link</a>, and some JavaScript.' +
    '<script src="stuff.js"></script>';
const matches = html.match(/area|a|link|script|source/ig);  // first attempt
```

The vertical bar (`|`) is a regex metacharacter that signals alternation. The `ig` signifies to ignore case (`i`) and to search globally (`g`). Without the `g`, only the first match would be returned. This would be read as "find all instances of the text *area*, *a*, *link*, *script*, or *source*, ignoring case." The astute reader might wonder why we put `area` before `a`; this is because regexes evaluate alternations from left to right. In other words, if the string has an `area` tag in it, it would match the `a` and then move on. The `a` is then consumed, and `rea` would not match anything. So you have to match `area` first, then `a`; otherwise, `area` will never match.

If you run this example, you'll find that you have many unintended matches: the word *link* (inside the `<a>` tag), and instances of the letter *a* that are *not* an HTML tag, just a regular part of English. One way to solve this would be to change the regex to `/<area|<a|<link|<script|<source/` (angle brackets are not regex metacharacters), but we're going to get even more sophisticated still.

## Matching HTML

In the previous example, we perform a very common task with regexes: matching HTML. Even though this is a common task, I must warn you that, while you can generally do useful things with HTML using regexes, you cannot *parse* HTML with regexes. *Parsing* means to completely break something down into its component parts. Regexes are capable of parsing *regular* languages only (hence the name). Regular languages are extremely simple, and most often you will be using regexes on more complex languages. Why the warning, then, if regexes can be used usefully on more complex languages? Because it's important to understand the limitations of regexes, and recognize when you need to use something more powerful. Even though we will be using regexes to do useful things with HTML, it's possible to construct HTML that will defeat our regex. To have a solution that works in 100% of the cases, you would have to employ a parser. Consider the following example:

```
const html = '<br> [!CDATA[[<br>]]';
const matches = html.match(/<br>/ig);
```

This regex will match twice; however, there is only one true `<br>` tag in this example; the other matching string is simply non-HTML character data (CDATA). Regexes are also extremely limited when it comes to matching hierarchical structures (such as an `<a>` tag within a `<p>` tag). The theoretical explanations for these limitations are beyond the scope of this book, but the takeaway is this: if you're struggling to make a regex to match something very complicated (such as HTML), consider that a regex simply might not be the right tool.

## Character Sets

Character sets provide a compact way to represent alternation of a *single character* (we will combine it with repetition later, and see how we can extend this to multiple characters). Let's say, for example, you wanted to find all the numbers in a string. You could use alternation:

```
const beer99 = "99 bottles of beer on the wall " +
   "take 1 down and pass it around -- " +
   "98 bottles of beer on the wall.";
const matches = beer99.match(/0|1|2|3|4|5|6|7|8|9/g);
```

How tedious! And what if we wanted to match not numbers but letters? Numbers *and* letters? Lastly, what if you wanted to match everything that's *not* a number? That's where character sets come in. At their simplest, they provide a more compact way of representing single-digit alternation. Even better, they allow you to specify *ranges*. Here's how we might rewrite the preceding:

```
const m1 = beer99.match(/[0123456789]/g);  // okay
const m2 = beer99.match(/[0-9]/g);         // better!
```

You can even combine ranges. Here's how we would match letters, numbers, and some miscellaneous punctuation (this will match everything in our original string except whitespace):

```
const match = beer99.match(/[\-0-9a-z.]/ig);
```

Note that order doesn't matter: we could just as easily have said `/[.a-z0-9\-]/`. We have to escape the dash to match it; otherwise, JavaScript would attempt to interpret it as part of a range (you can also put it right before the closing square bracket, unescaped).

Another very powerful feature of character sets is the ability to *negate* character sets. Negated character sets say "match everything *but* these characters." To negate a character set, use a caret (`^`) as the first character in the set:

```
const match = beer99.match(/[^\-0-9a-z.]/);
```

This will match only the whitespace in our original string (if we wanted to match only whitespace, there are better ways to do it, which we'll learn about shortly).

## Named Character Sets

Some character sets are so common—and so useful—that there are handy abbreviations for them:

| Named character set | Equivalent | Notes |
|---|---|---|
| `\d` | `[0-9]` | |
| `\D` | `[^0-9]` | |
| `\s` | `[ \t\v\n\r]` | Includes tabs, spaces, and vertical tabs. |
| `\S` | `[^ \t\v\n\r]` | |
| `\w` | `[a-zA-Z_]` | Note that dashes and periods are not included in this, making it unsuitable for things like domain names and CSS classes. |
| `\W` | `[^a-zA-Z_]` | |

Probably the most commonly used of these abbreviations is the whitespace set (`\s`). For example, whitespace is often used to line things up, but if you're trying to parse it programmatically, you want to be able to account for different amounts of whitespace:

```
const stuff =
    'hight:      9\n' +
    'medium:     5\n' +
    'low:        2\n';
const levels = stuff.match(/:\s*[0-9]/g);
```

(The `*` after the `\s` says "zero or more whitespace," which we'll learn about shortly.)

Don't overlook the usefulness of the negated character classes (`\D`, `\S`, and `\W`); they represent a great way of getting rid of unwanted cruft. For example, it's a great idea to normalize phone numbers before storing in a database. People have all kinds of fussy ways of entering phone numbers: dashes, periods, parentheses, and spaces. For searching, keying, and identification, wouldn't it be nice if they were just 10-digit numbers? (Or longer if we're talking about international phone numbers.) With `\D`, it's easy:

```
const messyPhone = '(505) 555-1515';
const neatPhone = messyPhone.replace(/\D/g, '');
```

Similarly, I often use `\S` to make sure there's data in required fields (they have to have at least one character that's not whitespace):

```
const field = '   something   ';
const valid = /\S/.test(field);
```

# Repetition

Repetition metacharacters allow you to specify how many times something matches. Consider our earlier example where we were matching single digits. What if, instead, we wanted to match *numbers* (which may consist of multiple contiguous digits)? We could use what we already know and do something like this:

```
const match = beer99.match(/[0-9][0-9][0-9]|[0-9][0-9]|[0-9]/);
```

Notice how we again have to match the most specific strings (three-digit numbers) before we match less specific ones (two-digit numbers). This will work for one-, two-, and three-digit numbers, but when we add four-digit numbers, we'd have to add to our alternation. Fortunately, there is a better way:

```
const match = beer99.match(/[0-9]+/);
```

Note the `+` following the character group: this signals that the *preceding element* should match *one or more times*. "Preceding element" often trips up beginners. The repetition metacharacters are *modifiers* that modify *what comes before them*. They do not (and cannot) stand on their own. There are five repetition modifiers:

| Repetition modifier | Description | Example |
|---|---|---|
| `{n}` | Exactly *n*. | `/d{5}/` matches only five-digit numbers (such as a zip code). |
| `{n,}` | At least *n*. | `/\d{5,}/` matches only five-digit numbers or longer. |
| `{n, m}` | At least *n*, at most *m*. | `/\d{2,5}/` matches only numbers that are at least two digits, but no more than five. |

| Repetition modifier | Description | Example |
|---|---|---|
| ? | Zero or one. Equivalent to {0,1}. | /[a-z]\d?/i matches letter followed by an *optional* digit. |
| * | Zero or more (sometimes called a "Klene star" or "Klene closure"). | /[a-z]\d*/i matches a letter followed by an optional number, possibly consisting of multiple digits. |
| + | One or more. | /[a-z]\d+/i matches a letter followed by a required number, possibly containing multiple digits. |

## The Period Metacharacter and Escaping

In regex, the period is a special character that means "match anything" (except newlines). Very often, this catch-all metacharacter is used to consume parts of the input that you don't care about. Let's consider an example where you're looking for a single five-digit zip code, and then you don't care about anything else on the rest of the line:

```
const input = "Address: 333 Main St., Anywhere, NY, 55532.  Phone: 555-555-2525.";
const match = input.match(/\d{5}.*/);
```

You might find yourself commonly matching a literal period, such as the periods in a domain name or IP address. Likewise, you may often want to match things that are regex metacharacters, such as asterisks and parentheses. To escape *any* special regex character, simply prefix it with a backslash:

```
const equation = "(2 + 3.5) * 7";
const match = equation.match(/\(\d \+ \d\.\d\) \* \d/);
```

Many readers may have experience with *filename globbing*, or being able to use `*.txt` to search for "any text files." The `*` here is a "wildcard" metacharacter, meaning it matches anything. If this is familiar to you, the use of `*` in regexes may confuse you, because it means something completely different, and cannot stand alone. The period in a regex is more closely related to the `*` in filename globbing, except that it only matches a single character instead of a whole string.

### A True Wildcard

Because the period matches any character *except* newlines, how do you match any character *including* newlines? (This comes up more often than you might think.) There are lots of ways to do this, but probably the most common is `[\s\S]`. This matches everything that's whitespace...and everything that's not whitespace. In short, everything.

## Grouping

So far, the constructs we've learned about allow us to identify single characters (repetition allows us to repeat that character match, but it's still a single-character match). *Grouping* allows us to construct *subexpressions*, which can then be treated like a single unit.

In addition to being able to create subexpressions, grouping can also "capture" the results of the groups so you can use them later. This is the default, but there is a way to create a "noncapturing group," which is how we're going to start. If you have some regex experience already, this may be new to you, but I encourage you to use noncapturing groups by default; they have performance advantages, and if you don't need to use the group results later, you should be using noncapturing groups. Groups are specified by parentheses, and noncapturing groups look like `(?:<subexpression>)`, where `<subexpression>` is what you're trying to match. Let's look at some examples. Imagine you're trying to match domain names, but only *.com*, *.org*, and *.edu*:

```
const text = "Visit oreilly.com today!";
const match = text.match(/[a-z]+(?:\.com|\.org|\.edu)/i);
```

Another advantage of groups is that you can apply repetition to them. Normally, repetition applies only to the *single character* to the left of the repetition metacharacter. Groups allow you to apply repetition to whole strings. Here's a common example. If you want to match URLs, and you want to include URLs that start with *http://*, *https://*, and simply *//* (protocol-independent URLs), you can use a group with a zero-or-one (`?`) repetition:

```
const html = '<link rel="stylesheet" href="http://insecure.com/stuff.css">\n' +
   '<link rel="stylesheet" href="https://secure.com/securestuff.css">\n' +
   '<link rel="stylesheet" href="//anything.com/flexible.css">';

const matches = html.match(/(?:https?)?\/\/[a-z][a-z0-9-]+[a-z0-9]+/ig);
```

Look like alphabet soup to you? It does to me too. But there's a lot of power packed into this example, and it's worth your while to slow down and really consider it. We start off with a noncapturing group: `(?:https?)?`. Note there are two zero-or-one repetition metacharacters here. The first one says "the *s* is optional." Remember that repetition characters normally refer only to the character to their immediate left. The second one refers to the whole *group* to its left. So taken all together, this will match the empty string (zero instances of `https?`), `http`, or `https`. Moving on, we match two slashes (note we have to escape them: `\/\/`). Then we get a rather complicated character class. Obviously domain names can have letters and numbers in them, but they can also have dashes (but they have to start with a letter, and they can't end with a dash).

This example isn't perfect. For example, it would match the URL *//gotcha* (no TLD) just as it would match *//valid.com*. However, to match completely valid URLs is a much more complicated task, and not necessary for this example.

If you're feeling a little fed up with all the caveats ("this will match invalid URLs"), remember that you don't have to do everything all the time, all at once. As a matter of fact, I use a very similar regex to the previous one all the time when scanning websites. I just want to pull out *all* the URLs—or suspect URLs—and then do a second analysis pass to look for invalid URLs, broken URLs, and so on. Don't get too caught up in making perfect regexes that cover every case imaginable. Not only is that sometimes impossible, but it is often unnecessary effort when it is possible. Obviously, there is a time and place to consider all the possibilities—for example, when you are screening user input to prevent injection attacks. In this case, you will want to take the extra care and make your regex ironclad.

## Lazy Matches, Greedy Matches

What separates the regex dilettantes from the pros is understanding lazy versus greedy matching. Regular expressions, by default, are *greedy*, meaning they will match as much as possible before stopping. Consider this classic example.

You have some HTML, and you want to replace, for example, `<i>` text with `<strong>` text. Here's our first attempt:

```
const input = "Regex pros know the difference between\n" +
   "<i>greedy</i> and <i>lazy</i> matching.";
input.replace(/<i>(.*)<\/i>/ig, '<strong>$1</strong>');
```

The `$1` in the replacement string will be replaced by the contents of the group `(.*)` in the regex (more on this later).

Go ahead and try it. You'll find the following disappointing result:

```
"Regex pros know the difference between
<strong>greedy</i> and <i>lazy</strong> matching."
```

To understand what's going on here, think back to how the regex engine works: it consumes input until it satisfies the match before moving on. By default, it does so in a *greedy* fashion: it finds the first `<i>` and then says, "I'm not going to stop until I see an `</i>` and *I can't find any more past that*." Because there are two instances of `</i>`, it ends at the second one, not the first.

There's more than one way to fix this example, but because we're talking about greedy versus lazy matching, we'll solve it by making the repetition metacharacter (*) lazy instead. We do so by following it with a question mark:

```
input.replace(/<i>(.*?)<\/i>/ig, '<strong>$1</strong>');
```

The regex is exactly the same except for the question mark following the * metacharacter. Now the regex engine thinks about this regex this way: "I'm going to stop as soon as I see an </i>." So it lazily stops matching every time it sees an </i> without scanning further to see if it could match later. While we normally have a negative association with the word *lazy*, that behavior is what we want in this case.

All of the repetition metacharacters—*, +, ?, {n}, {n,} and {n,m}—can be followed with a question mark to make them lazy (though in practice, I've only ever used it for * and +).

# Backreferences

Grouping enables another technique called *backreferences*. In my experience, this is one of the least used regex features, but there is one instance where it comes in handy. Let's consider a very silly example before we consider a truly useful one.

Imagine you want to match band names that follow the pattern XYYX (I bet you can think of a real band name that follows this pattern). So we want to match PJJP, GOOG, and ANNA. This is where backreferences come in. Each group (including subgroups) in a regex is assigned a number, from left to right, starting with 1. You can refer to that group in a regex with a backslash followed by a number. In other words, \1 means "whatever group #1 matched." Confused? Let's see the example:

```
const promo = "Opening for XAAX is the dynamic GOOG!  At the box office now!";
const bands = promo.match(/(?:[A-Z])(?:[A-Z])\2\1/g);
```

Reading from left to right, we see there are two groups, then \2\1. So if the first group matches X and the second group matches A, then \2 must match A and \1 must match X.

If this sounds cool to you but not very useful, you're not alone. The only time I think I have ever needed to use backreferences (other than solving puzzles) is matching quotation marks.

In HTML, you can use either single or double quotes for attribute values. This enables us to easily do things like this:

```
// we use backticks here because we're using single and
// double quotation marks:
const html = `<img alt='A "simple" example.'>` +
        `<img alt="Don't abuse it!">`;
const matches = html.match(/<img alt=(?:['"]).*?\1/g);
```

Note that there's some simplifying going on in this example; if the `alt` attribute didn't come first, this wouldn't work, nor would it if there were extra whitespace. We'll see this example revisited later with these problems addressed.

Just as before, the first group will match either a single or double quote, followed by zero or more characters (note the question mark that makes the match lazy), followed by `\1`—which will be whatever the first match was, either a single quote or a double quote.

Let's take a moment to reinforce our understanding of lazy versus greedy matching. Go ahead and remove the question mark after the `*`, making the match greedy. Run the expression again; what do you see? Do you understand why? This is a very important concept to understand if you want to master regular expressions, so if this is not clear to you, I encourage you to revisit the section on lazy versus greedy matching.

# Replacing Groups

One of the benefits grouping brings is the ability to make more sophisticated replacements. Continuing with our HTML example, let's say that we want to strip out everything but the `href` from an <a> tag:

```
let html = '<a class="nope" href="/yep">Yep</a>';
html = html.replace(/<a .*?(href=".*?").*?>/, '<a $1>');
```

Just as with backreferences, all groups are assigned a number starting with 1. In the regex itself, we refer to the first group with `\1`; in the replacement string, we use `$1`. Note the use of lazy quantifiers in this regex to prevent it from spanning multiple <a> tags. This regex will also fail if the `href` attribute uses single quotes instead of double quotes.

Now we'll extend the example. We want to preserve the `class` attribute and the `href` attribute, but nothing else:

```
let html = '<a class="yep" href="/yep" id="nope">Yep</a>';
html = html.replace(/<a .*?(class=".*?").*?(href=".*?").*?>/, '<a $2 $1>');
```

Note in this regex we reverse the order of `class` and `href` so that `href` always occurs first. The problem with this regex is that `class` and `href` always have to be in the same order and (as mentioned before) it will fail if we use single quotes instead of double. We'll see an even more sophisticated solution in the next section.

In addition to `$1`, `$2`, and so on, there are also `` $` `` (everything before the match), `$&` (the match itself), and `$'` (everything after the match). If you want to use a literal dollar sign, use `$$`:

```
const input = "One two three";
input.replace(/two/, '($`)');     // "One (One ) three"
input.replace(/\w+/g, '($&)');    // "(One) (two) (three)"
```

```
input.replace(/two/, "($')");     // "One ( three) three"
input.replace(/two/, "($$)");     // "One ($) three"
```

These replacement macros are often neglected, but I've seen them used in very clever solutions, so don't forget about them!

# Function Replacements

This is my favorite feature of regexes, which often allows you to break down a very complex regex into some simpler regexes.

Let's consider again the practical example of modifying HTML elements. Imagine you're writing a program that converts all `<a>` links into a very specific format: you want to preserve the `class`, `id`, and `href` attributes, but remove everything else. The problem is, your input is possibly messy. The attributes aren't always present, and when they are, you can't guarantee they'll be in the same order. So you have to consider the following input variations (among many):

```
const html =
   `<a class="foo" href="/foo" id="foo">Foo</a>\n` +
   `<A href='/foo' Class="foo">Foo</a>\n` +
   `<a href="/foo">Foo</a>\n` +
   `<a onclick="javascript:alert('foo!')" href="/foo">Foo</a>`;
```

By now, you should be realizing that this is a daunting task to accomplish with a regex: there are just too many possible variations! However, we can significantly reduce the number of variations by breaking this up into *two* regexes: one to recognize `<a>` tags, and another to replace the contents of an `<a>` tag with only what you want.

Let's consider the second problem first. If all you had was a single `<a>` tag, and you wanted to discard all attributes other than `class`, `id`, and `href`, the problem is easier. Even still, as we saw earlier, this can cause problems if we can't guarantee the attributes come in a particular order. There are multiple ways to solve this problem, but we'll use `String.prototype.split` so we can consider attributes one at a time:

```
function sanitizeATag(aTag) {
   // get the parts of the tag...
   const parts = aTag.match(/<a\s+(.*?)>(.*?)<\/a>/i);
   // parts[1] are the attributes of the opening <a> tag
   // parts[2] are what's between the <a> and </a> tags
   const attributes = parts[1]
      // then we split into individual attributes
      .split(/\s+/);
   return '<a ' + attributes
      // we only want class, id, and href attributes
      .filter(attr => /^(?:class|id|href)[\s=]/i.test(attr))
      // joined by spaces
      .join(' ')
```

```
        // close the opening <a> tag
        + '>'
        // add the contents
        + parts[2]
        // and the closing tag
        + '</a>';
}
```

This function is longer than it needs to be, but we've broken it down for clarity. Note that even in this function, we're using multiple regexes: one to match the parts of the `<a>` tag, one to do the split (using a regex to identify one or more whitespace characters), and one to filter only the attributes we want. It would be much more difficult to do all of this with a single regex.

Now for the interesting part: using `sanitizeATag` on a block of HTML that might contain many `<a>` tags, among other HTML. It's easy enough to write a regex to match just the `<a>` tags:

```
html.match(/<a .*?>(.*?)<\/a>/ig);
```

But what do we do with it? As it happens, you can pass a *function* to `String.prototype.replace` as the replacement parameter. So far, we've only be using strings as the replacement parameter. Using a function allows you to take special action for *each replacement*. Before we finish our example, let's use `console.log` to see how it works:

```
html.replace(/<a .*?>(.*?)<\/a>/ig, function(m, g1, offset) {
   console.log(`<a> tag found at ${offset}.  contents: ${g1}`);
});
```

The function you pass to `String.prototype.replace` receives the following arguments in order:

- The entire matched string (equivalent to `$&`).
- The matched groups (if any). There will be as many of these arguments as there are groups.
- The offset of the match within the original string (a number).
- The original string (rarely used).

The return value of the function is what gets replaced in the returned string. In the example we just considered, we weren't returning anything, so `undefined` will be returned, converted into a string, and used as a replacement. The point of that example was the mechanics, not the actual replacement, so we simply discard the resultant string.

Now back to our example.... We already have our function to sanitize an individual `<a>` tag, and a way to find `<a>` tags in a block of HTML, so we can simply put them together:

```
html.replace(/<a .*?<\/a>/ig, function(m) {
  return sanitizeATag(m);
});
```

We can simplify this even further—considering that the function `sanitizeATag` matches exactly what `String.prototype.replace` expects, we can rid ourselves of the anonymous function, and use `sanitizeATag` directly:

```
html.replace(/<a .*?<\/a>/ig, sanitizeATag);
```

Hopefully the power of this functionality is clear. Whenever you find yourself faced with a problem involving matching small strings within a bigger string, and you need to do processing on the smaller strings, remember that you can pass a function to `String.prototype.replace`!

## Anchoring

Very often, you'll care about things at the beginning or end of a string, or the entire string (as opposed to just a part of it). That's where *anchors* come in. There are two anchors—`^`, which matches the beginning of the line, and `$`, which matches the end of the line:

```
const input = "It was the best of times, it was the worst of times";
const beginning = input.match(/^\w+/g);   // "It"
const end = input.match(/\w+$/g);         // "times"
const everything = input.match(/^.*$/g);  // sames as input
const nomatch1 = input.match(/^best/ig);
const nomatch2 = input.match(/worst$/ig);
```

There's one more nuance to anchors that you need to be aware of. Normally, they match the beginning and end of the *whole string*, even if you have newlines in it. If you want to treat a string as multiline (as separated by newlines), you need to use the `m` (multiline) option:

```
const input = "One line\nTwo lines\nThree lines\nFour";
const beginnings = input.match(/^\w+/mg);   // ["One", "Two", "Three", "Four"]
const endings = input.match(/\w+$/mg);      // ["line", "lines", "lines", "Four"]
```

## Word Boundary Matching

One of the often-overlooked useful gems of regexes is *word boundary matches*. Like beginning and end-of-line anchors, the word boundary metacharacter, `\b`, and its inverse, `\B`, *do not consume input*. This can be a very handy property, as we'll see shortly.

A word boundary is defined where a `\w` match is either preceded by or followed by a `\W` (nonword) character, or the beginning or end of the string. Imagine you're trying to replace email addresses in English text with hyperlinks (for the purposes of this discussion, we'll assume email addresses start with a letter and end with a letter). Think of the situations you have to consider:

```
const inputs = [
    "john@doe.com",                   // nothing but the email
    "john@doe.com is my email",       // email at the beginning
    "my email is john@doe.com",       // email at the end
    "use john@doe.com, my email",     // email in the middle, with comma afterward
    "my email:john@doe.com.",         // email surrounded with punctuation
];
```

It's a lot to consider, but all of these email addresses have one thing in common: they exist at word boundaries. The other advantage of word boundary markers is that, because they don't consume input, we don't need to worry about "putting them back" in the replacement string:

```
const emailMatcher =
   /\b[a-z][a-z0-9._-]*@[a-z][a-z0-9_-]+\.[a-z]+(?:\.[a-z]+)?\b/ig;
inputs.map(s => s.replace(emailMatcher, '<a href="mailto:$&">$&</a>'));
// returns [
//    "<a href="mailto:john@doe.com">john@doe.com</a>",
//    "<a href="mailto:john@doe.com">john@doe.com</a> is my email",
//    "my email is <a href="mailto:john@doe.com">john@doe.com</a>",
//    "use <a href="mailto:john@doe.com">john@doe.com</a>, my email",
//    "my email:<a href="mailto:john@doe.com>john@doe.com</a>.",
// ]
```

In addition to using word boundary markers, this regex is using a lot of the features we've covered in this chapter: it may seem daunting at first glance, but if you take the time to work through it, you're well on your way to regex mastery (note especially that the replacement macro, `$&`, does *not* include the characters surrounding the email address...because they were not consumed).

Word boundaries are also handy when you're trying to search for text that begins with, ends with, or contains another word. For example, `/\bcount/` will find *count* and *countdown*, but not *discount*, *recount*, or *accountable*. `/\bcount\B/` will only find *countdown*, `/\Bcount\b/` will find *discount* and *recount*, and `/\Bcount\B/` will only find *accountable*.

## Lookaheads

If greedy versus lazy matching is what separates the dilettantes from the pros, *lookaheads* are what separate the pros from the gurus. Lookaheads—like anchor and word boundary metacharacters—don't consume input. Unlike anchors and word boundaries, however, they are general purpose: you can match any subexpression without consuming it. As with word boundary metacharacters, the fact that lookaheads don't match can save you from having to "put things back" in a replacement. While that can be a nice trick, it's not required. Lookaheads are necessary whenever there is overlapping content, and they can simplify certain types of matching.

A classic example is validating that a password matches some policy. To keep it simple, let's say our password must contain at least one uppercase letter, number, and lowercase letter, and no nonletter, nonnumber characters. We could, of course, use multiple regexes:

```
function validPassword(p) {
    return /[A-Z]/.test(p) &&           // at least one uppercase letter
        /[0-9]/.test(p) &&              // at least one number
        /[a-z]/.test(p) &&              // at least one lowercase letters
        ![^a-zA-Z0-9]/.test(p);         // only letters and numbers
}
```

Let's say we want to combine that into one regular expression. Our first attempt fails:

```
function validPassword(p) {
    return /[A-Z].*[0-9][a-z]/.test(p);
}
```

Not only does this require the capital letter to come before the numbers to come before the two lowercase letters, but we haven't tested for the invalid characters at all. And there's really no sensible way to do it, either, because characters are consumed as the regex is processed.

Lookaheads come to the rescue by not consuming input; essentially each lookahead is an independent regex that doesn't consume any input. Lookaheads in JavaScript look like `(?=<subexpression>)`. They also have a "negative lookahead": `(?!<subexpression>)` will match only things that *aren't* followed by the subexpression. Now we can write a single regex to validate our passwords:

```
function validPassword(p) {
    return /(?=.*[A-Z])(?=.*[0-9])(?=.*[a-z])(?!.*[^a-zA-Z0-9])/.test(p);
}
```

You might be looking at this soup of letters and characters and thinking that our multiregex function is better—or at least easier to read. And in this example, I would probably agree. However, it demonstrates one of the important uses of lookaheads (and negative lookaheads). Lookaheads definitely fall into the category of "advanced regex," but are important for solving certain problems.

# Constructing Regexes Dynamically

We started off this chapter by saying that you should prefer the regex literal over the `RegExp` constructor. In addition to having to type four fewer letters, we prefer the regex literal because we don't have to escape backslashes as we do in JavaScript strings. Where we do need to use the `RegExp` constructor is when we want to construct regexes *dynamically*. For example, you might have an array of usernames you want to match in a string; there's no (sensible) way to get those usernames into a regex literal. This is where the `RegExp` constructor comes in, because it constructs the regex from a string—which *can* be constructed dynamically. Let's consider this example:

```
const users = ["mary", "nick", "arthur", "sam", "yvette"];
const text = "User @arthur started the backup and 15:15, " +
   "and @nick and @yvette restored it at 18:35.";
const userRegex = new RegExp(`@(?:${users.join('|')})\\b`, 'g');
text.match(userRegex);  // [ "@arthur", "@nick", "@yvette" ]
```

The equivalent literal regex in this example would be `/@(?:mary|nick|arthur|sam|yvette)\b/g`, but we've managed to construct it dynamically. Note that we have to use double backslashes before the `b` (word boundary metacharacter); the first backslash is to escape the second backslash in the string.

# Conclusion

While this chapter has touched on the major points of regexes, it only scratches the surface of the techniques, examples, and complexities inherent in regexes. Becoming proficient at regexes is about 20% understanding the theory, and 80% practice. Using a robust regex tester (such as regular expressions 101 (*https://regex101.com/#javascript*)) can be very helpful when you're starting out (and even when you're experienced!). The most important thing you can take away from this chapter is an understanding of how a regex engine consumes input; a lack of understanding in that area is the source of a lot of frustration.

CHAPTER 18

# JavaScript in the Browser

JavaScript began its life as a browser scripting language, and now holds a near-complete monopoly in that role. This chapter is for anyone who's working with JavaScript in the browser. The language may be the same, but there are some special considerations and APIs for this scenario.

Fully covering browser-based JavaScript development is a whole book in itself. The goal of this chapter is to introduce you to the important core concepts in browser development, which will give you a solid foundation. At the end of this chapter, I will recommend some additional learning resources.

## ES5 or ES6?

Hopefully by now you are convinced of the utility of the enhancements ES6 brings. Unfortunately, it will be a while before you can rely on strong and consistent ES6 support on the Web.

On the server side, you can know with certainty which ES6 features are supported (assuming you have control of the JavaScript engine). On the Web, you send your precious code out into the ether, over HTTP(S), where it's executed by some JavaScript engine that you don't control. Worse, you may not even have reliable information about what browser is being used.

So-called "evergreen" browsers are cutting into this problem; by automatically updating (without asking the user), they are allowing new web standards to be rolled out more quickly and consistently. However, this only reduces the problem instead of eliminating it.

Unless you can somehow control your user's environment, you will have to ship ES5 for the foreseeable future. This isn't the end of the world: transcompilation still provides a path for writing ES6 today. It can make deployment and debugging more painful, but such is the price of progress.

In this chapter, we will assume the use of a transcompiler, as covered in Chapter 2. The examples in this chapter all run correctly in the latest version of Firefox without transcompilation. If you are publishing your code for a wider audience, you will need to transcompile to ensure your code works reliably across many browsers.

# The Document Object Model

The *Document Object Model*, or DOM, is a convention for describing the structure of an HTML document, and it's at the heart of interacting with the browser.

Conceptually, the DOM is a tree. A tree consists of *nodes*: every node has a parent (except for the root node), and zero or more *child nodes*. The root node is the *document*, and it consists of a single child, which is the `<html>` element. The `<html>` element, in turn, has two children: the `<head>` element and the `<body>` element (Figure 18-1 is an example DOM).

Every node in the DOM tree (including the document itself) is an instance of the `Node` class (not to be confused with Node.js, the subject of the next chapter). `Node` objects have a `parentNode` and `childNodes` properties, as well as identifying properties such as `nodeName` and `nodeType`.

The DOM consists entirely of nodes, only *some of which* are HTML *elements*. For example, a paragraph tag (`<p>`) is an HTML *element*, but the text it contains is a *text node*. Very often, the terms *node* and *element* are used interchangeably, which is rarely confusing, but not technically correct. In this chapter, we'll mostly be dealing with nodes that are HTML elements, and when we say "element" we mean "element node."

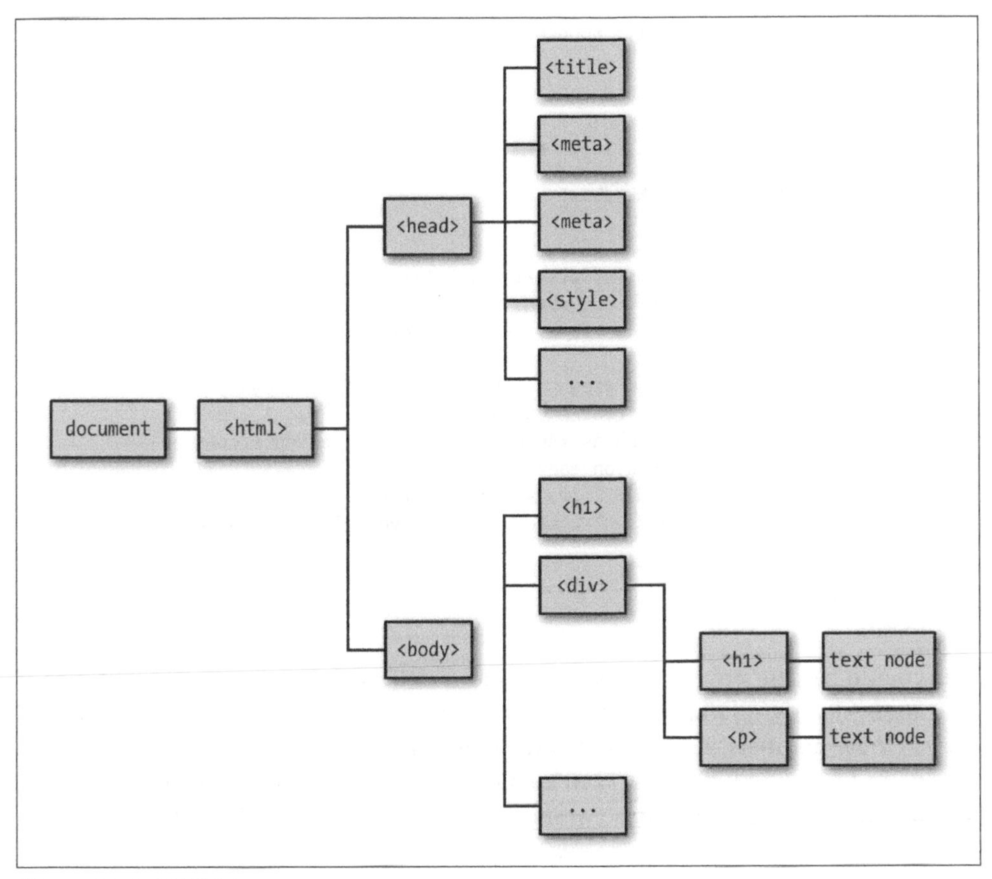


*Figure 18-1. DOM tree*

For the following examples, we'll use a very simple HTML file to demonstrate these features. Create a file called *simple.html*:

```
<!doctype html>
<html>
    <head>
        <meta charset="utf-8">
        <title>Simple HTML</title>
        <style>
            .callout {
                border: solid 1px #ff0080;
                margin: 2px 4px;
                padding: 2px 6px;
            }
            .code {
                background: #ccc;
                margin: 1px 2px;
                padding: 1px 4px;
```

```
                font-family: monospace;
            }
        </style>
    </head>
    <body>
        <header>
            <h1>Simple HTML</h1>
        </header>
        <div id="content">
            <p>This is a <i>simple</i> HTML file.</p>
            <div class="callout">
                <p>This is as fancy as we'll get!</p>
            </div>
            <p>IDs (such as <span class="code">#content</span>)
                are unique (there can only be one per page).</p>
            <p>Classes (such as <span class="code">.callout</span>)
                can be used on many elements.</p>
            <div id="callout2" class="callout fancy">
                <p>A single HTML element can have multiple classes.</p>
            </div>
        </div>
    </body>
</html>
```

Every node has the properties `nodeType` and `nodeName` (among others). `nodeType` is an integer identifying what type of node it is. The `Node` object contains constants that map to these numbers. The types of node we'll be primarily dealing with in this chapter are `Node.ELEMENT_NODE` (HTML elements) and `Node.TEXT_NODE` (text contents, usually within HTML elements). For more information, see the MDN documentation for `nodeType` (*https://developer.mozilla.org/en-US/docs/Web/API/Node/nodeType*).

It's an instructive exercise to write a function that *traverses* the entire DOM and prints it to the console, starting with `document`:

```
function printDOM(node, prefix) {
    console.log(prefix + node.nodeName);
    for(let i=0; i<node.childNodes.length; i++) {
        printDOM(node.childNodes[i], prefix + '\t');
    }
}
printDOM(document, '');
```

This recursive function does what's known as a *depth-first, pre-order traversal* of a tree. That is, it follows branches all the way before moving on to the next branch. If you run it in a browser with a page loaded, you will see the entire structure of the page printed out to the console.

While this is an instructive exercise, it would be a tedious and inefficient way to manipulate HTML (having to traverse the entire DOM to find what you're looking for). Fortunately, the DOM provides methods to locate HTML elements more directly.

While writing your own traversal function is a good exercise, the DOM API provides the `TreeWalker` object, which allows you to iterate through all of the elements in the DOM (optionally filtering by certain element types). For more information, see the MDN documentation for `document.createTreeWalker` (*https://developer.mozilla.org/en-US/docs/Web/API/Document/createTreeWalker*).

## Some Tree Terminology

The concept of a tree is straightforward and intuitive, and lends itself to similarly intuitive terminology. A node's parent is its *direct* parent (that is, not a "grandparent") and a child is a *direct* child (not a "grandchild"). The term *descendant* is used to refer to a child, or a child's child, or so on. The term *ancestor* is used to refer to a parent, the parent's parent, and so on.

## DOM "Get" Methods

The DOM provides "get" methods that allow you to quickly locate specific HTML elements.

The first of these is `document.getElementById`. Every HTML element on a page may be assigned a unique ID, and `document.getElementById` can retrieve an element by its ID:

```
document.getElementById('content');       // <div id="content">...</div>
```

Browsers don't do anything to enforce the uniqueness of IDs (though an HTML validator will catch these issues), so it is incumbent on you to ensure that IDs are unique. As the construction of web pages gets more complicated (with components coming from multiple sources), it's becoming increasingly difficult to avoid duplicate IDs. For this reason, I recommend using them carefully and sparingly.

`document.getElementsByClassName` returns a collection of elements that have the given class name:

```
const callouts = document.getElementsByClassName('callout');
```

And `document.getElementsByTagName` returns a collection of elements that have the given tag name:

```
const paragraphs = document.getElementsByTagName('p');
```

All of the DOM methods that return a collection do not return a JavaScript array, but an instance of `HTMLCollection`, which is an "array-like" object. You can iterate over it with a `for` loop, but the `Array.prototype` methods (such as `map`, `filter`, and `reduce`) won't be available. You can convert an `HTMLCollection` to an array by using the spread operator: `[...document.getElementsByTagName(p)]`.

# Querying DOM Elements

`getElementById`, `getElementsByClassName`, and `getElementsByTagName` are useful, but there's a much more general (and powerful) method that can locate elements not just by a single condition (ID, class, or name), but also by the element's *relationship to other elements*. The `document` methods `querySelector` and `querySelectorAll` allow you to use *CSS selectors*.

CSS selectors allow you to identify elements by their name (`<p>`, `<div>`, etc.), their ID, their class (or combination of classes), or any combination thereof. To identify elements by name, simply use the name of the element (without angle brackets). So `a` will match all `<a>` tags in the DOM, and `br` will match all the `<br>` tags. To identify elements by their class, use a period before the class name: `.callout` will match all elements that have the class `callout`. To match multiple classes, just separate them with periods: `.callout.fancy` will match all elements that have the class `callout` *and* the class `fancy`. Lastly, they can be combined: for example, `a#callout2.callout.fancy` will match `<a>` elements with ID `callout2`, and classes `callout` and `fancy` (it's very rare to see a selector that uses element name, ID, and class(es)...but it is possible).

The best way to get the hang of CSS selectors is to load the sample HTML provided in this chapter in a browser, open the browser's console, and try them out with `querySelectorAll`. For example, in the console, type **`document.querySelectorAll('.callout')`**. All of the examples in this section will produce at least one result with `querySelectorAll`.

So far, we've been talking about identifying specific elements no matter where they appear in the DOM. CSS selectors also enable us to locate elements according to their position in the DOM.

If you separate multiple element selectors with a space, you can select nodes with a specific ancestry. For example, `#content p` will select `<p>` elements that are *descendants* of whatever element has the ID `content`. Likewise, `#content div p` will select `<p>` elements that are inside a `<div>` that are inside an element with the ID `content`.

If you separate multiple elements selectors with a greater-than sign (>), you can select nodes that are *direct children*. For example, `#content > p` will select `<p>` elements that are children of an element with ID `content` (contrast this with "`#content p`").

Note that you can combine ancestry and direct child selectors. For example, `body .content > p` will select `<p>` tags that are direct children of elements with class `content` that are descendants of `<body>`.

There are more sophisticated selectors, but the ones covered here are the most common. To learn more about all the selectors available, see the MDN documentation on selectors (*http://mzl.la/1Pxcg2f*).

# Manipulating DOM Elements

Now that we know how to traverse, get, and query elements, what do we *do* with them? Let's start with content modification. Each element has two properties, `textContent` and `innerHTML`, that allow you to access (and change) the element's content. `textContent` strips out all HTML tags and provides text data only, whereas `innerHTML` allows you to create HTML (which results in new DOM nodes). Let's see how we can access and modify the first paragraph in our example:

```
const para1 = document.getElementsByTagName('p')[0];
para1.textContent;     // "This is a simple HTML file."
para1.innerHTML;       // "This is a <i>simple</i> HTML file."
para1.textContent = "Modified HTML file";        // look for change in browser
para1.innerHTML = "<i>Modified</i> HTML file";   // look for change in browser
```

Assigning to `textContent` and `innerHTML` is a *destructive* operation: it will replace whatever is in that element, no matter how big or complex. For example, you could replace the entire page contents by setting `innerHTML` on the `<body>` element!

# Creating New DOM Elements

We've already seen how to implicitly create new DOM nodes by setting an element's `innerHTML` property. We can also explicitly create new nodes with `document.createElement`. This function creates a new element, but it doesn't add it to the DOM; you'll have to do that in a separate step. Let's create two new paragraph elements; one will become the first paragraph in `<div id="content">`, and the other will become the last:

```
const p1 = document.createElement('p');
const p2 = document.createElement('p');
p1.textContent = "I was created dynamically!";
p2.textContent = "I was also created dynamically!";
```

To add these newly created elements to the DOM, we'll use the `insertBefore` and `appendChild` methods. We'll need to get references to the parent DOM element (`<div id="content">`), and its first child:

```
const parent = document.getElementById('content');
const firstChild = parent.childNodes[0];
```

Now we can insert the newly created elements:

```
parent.insertBefore(p1, firstChild);
parent.appendChild(p2);
```

`insertBefore` takes the element to inset first, and then a "reference node," which is the node to insert before. `appendChild` is very simple, appending the specified element as the last child.

## Styling Elements

With the DOM API, you have complete and fine-grained control over element styling. However, it is generally considered good practice to use CSS classes instead of modifying the individual properties of an element. That is, if you want to change the style of an element, create a new CSS class, and then apply that class to the element(s) you wish to style. Using JavaScript, it is easy to apply an existing CSS class to an element. For example, if we wanted to highlight all paragraphs that contain the word *unique*, we would first create a new CSS class:

```
.highlight {
    background: #ff0;
    font-style: italic;
}
```

With that in place, we can find all `<p>` tags, and if they contain the word *unique*, add the `highlight` class. Every element has a property `classList`, which contains all of the classes (if any) the element has. `classList` has an `add` method that allows you to add further classes. We'll be using this example later in this chapter, so we put it in a function called `highlightParas`:

```
function highlightParas(containing) {
    if(typeof containing === 'string')
        containing = new RegExp(`\\b${containing}\\b`, 'i');
    const paras = document.getElementsByTagName('p');
    console.log(paras);
    for(let p of paras) {
        if(!containing.test(p.textContent)) continue;
        p.classList.add('highlight');
    }
}
highlightParas('unique');
```

And then if we want to remove the highlights, we can use `classList.remove`:

```
function removeParaHighlights() {
    const paras = document.querySelectorAll('p.highlight');
    for(let p of paras) {
        p.classList.remove('highlight');
    }
}
```

When removing the highlight class, we could have reused the same paras variable, and simply called remove('highlight') on every paragraph element; it will do nothing if the element doesn't already have the class. However, it's likely that the removal will come at some later point in time, and there may have been highlighted paragraphs added by other code: if our intention is to clear all highlighting, performing a query is the safer method.

## Data Attributes

HTML5 introduced *data attributes*, which allow you to add arbitrary data to HTML elements; this data isn't rendered by the browser, but it does allow you to add information to elements that can easily be read and modified by JavaScript. Let's modify our HTML by adding a button that we will eventually hook up to our highlightParas function, and another one that we'll hook up to removeParaHighlights:

```
<button data-action="highlight" data-containing="unique">
    Highlight paragraphs containing "unique"
</button>
<button data-action="removeHighlights">
    Remove highlights
</button>
```

We've called our data attributes action and contains (the names are up to us), and we can use document.querySelectorAll to find all elements that have "highlight" as their action:

```
const highlightActions = document.querySelectorAll('[data-action="highlight"]');
```

This introduces a new type of CSS selector. So far, we've seen selectors that can match specific tags, classes, and IDs. The square bracket syntax allows us to match elements by any attribute…in this case, a specific data attribute.

Because we only have one button, we could have used querySelector instead of querySelectorAll, but this allows us to have multiple elements that are designed to trigger the same action (which is quite common: think about actions that you can access through a menu, link, or toolbar, all on the same page). If we take a look at one of the elements in highlightActions, we note that it has a dataset property:

```
highlightActions[0].dataset;
// DOMStringMap { containing: "unique", action: "highlight" }
```

The DOM API stores data attribute values as strings (as implied by the class `DOMStringMap`), meaning you cannot store object data. jQuery extends the functionality of data attributes by providing an interface that allows you to store objects as data attributes, which we will be learning about in Chapter 19.

We can also modify or add data attributes with JavaScript. For example, if we wanted to highlight paragraphs with the word *giraffe* and indicate that we want case-sensitive matches, we might do this:

```
highlightActions[0].dataset.containing = "giraffe";
highlightActions[0].dataset.caseSensitive = "true";
```

# Events

The DOM API describes almost 200 events, and each browser further implements nonstandard events, so we certainly won't discuss all events here, but we will cover what you need to know about them. Let's start with a very easy-to-understand event: `click`. We'll use the `click` event to hook up our "highlight" button to our `highlightParas` function:

```
const highlightActions = document.querySelectorAll('[data-action="highlight"]');
for(let a of highlightActions) {
    a.addEventListener('click', evt => {
        evt.preventDefault();
        highlightParas(a.dataset.containing);
    });
}

const removeHighlightActions =
    document.querySelectorAll('[data-action="removeHighlights"]');
for(let a of removeHighlightActions) {
    a.addEventListener('click', evt => {
        evt.preventDefault();
        removeParaHighlights();
    });
}
```

Every element has a method named `addEventListener` that allows you to specify a function that will be called when that event occurs. That function takes a single argument, an object of type `Event`. The event object contains all the relevant information about the event, which will be specific to the type of event. For example, `click` events will have the properties `clientX` and `clientY`, which tell you the coordinates where the click occurred, as well as `target`, which is the element that raised the `click` event.

The event model is designed to allow multiple handlers to handle the same event. Many events have default handlers; for example, if the user clicks on an `<a>` link, the browser will handle the event by loading the requested page. If you want to prevent this behavior, call `preventDefault()` on the event object. Most of the event handlers you write will call `preventDefault()` (unless you explicitly want to do something *in addition* to the default handler).

To add our highlights, we call `highlightParas`, passing in the value of the button's `containing` data element: this allows us to change the text we're looking for simply by changing the HTML!

## Event Capturing and Bubbling

Because HTML is hierarchical, events can be handled in multiple places. For example, if you click on a button, the button itself could handle the event, the button's parent, parent's parent, and so on. Because multiple elements have the opportunity to handle the event, the question becomes "in what order do elements get the opportunity to respond to the event?"

There are essentially two options. One is to start at the most distant ancestor. This is called *capturing*. In our example, our buttons are children of `<div id="content">` which is, in turn, a child of `<body>`. Therefore, `<body>` has the opportunity to "capture" events destined for the buttons.

The other option is to start at the element where the event occurred, and then walk up the hierarchy so all ancestors have a chance to respond. This is called *bubbling*.

To support both options, HTML5 event propagation starts by allowing handlers to capture the event (starting at the most distant ancestor and working down to the target element) and then the event bubbles back up from the target element to the most distant ancestor.

Any handler can optionally do one of three things to affect how (and if) additional handlers will get called. The first and most common, which we've already seen, is `preventDefault`, which *cancels* the event. Canceled events continue propagating, but their `defaultPrevented` property is set to `true`. Event handlers built into the browser will respect the `defaultPrevented` property and take no action. Event handlers that you write can (and usually do) choose to ignore this property. The second approach is to call `stopPropagation`, which prevents further propagation past the current element (all handlers attached to the current element will be called, but no handlers attached to other elements). Finally—the big gun—`stopImmediatePropagation` will prevent any further handlers from getting called (even if they're on the current element).

To see all of this in action, consider the following HTML:

```
<!doctype html>
<html>
    <head>
        <title>Event Propagation</title>
```

```
        <meta charset="utf-8">
    </head>
    <body>
        <div>
            <button>Click Me!</button>
        </div>
        <script>

            // this creates an event handler and returns it
            function logEvent(handlerName, type, cancel,
                    stop, stopImmediate) {
                // this is the actual event handler
                return function(evt) {
                    if(cancel) evt.preventDefault();
                    if(stop) evt.stopPropagation();
                    if(stopImmediate) evt.stopImmediatePropagation();
                    console.log(`${type}: ${handlerName}` +
                        (evt.defaultPrevented ? ' (canceled)' : ''));
                }
            }

            // this adds an event logger to an element
            function addEventLogger(elt, type, action) {
                const capture = type === 'capture';
                elt.addEventListener('click',
                    logEvent(elt.tagName, type, action==='cancel',
                    action==='stop', action==='stop!'), capture);
            }

            const body = document.querySelector('body');
            const div = document.querySelector('div');
            const button = document.querySelector('button');

            addEventLogger(body, 'capture');
            addEventLogger(body, 'bubble');
            addEventLogger(div, 'capture');
            addEventLogger(div, 'bubble');
            addEventLogger(button, 'capture');
            addEventLogger(button, 'bubble');

        </script>
    </body>
</html>
```

If you click the button, this is what you will see on the console:

```
capture: BODY
capture: DIV
capture: BUTTON
bubble: BUTTON
bubble: DIV
bubble: BODY
```

Here we clearly see the capture propagation followed by the bubble propagation. Note that on the element on which the event was actually raised, handlers will be called in the order they were added, whether they were capture or propagation events (if we reversed the order in which we added the capture and bubble event handlers, we would see the bubble called before the capture).

Now let's see what happens if we cancel propagation. Modify the example to cancel propagation on the `<div>` capture:

```
addEventLogger(body, 'capture');
addEventLogger(body, 'bubble');
addEventLogger(div, 'capture', 'cancel');
addEventLogger(div, 'bubble');
addEventLogger(button, 'capture');
addEventLogger(button, 'bubble');
```

We now see that the propagation continues, but the event is marked as canceled:

```
capture: BODY
capture: DIV (canceled)
capture: BUTTON (canceled)
bubble: BUTTON (canceled)
bubble: DIV (canceled)
bubble: BODY (canceled)
```

Now stop the propagation at the `<button>` capture:

```
addEventLogger(body, 'capture');
addEventLogger(body, 'bubble');
addEventLogger(div, 'capture', 'cancel');
addEventLogger(div, 'bubble');
addEventLogger(button, 'capture', 'stop');
addEventLogger(button, 'bubble');
```

We see that propagation stops after the `<button>` element. The `<button>` bubble event still fires, even though the capture fired first and stopped the propagation. The `<div>` and `<body>` elements do not receive their bubbled events, however:

```
capture: BODY
capture: DIV (canceled)
capture: BUTTON (canceled)
bubble: BUTTON (canceled)
```

Lastly, we stop immediately on the `<button>` capture:

```
addEventLogger(body, 'capture');
addEventLogger(body, 'bubble');
addEventLogger(div, 'capture', 'cancel');
addEventLogger(div, 'bubble');
addEventLogger(button, 'capture', 'stop!');
addEventLogger(button, 'bubble');
```

Now we see that propagation stops totally at the <button> capture, and no further propagation occurs:

```
capture: BODY
capture: DIV (canceled)
capture: BUTTON (canceled)
```

`addEventListener` replaces a much older way to add events: using "on" properties. For example, a click handler would have been added on the element `elt` with `elt.onclick = function(evt) { /* handler */ }`. The primary disadvantage of this method is that only one handler could be registered at a time.

While it is unlikely that you will have to do advanced control of event propagation very often, it is a subject that causes much confusion among beginners. Having a firm grasp on the details of event propagation will set you apart from the crowd.

With jQuery event listeners, explicitly returning `false` from the handler is equivalent to calling `stopPropagation`; this is a jQuery convention, and this shortcut does not work in the DOM API.

## Event Categories

MDN has an excellent reference of all DOM events grouped into categories (*https://developer.mozilla.org/en-US/docs/Web/Events#Categories*). Some commonly used event categories include:

*Drag events*
: Allow the implementation of a drag-and-drop interface with events like `dragstart`, `drag`, `dragend`, `drop`, and others.

*Focus events*
: Allow you to take action when a user interacts with editable elements (such as form fields). `focus` is raised when a user "enters" a field (by clicking, pressing Tab, or touching), and `blur` is raised when the user "leaves" a field (by clicking somewhere else, pressing Tab, or touching elsewhere). The `change` event is raised when a user makes a change to a field.

*Form events*
: When a user submits a form (by pressing a Submit button, or pressing Enter in the right context), the `submit` event is raised on the form.

*Input device events*
: We've already seen `click`, but there are additional mouse events (`mousedown`, `move`, `mouseup`, `mouseenter`, `mouseleave`, `mouseover`, `mousewheel`) and keyboard events (`keydown`, `keypress`, `keyup`). Note that "touch" events (for touch-enabled devices) take precedence over mouse events, but if touch events aren't handled, they result in mouse events. For example, if a user touches a button, and touch events aren't handled explicitly, a `click` event will be raised.

*Media events*
: Allow you to track a user's interaction with HTML5 video and audio players (`pause`, `play`, etc.).

*Progress events*
: Inform you about the browser's progress loading content. The most common is `load`, which fires once the browser has loaded the element and all its dependent resources. `error` is also useful, allowing you to take action when an element is unavailable (for example, a broken image link).

*Touch events*
: Touch events provide sophisticated support for devices that allow touch. Multiple simultaneous touches are permitted (look for the `touches` property in the event), enabling sophisticated touch handling, such as support for gestures (pinch, swipe, etc.).

# Ajax

Ajax (which was originally an acronym for "Asynchronous JavaScript and XML") enables asynchronous communication with a server—allowing elements on your page to be refreshed with data from the server without reloading the entire page. This innovation was made possible with the introduction of the `XMLHttpRequest` object in the early 2000s, and ushered in what became known as "Web 2.0."

The core concept of Ajax is simple: browser-side JavaScript makes HTTP requests programatically to a server, which returns data, usually in JSON format (which is much easier to work with in JavaScript than XML). That data is used to enable functionality on the browser. While Ajax is based on HTTP (just like non-Ajax web pages), the overhead of transferring and rendering a page is reduced, enabling web applications that perform much faster—or at least appear to from the user's perspective.

To use Ajax, we need to have a *server*. We'll write an extremely simple server in Node.js (this is a preview of Chapter 20) that exposes an Ajax *endpoint* (a specific service that is exposed for use in other services or applications). Create a file called *ajaxServer.js*:

```
const http = require('http');

const server = http.createServer(function(req, res) {
    res.setHeader('Content-Type', 'application/json');
    res.setHeader('Access-Control-Allow-Origin', '*');
    res.end(JSON.stringify({
        platform: process.platform,
        nodeVersion: process.version,
        uptime: Math.round(process.uptime()),
    }));
});

const port = 7070;
server.listen(port, function() {
    console.log(`Ajax server started on port ${port}`);
});
```

This creates a very simple server that reports the platform ("linux," "darwin," "win32," etc.), the version of Node.js, and the server uptime.

Ajax introduced the possibility of a security vulnerability called *cross-origin resource sharing* (CORS). In this example, we are adding a header of `Access-Control-Allow-Origin` with a value of `*`, which signals to the client (the browser) not to prevent the call for security reasons. On a production server, you would either want to use the same protocol, domain, and port (which will be allowed by default), or specify explicitly what protocol, domain, and port can access the endpoint. For demonstration purposes, though, it is safe to disable CORS checking like this.

To start this server, simply run:

```
$ babel-node ajaxServer.js
```

If you load *http://localhost:7070* in a browser, you will see the output of the server. Now that we have a server, we can make an Ajax code from our sample HTML page (you can use the same one that we've been using through this chapter). We'll start by adding a placeholder somewhere in the body that will receive the information:

```
<div class="serverInfo">
    Server is running on <span data-replace="platform">???</span>
    with Node <span data-replace="nodeVersion">???</span>.  It has
    been up for <span data-replace="uptime">???</span> seconds.
</div>
```

Now that we have a place to put the data that's coming from the server, we can use `XMLHttpRequest` to perform an Ajax call. At the bottom of your HTML file (right before the closing `</body>` tag), add the following script:

```
<script type="application/javascript;version=1.8">
    function refreshServerInfo() {
        const req = new XMLHttpRequest();
        req.addEventListener('load', function() {
            // TODO: put these values into HTML
            console.log(this.responseText);
        });
        req.open('GET', 'http://localhost:7070', true);
        req.send();
    }
    refreshServerInfo();
</script>
```

This script executes a basic Ajax call. We first create a new `XMLHttpRequest` object, and then we add a listener that listens for the `load` event (which is what will get called if the Ajax call was successful). For now, we just print the server response (which is in `this.responseText`) to the console. Then we call `open`, which is what actually establishes the connection to the server. We specify that it's an HTTP *GET* request, which is the same method used when you visit a web page with your browser (there are also *POST* and *DELETE* methods, among others), and we provide the URL to the server. Finally, we call `send`, which actually executes the request. In this example, we're not explicitly sending any data to the server, but we could.

If you run this example, you'll see the data that's returned from the server show up on the console. Our next step is inserting this data into our HTML. We structured our HTML so that we could simply look for any element that has the data attribute `replace`, and replace that element's contents with the data from the object that was returned. To accomplish this, we iterate over the properties that were returned from the server (using `Object.keys`), and if there are any elements with matching `replace` data attributes, we replace their contents:

```
req.addEventListener('load', function() {
    // this.responseText is a string containing JSON; we use
    // JSON.parse to convert it to an object
    const data = JSON.parse(this.responseText);

    // In this example, we only want to replace text within the <div>
    // that has class "serverInfo"
    const serverInfo = document.querySelector('.serverInfo');

    // Iterate over the keys in the object returned from the server
    // ("platform", "nodeVersion", and "uptime"):
    Object.keys(data).forEach(p => {
        // Find elements to replace for this property (if any)
        const replacements =
            serverInfo.querySelectorAll(`[data-replace="${p}"]`);
        // replace all elements with the value returned from the server
        for(let r of replacements) {
            r.textContent = data[p];
```

```
        }
    });
});
```

Because `refreshServerInfo` is a function, we can call it at any time. In particular, we may wish to update the server info periodically (which is one reason we added the `uptime` field). For example, if we want to update the server five times a second (every 200 milliseconds), we can add the following code:

```
setInterval(refreshServerInfo, 200);
```

By doing this, we will see the server uptime increase live in the browser!

In this example, when the page initially loads, `<div class=".serverInfo">` contains placeholder text with question marks in it. On a slow Internet connection, the user may see those question marks for an instant before they're replaced with the information from the server. This is a variation of the "flash of unstyled content" (FOUC) problem. One solution is to have the server render the initial page with the correct values. Another solution is to hide the entire element until its contents have been updated; it could still be a jarring effect, but might be more acceptable than meaningless question marks.

This covers only the basic concepts involved in making Ajax requests; to learn more, see the MDN article "Using XMLHttpRequest" (*https://developer.mozilla.org/en-US/docs/Web/API/XMLHttpRequest/Using_XMLHttpRequest*).

# Conclusion

As you can see from this chapter, web development introduces a lot of concepts and complexities in addition to the JavaScript language itself. We've only scratched the surface here, and if you are a web developer, I recommend Semmy Purewal's *Learning Web App Development*. If you'd like to learn more about CSS, any of Eric A. Meyer's books are excellent.

# CHAPTER 19
# jQuery

jQuery is a popular library for manipulating the DOM and executing Ajax requests. There's nothing you can do with jQuery that you can't do with the DOM API (jQuery is, after all, built on the DOM API itself), but it offers three main advantages:

- jQuery protects you from idiosyncrasies in the way different browsers implement the DOM API (especially older browsers).
- jQuery provides a simpler Ajax API (which is welcome because Ajax is used heavily in today's websites).
- jQuery provides many powerful and compact enhancements on the built-in DOM API.

There is a growing community of web developers who feel that jQuery is no longer necessary with the improvements in the DOM API and browser quality. This community touts the performance and purity of "vanilla JavaScript." It's true that the first point (browser idiosyncrasies) is becoming less true over time, but it has not vanished altogether. I feel that jQuery remains relevant, and provides many features that would be extremely time-consuming to reimplement in the DOM API. Whether or not you choose to use jQuery, its ubiquity makes it hard to avoid entirely, and the wise web developer will know the basics.

## The Almighty Dollar (Sign)

jQuery was one of the first libraries to take advantage of JavaScript's inclusion of the dollar sign as an identifier. Perhaps it was hubris when the decision was first made, but given jQuery's ubiquity today, the decision seems prescient. When you include jQuery in your project, you can either use the variable `jQuery` or the much shorter `$`.[1] In this text, we'll use the `$` alias.

## Including jQuery

The easiest way to include jQuery is by using a CDN:

```
<script src="//code.jquery.com/jquery-2.1.4.min.js"></script>
```

jQuery 2.x dropped support for Internet Explorer 6, 7, and 8. If you need to support those browsers, you will have to use jQuery 1.x. jQuery 2.x is considerably smaller and simpler because it doesn't need to support these aging browsers.

## Waiting for the DOM to Load

The way a browser reads, interprets, and renders an HTML file is complicated, and many an unwary web developer has been caught off-guard by attempting to programmatically access DOM elements before the browser has had a chance to load them.

jQuery allows you to put your code in a callback that will only be invoked once the browser has fully loaded the page and the DOM has been constructed:

```
$(document).ready(function() {
    // code here is run after all HTML has been
    // loaded and the DOM is constructed
});
```

It is safe to use this technique multiple times, allowing you to place jQuery code in different places and still have it safely wait for the DOM to load. There is also a shortcut version that is equivalent:

```
$(function() {
    // code here is run after all HTML has been
    // loaded and the DOM is constructed
});
```

When using jQuery, putting all of your code in such a block is a ubiquitous practice.

1 There is a way to prevent jQuery from using `$` if it conflicts with another library; see jQuery.noConflict (*https://api.jquery.com/jquery.noconflict/*).

# jQuery-Wrapped DOM Elements

The primary technique for manipulating the DOM with jQuery is using *jQuery-wrapped DOM elements*. Any DOM manipulation you do with jQuery starts with creating a jQuery object that's "wrapped around" a set of DOM elements (keep in mind the set could be empty or have only one element in it).

The jQuery function (`$` or `jQuery`) creates a jQuery-wrapped set of DOM elements (which we will simply be referring to as a "jQuery object" from here on out—just remember that a jQuery object holds a set of DOM elements!). The jQuery function is primarily called in one of two ways: with a CSS selector or with HTML.

Calling jQuery with a CSS selector returns a jQuery object matching that selector (similar to what's returned from `document.querySelectorAll`). For example, to get a jQuery object that matches all <p> tags, simply do:

```
const $paras = $('p');
$paras.length;                // number of paragraph tags matched
typeof $paras;                // "object"
$paras instanceof $;          // true
$paras instanceof jQuery;     // true
```

Calling jQuery with HTML, on the other hand, creates new DOM elements based on the HTML you provide (similar to what happens when you set an element's `innerHTML` property):

```
const $newPara = $('<p>Newly created paragraph...</p>');
```

You'll notice that, in both of these examples, the variable we assign the jQuery object to starts with a dollar sign. This is not necessary, but it is a good convention to follow. It allows you to quickly recognize variables that are jQuery objects.

# Manipulating Elements

Now that we have some jQuery objects, what can we do with them? jQuery makes it very easy to add and remove content. The best way to work through these examples is to load our sample HTML in a browser, and execute these examples on the console. Be prepared to reload the file; we'll be wantonly removing, adding, and modifying content.

jQuery provides `text` and `html` methods that are rough equivalents of assigning to a DOM element's `textContent` and `innerHTML` properties. For example, to replace every paragraph with the same text:

```
$('p').text('ALL PARAGRAPHS REPLACED');
```

Likewise, we can use `html` to use HTML content:

```
$('p').html('<i>ALL</i> PARAGRAPHS REPLACED');
```

This brings us to an important point about jQuery: jQuery makes it very easy to operate on many elements at once. With the DOM API, `document.querySelectorAll()` will return multiple elements, but it's up to us to iterate through them and perform whatever operations we want to. jQuery handles all the iteration for you, and by default assumes that you want to perform actions on every element in the jQuery object. What if you only want to modify the third paragraph? jQuery provides a method `eq` that returns a new jQuery object containing a single element:

```
$('p')          // matches all paragraphs
    .eq(2)      // third paragraph (zero-based indices)
    .html('<i>THIRD</i> PARAGRAPH REPLACED');
```

To remove elements, simply call `remove` on a jQuery object. To remove all paragraphs:

```
$('p').remove();
```

This demonstrates another important paradigm in jQuery development: *chaining*. All jQuery methods return a jQuery object, which allows you to *chain* calls as we just did. Chaining allows for very powerful and compact manipulation of multiple elements.

jQuery provides many methods for adding new content. One of these methods is `append`, which simply appends the provided content to every element in the jQuery object. For example, if we wanted to add a footnote to every paragraph, we can do so very easily:

```
$('p')
    .append('<sup>*</sup>');
```

`append` adds a child to the matched elements; we can also insert siblings with `before` or `after`. Here is an example that adds <hr> elements before and after every paragraph:

```
$('p')
    .after('<hr>')
    .before('<hr>');
```

These insertion methods also include counterparts `appendTo`, `insertBefore`, and `insertAfter` that reverse the order of the insertion, which can be helpful in certain situations. For example:

```
$('<sup>*</sup>').appendTo('p');  // equivalent to $('p').append('<sup>*</sup>')
$('<hr>').insertBefore('p');      // equivalent to $('p').before('<hr>')
$('<hr>').insertAfter('p');       // equivalent to $('p').after('<hr>');
```

jQuery also makes it very easy to modify the styling of an element. You can add classes with `addClass`, remove classes with `removeClass`, or *toggle* classes with `toggleClass` (which will add the class if the element doesn't have it, and remove the class if it does). You can also manipulate style directly with the `css` method. We'll also introduce the `:even` and `:odd` selectors, which allow you to select every other element. For example, if we wanted to make every other paragraph red, we could do the following:

```
$('p:odd').css('color', 'red');
```

Inside a jQuery chain, it's sometimes desirable to select a subset of the matched elements. We've already seen `eq`, which allows us to reduce the jQuery object to a single element, but we can also use `filter`, `not`, and `find` to modify the selected elements. `filter` reduces the set to elements that match the specified selector. For example, we can use `filter` in a chain to make every other paragraph red *after* we've modified each paragraph:

```
$('p')
    .after('<hr>')
    .append('<sup>*</sup>')
    .filter(':odd')
    .css('color', 'red');
```

`not` is essentially the inverse of `filter`. For example, if we want to add an `<hr>` after every paragraph, and then indent any paragraph that doesn't have the class `highlight`:

```
$('p')
    .after('<hr>')
    .not('.highlight')
    .css('margin-left', '20px');
```

Finally, `find` returns the set of *descendant* elements that match the given query (as opposed to `filter`, which filters the existing set). For example, if we wanted to add an `<hr>` before every paragraph and then increase the font size of elements with the class `code` (which, in our example, are descendants of the paragraphs):

```
$('p')
    .before('<hr>')
    .find('.code')
    .css('font-size', '30px');
```

## Unwrapping jQuery Objects

If we need to "unwrap" a jQuery object (get access to the underlying DOM elements), we can do so with the `get` method. To get the second paragraph DOM element:

```
const para2 = $('p').get(1);        // second <p> (zero-based indices)
```

To get an array containing all paragraph DOM elements:

```
const paras = $('p').get();         // array of all <p> elements
```

## Ajax

jQuery provides convenience methods that make Ajax calls easier. jQuery exposes an `ajax` method that allows sophisticated control over an Ajax call. It also provides convenience methods, `get` and `post`, that perform the most common types of Ajax calls. While these methods support callbacks, they also return promises, which is the recommended way to handle the server response. For example, we can use `get` to rewrite our `refreshServerInfo` example from before:

```
function refreshServerInfo() {
    const $serverInfo = $('.serverInfo');
    $.get('http://localhost:7070').then(
        // successful return
        function(data) {
            Object.keys(data).forEach(p => {
                $(`[data-replace="${p}"]`).text(data[p]);
            });
        },
        function(jqXHR, textStatus, err) {
            console.error(err);
            $serverInfo.addClass('error')
                .html('Error connecting to server.');
        }
    );
}
```

As you can see, we have significantly simplified our Ajax code by using jQuery.

## Conclusion

The future of jQuery is unclear. Will improvements to JavaScript and browser APIs render jQuery obsolete? Will the "vanilla JavaScript" purists be vindicated? Only time will tell. I feel that jQuery remains useful and relevant, and will so for the foreseeable future. Certainly the usage of jQuery remains quite high, and any aspiring developer would do well to at least understand the basics.

If you want to learn more about jQuery, I recommend *jQuery: Novice to Ninja* by Earle Castledine and Craig Sharkie. The online jQuery documentation (*http://api.jquery.com/*) is also quite good.

CHAPTER 20

# Node

Up until 2009, JavaScript was almost exclusively a browser scripting language.[1] In 2009, frustrated by the state of server-side options, a Joyent developer named Ryan Dahl created Node. Node's adoption was meteoric, and it even achieved success in the notoriously slow-to-adopt enterprise markets.

For those who liked JavaScript as a language, Node made it possible to use the language for tasks traditionally relegated to other languages. For web developers, the appeal is stronger than just the choice of language. Being able to write JavaScript on the server means a *consistent* language choice—no mental context-switching, a reduced reliance on specialists, and (perhaps most importantly) the ability to run the same code on the server and the client.

While Node was introduced to enable web application development, its jump to the server inadvertently enabled other nontraditional uses, such as desktop application development and system scripting. In a sense, Node allowed JavaScript to grow up and join the party.

## Node Fundamentals

If you can write JavaScript, you can write Node applications. That's not to say that you can simply take any browser-based JavaScript program and run it on Node: browser-based JavaScript uses APIs that are specific to the browser. In particular, in Node, there is no DOM (which makes sense: there's no HTML). Likewise, there are APIs that are specific to Node that don't exist in the browser. Some, like operating system

1 There were attempts at server-side JavaScript before Node; notably, the Netscape Enterprise Server supported server-side JavaScript as early as 1995. However, server-side JavaScript didn't start to gain traction until the 2009 introduction of Node.

and filesystem support, are not available in the browser for security reasons (can you imagine the damage hackers could do if they could delete your files from the browser?). Others, such as the ability to create a web server, simply aren't very useful in a browser.

It's important to understand what's *JavaScript*, and what's *part of an API*. A programmer who has always written browser-based code might reasonably assume that `window` and `document` are simply part of JavaScript. However, those are *APIs* provided in the browser environment (which were covered in Chapter 18). In this chapter, we'll cover the APIs provided in Node.

If you haven't already, make sure Node and npm are installed (see Chapter 2).

# Modules

*Modules* are a mechanism for packaging and *namespacing* code. Namespacing is a way to prevent *name collisions*. For example, if Amanda and Tyler both write a function called `calculate`, and you simply cut and paste their functions into your program, the second one will replace the first. Namespacing allows you to somehow refer to "Amanda's `calculate`" and "Tyler's `calculate`." Let's see how Node modules solve this problem. Create a file called *amanda.js*:

```
function calculate(a, x, n) {
    if(x === 1) return a*n;
    return a*(1 - Math.pow(x, n))/(1 - x);
}

module.exports = calculate;
```

And a file called *tyler.js*:

```
function calculate(r) {
    return 4/3*Math.PI*Math.pow(r, 3);
}

module.exports = calculate;
```

We could legitimately make the argument that Amanda and Tyler were both lazy in naming their functions something so nondescript, but we'll let it slide for the sake of this example. The important line in both of these files is `modules.export = calculate`. `module` is a special object that Node makes available to implement modules. Whatever you assign to its `exports` property will be what is *exported* from the module. Now that we've written a couple of modules, let's see how we use them in a third program. Create a file called *app.js*, and we'll *import* these modules:

```
const amanda_calculate = require('./amanda.js');
const tyler_calculate = require('./tyler.js');
```

```
console.log(amanda_calculate(1, 2, 5));    // logs 31
console.log(tyler_calculate(2));           // logs 33.510321638291124
```

Note that the names we chose (`amanda_calculate` and `tyler_calculate`) are totally arbitrary; they are just variables. The value they're receiving is the result of Node processing the `require` function.

The mathematically inclined reader may have already recognized these two calculations: Amanda is providing the sum of the geometric series $a + ax + ax^2 + . . . + ax^{n-1}$, and Tyler is providing the volume of a sphere of radius $r$. Now that we know this, we can shake our heads at Amanda and Tyler's poor naming practices, and choose appropriate names in *app.js*:

```
const geometricSum = require('./amanda.js');
const sphereVolume = require('./tyler.js');

console.log(geometricSum(1, 2, 5));       // logs 31
console.log(sphereVolume(2));             // logs 33.510321638291124
```

Modules can export a value of any type (even a primitive, though there's little reason for that). Very commonly, you want your module to contain not just one function, but many, in which case you could export an object with function properties. Imagine that Amanda is an algebraist who is providing us many useful algebraic functions in addition to a geometric sum:

```
module.exports = {
    geometricSum(a, x, n) {
        if(x === 1) return a*n;
        return a*(1 - Math.pow(x, n))/(1 - x);
    },
    arithmeticSum(n) {
        return (n + 1)*n/2;
    },
    quadraticFormula(a, b, c) {
        const D = Math.sqrt(b*b - 4*a*c);
        return [(-b + D)/(2*a), (-b - D)/(2*a)];
    },
};
```

This results in a more traditional approach to namespacing—we name what's returned, but what's returned (an object) contains its own names:

```
const amanda = require('./amanda.js');
console.log(amanda.geometricSum(1, 2, 5));          // logs 31
console.log(amanda.quadraticFormula(1, 2, -15));    // logs [ 3, -5 ]
```

There's no magic here: the module is simply exporting an ordinary object with function properties (don't let the abbreviated ES6 syntax confuse you; they're just functions). This paradigm is so common that there's a shorthand syntax for it, using a special variable simply called `exports`. We can rewrite Amanda's exports in a more compact (but equivalent) way:

```
exports.geometricSum = function(a, x, n) {
    if(x === 1) return a*n;
    return a*(1 - Math.pow(x, n))/(1 - x);
};

exports.arithmeticSum = function(n) {
    return (n + 1)*n/2;
};

exports.quadraticFormula = function(a, b, c) {
    const D = Math.sqrt(b*b - 4*a*c);
    return [(-b + D)/(2*a), (-b - D)/(2*a)];
};
```

The `exports` shorthand only works for exporting objects; if you want to export a function or some other value, you must use `module.exports`. Furthermore, you can't meaningfully mix the two: use one or the other.

## Core Modules, File Modules, and npm Modules

Modules fall into three categories, *core modules*, *file modules*, and *npm modules*. Core modules are reserved module names that are provided by Node itself, such as `fs` and `os` (which we'll discuss later in this chapter). File modules we've already seen: we create a file that assigns to `module.exports`, and then require that file. npm modules are just file modules that are located in a special directory called *node_modules*. When you use the `require` function, Node determines the type of module (listed in Table 20-1) from the string you pass in.

*Table 20-1. Module types*

| Type | String passed to require | Examples |
|---|---|---|
| Core | Doesn't start with /, ./, or ../ | `require('fs')`<br>`require('os')`<br>`require('http')`<br>`require('child_process')` |
| File | Starts with /, ./, or ../ | `require('./debug.js')`<br>`require('/full/path/to/module.js')`<br>`require('../a.js')`<br>`require('../../a.js')` |
| npm | Not a core module and doesn't start with /, ./, or ../ | `require('debug')`<br>`require('express')`<br>`require('chalk')`<br>`require('koa')`<br>`require('q')` |

Some core modules, such as `process` and `buffer`, are *global*, are always available, and do not require an explicit `require` statement. The core modules are listed in Table 20-2.

*Table 20-2. Core modules*

| Module | Global | Description |
|---|---|---|
| `assert` | No | Used for testing purposes. |
| `buffer` | Yes | For input/output (I/O) operations (primarily file and network). |
| `child_process` | No | Functions for running external programs (Node and otherwise). |
| `cluster` | No | Allows you to take advantage of multiple processes for performance. |
| `crypto` | No | Built-in cryptography libraries. |
| `dns` | No | Domain name system (DNS) functions for network name resolution. |
| `domain` | No | Allows grouping of I/O and other asynchronous operations to isolate errors. |
| `events` | No | Utilities to support asynchronous events. |
| `fs` | No | Filesystem operations. |
| `http` | No | HTTP server and related utilities. |
| `https` | No | HTTPS server and related utilities. |
| `net` | No | Asynchronous socket-based network API. |
| `os` | No | Operating system utilities. |
| `path` | No | Filesystem pathname utilities. |
| `punycode` | No | Encoding of Unicode using a limited ASCII subset. |
| `querystring` | No | Utilities for parsing and constructing URL querystrings. |
| `readline` | No | Interactive I/O utilities; primarily used for command-line programs. |
| `smalloc` | No | Allows for explicit allocation of memory for buffers. |
| `stream` | Yes | Stream-based data transfer. |
| `string_decoder` | No | Converts buffers to strings. |

| Module | Global | Description |
| --- | --- | --- |
| `tls` | No | Transport Layer Security (TLS) communication utilities. |
| `tty` | No | Low-level TeleTYpewriter (TTY) functions. |
| `dgram` | No | User Datagram Protocol (UDP) networking utilities. |
| `url` | Yes | URL prasing utilities. |
| `util` | No | Internal Node utilities. |
| `vm` | No | Virtual (JavaScript) Machine: allows for metaprogramming and context creation. |
| `zlib` | No | Compression utilities. |

It is beyond the scope of this book to cover all of these modules (we will discuss the most important ones in this chapter), but this list gives you a starting point to look for more information. Detailed documentation for these modules is available in the Node API documentation (*https://nodejs.org/api/*).

Finally, there are *npm modules*. npm modules are file modules with a specific naming convention. If you require some module `x` (where `x` is not a core module), Node will look in the current directory for a subdirectory called *node_modules*. If it finds it, it will look for `x` in that directory. If it doesn't find it, it will go up to the parent directory, look for a module called *node_modules* there, and repeat the process until it finds the module or reaches the root. For example, if your project is located in */home/jdoe/test_project*, and in your application file, you call `require('x')`, Node will look for the module `x` in the following locations (in this order):

- */home/jdoe/test_project/node_modules/x*
- */home/jdoe/node_modules/x*
- */home/node_modules/x*
- */node_modules/x*

For most projects, you'll have a single *node_modules* directory in the application root. Furthermore, you shouldn't add or remove things from that directory manually; you'll let npm do all the heavy lifting. Still, it's useful to know how Node resolves module imports, especially when it comes time to debug problems in third-party modules.

For modules that you write yourself, do not put them in *node_modules*. It will work, but the point of *node_modules* is that it's a directory that can be deleted at any time and re-created by npm from the dependencies listed in *package.json* (see Chapter 2).

You can, of course, publish your own npm module, and manage that module with npm, but you should avoid editing things directly in *node_modules*!

## Customizing Modules with Function Modules

Modules most commonly export objects, and sometimes a single function. There's another very common pattern: a module that exports a function that's intended to be invoked immediately. It's the return value of that function (which can be a function itself) that's intended to be used (in other words, you don't use the function that's returned; you invoke that function and use whatever it returns). This pattern is used when the module needs to be customized somehow or receive information about the enclosing context. Let's consider the real-world npm package `debug`. When you import `debug`, it takes a string that will be used as a log prefix so logging for different parts of your program can be distinguished. It's used like this:

```
const debug = require('debug')('main'); // note that we immediately call the
                                        // function that the module returns

debug("starting");                      // will log "main starting +0ms"
                                        // if debugging is enabled
```

To enable debugging with the `debug` library, set an environment variable called `DEBUG`. For our example, we would set `DEBUG=main`. You can also set `DEBUG=*` to enable all debug messages.

It's clear from this example that the `debug` module returns a function (because we immediately call it as a function)…and that function itself returns a function that "remembers" the string from the first function. In essence, we have "baked in" a value to that module. Let's see how we might implement our own `debug` module:

```
let lastMessage;

module.exports = function(prefix) {
    return function(message) {
        const now = Date.now();
        const sinceLastMessage = now - (lastMessage || now);
        console.log(`${prefix} ${message} +${sinceLastMessage}ms`);
        lastMessage = now;
    }
}
```

This module is exporting a function that is designed to be called right away so that the value for `prefix` can be baked into the module. Note we also have another value, `lastMessage`, which is the timestamp of the last message that was logged; we use that to calculate the time between messages.

This brings us to an important point: what happens when you import a module multiple times? For example, consider what happens if we import our home-grown debug module twice:

```
const debug1 = require('./debug')('one');
const debug2 = require('./debug')('two');

debug1('started first debugger!')
debug2('started second debugger!')

setTimeout(function() {
    debug1('after some time...');
    debug2('what happens?');
}, 200);
```

You might expect to see something like this:

```
one started first debugger! +0ms
two started second debugger! +0ms
one after some time... +200ms
two what happens? +200ms
```

But what you will actually see is this (plus or minus a few milliseconds):

```
one started first debugger! +0ms
two started second debugger! +0ms
one after some time... +200ms
two what happens? +0ms
```

As it turns out, Node only ever imports any given module once (every time a Node app is run). So even though we import our `debug` module twice, Node has "remembered" that we imported it before, and used the same instance. Thus, even though `debug1` and `debug2` are separate functions, they both share a reference to `lastMessage`.

This behavior is safe and desirable. For reasons of performance, memory usage, and maintainability, it's better for modules to only ever be included once.

The way we've written our home-grown `debug` module is similar to the way its npm namesake works. However, if we did want multiple debug logs that had independent timing, we could always move the `lastMessage` timestamp into the body of the function that the module returns; then it will receive a new, independent value every time a logger is created.

## Filesystem Access

Many introductory programming books cover *filesystem access* because it's considered a critical part of "normal" programming. Poor JavaScript: up until Node, it wasn't in the filesystem club.

The examples in this chapter assume your project root is */home/<jdoe>/fs*, which is a typical path on a Unix system (replace *<jdoe>* with your username). The same principles apply on a Windows system (where your project root might be *C:\Users\<John Doe>\Documents\fs*).

To create a file, use `fs.writeFile`. Create a file in your project root called *write.js*:

```
const fs = require('fs');

fs.writeFile('hello.txt', 'hello from Node!', function(err) {
    if(err) return console.log('Error writing to file.');
});
```

This will create a file in the directory you're in when you run *write.js* (assuming you have sufficient privileges in that directory, and there isn't a directory or read-only file called *hello.txt* already). Whenever you invoke a Node application, it inherits its *current working directory* from where you run it from (which may be different than where the file lives). For example:

```
$ cd /home/jdoe/fs
$ node write.js             # current working dir is /home/jdoe/fs
                            # creates /home/jdoe/fs/hello.txt

$ cd ..                     # current working dir is now /home/jdoe
$ node fs/write.js          # creates /home/jdoe/hello.txt
```

Node provides a special variable, `__dirname`, which is always set to the directory in which the source file resides. For example, we can change our example to:

```
const fs = require('fs');

fs.writeFile(__dirname + '/hello.txt',
        'hello from Node!', function(err) {
    if(err) return console.error('Error writing to file.');
});
```

Now *write.js* will always create *hello.txt* in */home/<jdoe>/fs* (where *write.js* is located). Using string concatenation to join `__dirname` and our filename isn't very platform-agnostic; this could cause problems on a Windows machine, for example. Node provides platform-independent pathname utilities in the module `path`, so we can rewrite this module to be more friendly on all platforms:

```
const fs = require('fs');
const path = require('path');
```

```
fs.writeFile(path.join(__dirname, 'hello.txt'),
        'hello from Node!', function(err) {
    if(err) return console.error('Error writing to file.');
});
```

`path.join` will join directory elements using whatever directory separator is appropriate for the operating system, and is generally a good practice.

What if we want to read the contents of that file back in? We use `fs.readFile`. Create *read.js*:

```
const fs = require('fs');
const path = require('path');

fs.readFile(path.join(__dirname, 'hello.txt'), function(err, data) {
    if(err) return console.error('Error reading file.');
    console.log('Read file contents:');
    console.log(data);
});
```

If you run this example, you may be unpleasantly surprised at the result:

```
Read file contents:
<Buffer 68 65 6c 6c 6f 20 66 72 6f 6d 20 4e 6f 64 65 21>
```

If you convert those hex codes to their ASCII/Unicode equivalents, you'll find it is indeed `hello from Node!`, but the program as it stands is not very friendly. If you don't tell `fs.readFile` what *encoding* was used, it will return a *buffer*, which contains raw binary data. Although we didn't explicitly specify an encoding in *write.js*, the default string encoding is UTF-8 (a Unicode encoding). We can modify *read.txt* to specify UTF-8 and get the result we expect:

```
const fs = require('fs');
const path = require('path');

fs.readFile(path.join(__dirname, 'hello.txt'),
        { encoding: 'utf8' }, function(err, data) {
    if(err) return console.error('Error reading file.');
    console.log('File contents:');
    console.log(data);
});
```

All of the functions in `fs` have synchronous equivalents (that end in "Sync"). In *write.js*, we can use the synchronous equivalent instead:

```
fs.writeFileSync(path.join(__dirname, 'hello.txt'), 'hello from Node!');
```

And in *read.js*:

```
const data = fs.readFileSync(path.join(__dirname, 'hello.txt'),
    { encoding: 'utf8' });
```

With the synchronous versions, error handling is accomplished with exceptions, so to make our examples robust, we would wrap them in try/catch blocks. For example:

```
try {
    fs.writeFileSync(path.join(__dirname, 'hello.txt'), 'hello from Node!');
} catch(err) {
    console.error('Error writing file.');
}
```

The synchronous filesystem functions are temptingly easy to use. However, if you are writing a webserver or networked application, remember that Node's performance derives from asynchronous execution; you should always use the asynchronous versions in those cases. If you are writing a command-line utility, it is usually not an issue to use the synchronous versions.

You can list the files in a directory with `fs.readdir`. Create a file called *ls.js*:

```
const fs = require('fs');

fs.readdir(__dirname, function(err, files) {
    if(err) return console.error('Unable to read directory contents');
    console.log(`Contents of ${__dirname}:`);
    console.log(files.map(f => '\t' + f).join('\n'));
});
```

The `fs` module contains many more filesystem functions; you can delete files (`fs.unlink`), move or rename files (`fs.rename`), get information about files and directories (`fs.stat`), and much more. Consult the Node API documentation (*https://nodejs.org/api/fs.html*) for more information.

# Process

Every running Node program has access to a variable called `process` that allows it to get information about—and control—its own execution. For example, if your application encounters an error so severe that it's inadvisable or senseless to continue executing (often called a *fatal error*), you can immediately stop execution by calling `process.exit`. You can also provide a numeric *exit code*, which is used by scripts to determine whether or not your program exited successfully. Conventionally, an exit code of 0 has indicated "no error," and a nonzero exit code indicates an error. Consider a script that processes *.txt* files in a subdirectory *data*: if there are no files to process, there's nothing to do, so the program exits immediately, but it's not an error. On the other hand, if the subdirectory *data* doesn't exist, we will consider this a more serious problem, and the program should exit with an error. Here's how that program might look:

```
const fs = require('fs');

fs.readdir('data', function(err, files) {
    if(err) {
        console.error("Fatal error: couldn't read data directory.");
        process.exit(1);
    }
    const txtFiles = files.filter(f => /\.txt$/i.test(f));
    if(txtFiles.length === 0) {
        console.log("No .txt files to process.");
        process.exit(0);
    }
    // process .txt files...
});
```

The `process` object also gives you access to an array containing the *command-line arguments* passed to the program. When you execute a Node application, you can provide optional command-line arguments. For example, we could write a program that takes multiple filenames as command-line arguments, and print out the number of lines of text in each file. We might invoke the program like this:

```
$ node linecount.js file1.txt file2.txt file3.txt
```

The command-line arguments are contained in the `process.argv` array.[2] Before we count the lines in our files, let's print out `process.argv` so we know what we're getting:

```
console.log(process.argv);
```

Along with *file1.txt*, *file2.txt*, and *file3.txt*, you'll see a couple of extra elements at the beginning of the array:

```
[ 'node',
  '/home/jdoe/linecount.js',
  'file1.txt',
  'file2.txt',
  'file3.txt' ]
```

The first element is the *interpreter*, or program that interpreted the source file (`node`, in our case). The second element is the full path to the script being executed, and the rest of the elements are any arguments passed to the program. Because we don't need this extra information, we'll just use `Array.slice` to get rid of it before counting the lines in our files:

```
const fs = require('fs');

const filenames = process.argv.slice(2);
```

2 The name `argv` is a nod to the C language. The *v* is for *vector*, which is similar to an array.

```
let counts = filenames.map(f => {
    try {
        const data = fs.readFileSync(f, { encoding: 'utf8' });
        return `${f}: ${data.split('\n').length}`;
    } catch(err) {
        return `${f}: couldn't read file`;
    }
});

console.log(counts.join('\n'));
```

`process` also gives you access to environment variables through the object `process.env`. Environment variables are named system variables that are primarily used for command-line programs. On most Unix systems, you can set an environment variable simply by typing `export VAR_NAME=`*`some value`* (environment variables are traditionally all caps). On Windows, you use `set VAR_NAME=some value`. Environment variables are often used to configure the behavior of some aspect of your program (without your having to provide the values on the command line every time you execute the program).

For example, we might want to use an environment variable to control whether or not our program logs debugging information or "runs silently." We'll control our debug behavior with an environment variable `DEBUG`, which we'll set to `1` if we want to debug (any other value will turn debugging off):

```
const debug = process.env.DEBUG === "1" ?
    console.log :
    function() {};

debug("Visible only if environment variable DEBUG is set!");
```

In this example, we create a function, `debug`, that is simply an alias for `console.log` if the environment variable `DEBUG` is set, and a *null function*—a function that does nothing—otherwise (if we left `debug` undefined, we would generate errors when we tried to use it!).

In the previous section, we talked about the current working directory, which defaults to the directory you execute the program from (not the directory where the program exists). `process.cwd` tells you what the current working directory is, and `process.chdir` allows you to change it. For example, if you wanted to print out the directory in which the program was started, then switch the current working directory to the directory where the program itself is located, you could do this:

```
console.log(`Current directory: ${process.cwd()}`);
process.chdir(__dirname);
console.log(`New current directory: ${process.cwd()}`);
```

## Operating System

The os module provides some platform-specific information about the computer on which the app is running. Here is an example that shows the most useful information that os exposes (and their values on my cloud-based dev machine):

```
const os = require('os');

console.log("Hostname: " + os.hostname());          // prometheus
console.log("OS type: " + os.type());               // Linux
console.log("OS platform: " + os.platform());       // linux
console.log("OS release: " + os.release());         // 3.13.0-52-generic
console.log("OS uptime: " +
    (os.uptime()/60/60/24).toFixed(1) + " days");   // 80.3 days
console.log("CPU architecture: " + os.arch());      // x64
console.log("Number of CPUs: " + os.cpus().length); // 1
console.log("Total memory: " +
    (os.totalmem()/1e6).toFixed(1) + " MB");        // 1042.3 MB
console.log("Free memory: " +
    (os.freemem()/1e6).toFixed(1) + " MB");         // 195.8 MB
```

## Child Processes

The child_process module allows your app to run other programs, whether it be another Node program, an executable, or a script in another language. It's beyond the scope of this book to cover all of the details of managing child processes, but we will consider a simple example.

The child_process module exposes three primary functions: exec, execFile, and fork. As with fs, there are synchronous versions of these functions (execSync, execFileSync, and forkSync). exec and execFile can run any executable supported by your operating system. exec invokes a *shell* (which is what underlies your operating system's command line; if you can run it from the command line, you can run it from exec). execFile allows you to execute an executable directly, which offers slightly improved memory and resource use, but generally requires greater care. Lastly, fork allows you to execute other Node scripts (which can also be done with exec).

fork does invoke a separate Node engine, so you're paying the same resource cost you would with exec; however, fork gives you access to some interprocess communication options. See the official documentation (*http://bit.ly/1PxcnL9*) for more information.

Because exec is the most general, and the most forgiving, we'll use it in this chapter.

For demonstration purposes, we'll execute the command `dir`, which displays a directory listing (while Unix users are more familiar with `ls`, `dir` is aliased to `ls` on most Unix systems):

```
const exec = require('child_process').exec;

exec('dir', function(err, stdout, stderr) {
    if(err) return console.error('Error executing "dir"');
    stdout = stdout.toString(); // convert Buffer to string
    console.log(stdout);
    stderr = stderr.toString();
    if(stderr !== '') {
        console.error('error:');
        console.error(stderr);
    }
});
```

Because `exec` spawns a shell, we don't need to provide the path to where the `dir` executable lives. If we were invoking a specific program that's not generally available from your system's shell, you would need to provide a full path to the executable.

The callback that gets invoked receives two `Buffer` objects for `stdout` (the normal output of a program) and `stderr` (error output, if any). In this example, since we don't expect any output on `stderr`, we check first to see if there was any error output before printing it out.

`exec` takes an optional `options` object, which allows us to specify things like the working directory, environment variables, and more. See the official documentation (*https://nodejs.org/api/child_process.html*) for more information.

Note the way we import `exec`. Instead of importing `child_process` with `const child_process = require('child_process')`, and then calling `exec` as `child_process.exec`, we simply alias `exec` right away. We could do it either way, but the way we've done it is quite common.

## Streams

The concept of a *stream* is an important one in Node. A stream is an object that deals with data—as the name implies—in a stream (the word *stream* should make you think of *flow*, and because flow is something that happens over time, it makes sense that it would be asynchronous).

Streams can be *read streams*, *write streams*, or both (called *duplex streams*). Streams make sense whenever the flow of data happens over time. Examples might be a user typing at a keyboard, or a web service that has back-and-forth communication with a client. File access, too, often uses streams (even though we can also read and write files without streams). We'll use file streams to demonstrate how to create read and write streams, and how to *pipe* streams to one another.

We'll start by creating a write stream and writing to it:

```
const ws = fs.createWriteStream('stream.txt', { encoding: 'utf8' });
ws.write('line 1\n');
ws.write('line 2\n');
ws.end();
```

The end method optionally takes a data argument that is equivalent to calling write. Thus, if you're sending data only once, you can simply call end with the data you want to send.

Our write stream (ws) can be written to with the write method until we call end, at which point the stream will be closed, and further calls to write will produce an error. Because you can call write as many times as you need before calling end, a write stream is ideal for writing data over a period of time.

Similarly, we can create a read stream to read data as it arrives:

```
const rs = fs.createReadStream('stream.txt', { encoding: 'utf8' });
rs.on('data', function(data) {
    console.log('>> data: ' + data.replace('\n', '\\n'));
});
rs.on('end', function(data) {
    console.log('>> end');
});
```

In this example, we're simply logging the file contents to the console (replacing newlines for neatness). You can put both of these examples in the same file: you can have a write stream writing to a file and a read stream reading it.

Duplex streams are not as common, and are beyond the scope of this book. As you might expect, you can call write to write data to a duplex stream, as well as listen for data and end events.

Because data "flows" through streams, it stands to reason that you could take the data coming out of a read stream and immediately write it to a write stream. This process is called *piping*. For example, we could pipe a read stream to a write stream to copy the contents of one file to another:

```
const rs = fs.createReadStream('stream.txt');
const ws = fs.createWriteStream('stream_copy.txt');
rs.pipe(ws);
```

Note that in this example, we don't have to specify encoding: `rs` is simply piping bytes from *stream.txt* to `ws` (which is writing them to *stream_copy.txt*); encoding only matters if we're trying to interpret the data.

Piping is a common technique for moving data. For example, you could pipe the contents of a file to a webserver's response. Or you could pipe compressed data into a decompression engine, which would in turn pipe data out to a file writer.

# Web Servers

While Node is being used in many applications now, its original purpose was to provide a web server, so we would be remiss not to cover this usage.

Those of you who have configured Apache—or IIS, or any other web server—may be startled at how easy it is to create a functioning web server. The `http` module (and its secure counterpart, the `https` module) exposes a `createServer` method that creates a basic web server. All you have to do is provide a callback function that will handle incoming requests. To start the server, you simply call its `listen` method and give it a port:

```
const http = require('http');

const server = http.createServer(function(req, res) {
    console.log(`${req.method} ${req.url}`);
    res.end('Hello world!');
});

const port = 8080;
server.listen(port, function() {
    // you can pass a callback to listen that lets you know
    // the server has started
    console.log(`server startd on port ${port}`);
});
```

Most operating systems prevent you from listening on the default HTTP port (80) without elevated privileges, for security reasons. As a matter of fact, you need elevated privileges to listen on any port below 1024. Of course this is easy to do: if you have sudo access, you can just run your server with sudo to gain elevated privileges, and listen on port 80 (as long as nothing else is). For development and testing purposes, it's common to listen on ports above 1024. Numbers like 3000, 8000, 3030, and 8080 are commonly picked because they are memorable.

If you run this program and visit *http://localhost:8080* in a browser, you will see `Hello world!`. On the console, we're logging all requests, which consist of a method (sometimes called a *verb*) and a URL path. You might be surprised to see two requests each time you go to that URL in the browser:

```
GET /
GET /favicon.ico
```

Most browsers will request an icon that they can display in the URL bar or tab; the browser will do this implicitly, which is why we see it logged on the console.

At the heart of Node's web server is the callback function that you provide, that will respond to all incoming requests. It takes two arguments, an `IncomingMessage` object (often abbreviated `req`) and a `ServerRequest` object (often abbreviated `res`). The `IncomingMessage` object contains all information about the HTTP request: what URL was requested, any headers that were sent, any data sent in the body, and more. The `ServerResponse` object contains properties and methods to control the response that will be sent back to the client (usually a browser). If you saw that we called `req.end` and wondered if `req` is a write stream, go to the head of the class. The `ServerResponse` object implements the writable stream interface, which is how you write data to the client. Because the `ServerResponse` object is a write stream, it makes it easy to send a file...we can just create a file read stream and pipe it to the HTTP response. For example, if you have a *favicon.ico* file to make your website look nicer, you could detect this request and send this file directly:

```
const server = http.createServer(function(req, res) {
    if(req.method === 'GET' && req.url === '/favicon.ico') {
        const fs = require('fs');
        fs.createReadStream('favicon.ico');
        fs.pipe(res);       // this replaces the call to 'end'
    } else {
        console.log(`${req.method} ${req.url}`);
        res.end('Hello world!');
    }
});
```

This a minimal web server, though not a very interesting one. With the information contained in `IncomingRequest`, you can expand this model to create any kind of website you wish.

If you're using Node to serve websites, you'll probably want to look into using a framework such as Express (*http://expressjs.com/*) or Koa (*http://koajs.com/*) that will take some of the drudgery out of building a web server from scratch.

Koa is something of a successor to the very popular Express, and it's no coincidence: both are the work of TJ Holowaychuk. If you're already familiar with Express, you will feel right at home with Koa —except that you get to enjoy a more ES6-centric approach to web development.

## Conclusion

We've scratched the surface of the most important Node APIs here. We've focused on the ones you'll probably see in almost any application (such as `fs`, `Buffer`, `process`, and `stream`), but there are many more APIs to learn about. The official documentation (*https://nodejs.org/en/docs/*) is comprehensive, but can be daunting for the beginner. Shelley Powers' *Learning Node* is a good place to start if you're interested in Node development.

CHAPTER 21

# Object Property Configuration and Proxies

## Accessor Properties: Getters and Setters

There are two types of object properties: *data properties* and *accessor properties*. We've already seen both, but the accessor properties have been hidden behind some ES6 syntactic sugar (we called them "dynamic properties" in Chapter 9).

We're familiar with function properties (or methods); accessor properties are similar except they have *two* functions—a *getter* and a *setter*—and when accessed, they act more like a data property than a function.

Let's review dynamic properties. Imagine you have a `User` class, with methods `setEmail` and `getEmail`. We opted to use a "get" and "set" method instead of just having a property called `email` because we want to prevent a user from getting an invalid email address. Our class is very simple (for simplicity, we'll treat any string with an at sign as a valid email address):

```
const USER_EMAIL = Symbol();
class User {
    setEmail(value) {
        if(!/@/.test(value)) throw new Error(`invalid email: ${value}`);
        this[USER_EMAIL] = value;
    }
    getEmail() {
        return this[USER_EMAIL];
    }
}
```

In this example, the only thing that's compelling us to use two methods (instead of a property) is to prevent the `USER_EMAIL` property from receiving an invalid email address. We're using a symbol property here to discourage accidental direct access of the property (if we used a string property called `email` or even `_email`, it would be easy to carelessly access it directly).

This is a common pattern, and it works well, but it's slightly more unwieldy than we might like. Here's an example of using this class:

```
const u = new User();
u.setEmail("john@doe.com");
console.log(`User email: ${u.getEmail()}`);
```

While this works, it would be more natural to write:

```
const u = new User();
u.email = "john@doe.com";
console.log(`User email: ${u.email}`);
```

Enter accessor properties: they allow us to have the benefits of the former with the natural syntax of the latter. Let's rewrite our class using accessor properties:

```
const USER_EMAIL = Symbol();
class User {
   set email(value) {
      if(!/@/.test(value)) throw new Error(`invalid email: ${value}`);
      this[USER_EMAIL] = value;
   }
   get email() {
      return this[USER_EMAIL];
   }
}
```

We've provided two distinct functions, but they are bundled into a single property called `email`. If the property is assigned to, then the *setter* is called (with the assignment value being passed in as the first argument), and if the property is evaluated, the *getter* is called.

You can provide a getter without a setter; for example, consider a getter that provides the perimeter of a rectangle:

```
class Rectangle {
    constructor(width, height) {
        this.width = width;
        this.height = height;
    }
    get perimeter() {
        return this.width*2 + this.height*2;
    }
}
```

We don't provide a setter for perimeter because there's no obvious way to infer the rectangle's width and height from the length of the perimeter; it makes sense for this to be a read-only property.

Likewise, you can provide a setter without a getter, though this is a much less common pattern.

## Object Property Attributes

At this point, we have a lot of experience with object properties. We know that they have a key (which can be a string or a symbol) and a value (which can be of any type). We also know that you cannot guarantee the order of properties in an object (the way you can in an array or `Map`). We know two ways of accessing object properties (member access with dot notation, and computed member access with square brackets). Lastly, we know three ways to create properties in the object literal notation (regular properties with keys that are identifiers, computed property names allowing nonidentifiers and symbols, and method shorthand).

There's more to know about properties, however. In particular, properties have *attributes* that control how the properties behave in the context of the object they belong to. Let's start by creating a property using one of the techniques we know; then we'll use `Object.getOwnPropertyDescriptor` to examine its attributes:

```
const obj = { foo: "bar" };
Object.getOwnPropertyDescriptor(obj, 'foo');
```

This will return the following:

```
{ value: "bar", writable: true, enumerable: true, configurable: true }
```

The terms *property attributes*, *property descriptor*, and *property configuration* are used interchangeably; they all refer to the same thing.

This exposes the three attributes of a property:

*Writable*
: Controls whether the value of the property can be changed.

*Enumerable*
: Controls whether the property will be included when the properties of the object are enumerated (with `for...in`, `Object.keys`, or the spread operator).

*Configurable*
: Controls whether the property can be deleted from the object or have its attributes modified.

We can control property attributes with `Object.defineProperty`, which allows you to create new properties or modify existing ones (as long as the property is configurable).

For example, if we want to make the `foo` property of `obj` read-only, we can use `Object.defineProperty`:

```
Object.defineProperty(obj, 'foo', { writable: false });
```

Now if we try to assign a value to `foo`, we get an error:

```
obj.foo = 3;
// TypeError: Cannot assign to read only property 'foo' of [object Object]
```

Attempting to set a read-only property will only result in an error in strict mode. In nonstrict mode, the assignment will not be successful, but there will be no error.

We can also use `Object.defineProperty` to add a new property to an object. This is especially useful for attribute properties because, unlike with data properties, there's no other way to add an accessor property after an object has been created. Let's add a `color` property to `o` (we won't bother with symbols or validation this time):

```
Object.defineProperty(obj, 'color', {
    get: function() { return this.color; },
    set: function(value) { this.color = value; },
});
```

To create a data property, you provide the `value` property to `Object.defineProperty`. We'll add `name` and `greet` properties to `obj`:

```
Object.defineProperty(obj, 'name', {
    value: 'Cynthia',
});
Object.defineProperty(obj, 'greet', {
    value: function() { return `Hello, my name is ${this.name}!`; }
});
```

One common use of `Object.defineProperty` is making properties not enumerable in an array. We've mentioned before that it's not wise to use string or symbol properties in an array (because it is contrary to the use of an array), but it can be useful if done carefully and thoughtfully. While the use of `for...in` or `Object.keys` on an array is also discouraged (instead prefer `for`, `for...of`, or `Array.prototype.forEach`), you can't prevent people from doing it. Therefore, if you add non-numeric properties to an array, you should make them non-enumerable in case someone (inadvisably) uses `for..in` or `Object.keys` on an array. Here's an example of adding `sum` and `avg` methods to an array:

```
const arr = [3, 1.5, 9, 2, 5.2];
arr.sum = function() { return this.reduce((a, x) => a+x); }
arr.avg = function() { return this.sum()/this.length; }
Object.defineProperty(arr, 'sum', { enumerable: false });
Object.defineProperty(arr, 'avg', { enumerable: false });
```

We could also do this in one step per property:

```
const arr = [3, 1.5, 9, 2, 5.2];
Object.defineProperty(arr, 'sum', {
    value: function() { return this.reduce((a, x) => a+x); },
    enumerable: false
 });
Object.defineProperty(arr, 'avg', {
    value: function() { return this.sum()/this.length; },
    enumerable: false
});
```

Lastly, there is also a `Object.defineProperties` (note the plural) that takes an object that maps property names to property definitions. So we can rewrite the previous example as:

```
const arr = [3, 1.5, 9, 2, 5.2];
Object.defineProperties(arr,
    sum: {
        value: function() { return this.reduce((a, x) => a+x); },
        enumerable: false
     }),
    avg: {
        value: function() { return this.sum()/this.length; },
        enumerable: false
    })
);
```

## Protecting Objects: Freezing, Sealing, and Preventing Extension

JavaScript's flexible nature is very powerful, but it can get you into trouble. Because any code anywhere can normally modify an object in any way it wishes, it's easy to write code that is unintentionally dangerous or—even worse—intentionally malicious.

JavaScript does provide three mechanisms for preventing unintentional modifications (and making intentional ones more difficult): freezing, sealing, and preventing extension.

Freezing prevents *any* changes to an object. Once you freeze an object, you cannot:

- Set the value of properties on the object.
- Call methods that modify the value of properties on the object.

- Invoke setters on the object (that modify the value of properties on the object).
- Add new properties.
- Add new methods.
- Change the configuration of existing properties or methods.

In essence, freezing an object makes it immutable. It's most useful for data-only objects, as freezing an object with methods will render useless any methods that modify the state of the object.

To freeze an object, use `Object.freeze` (you can tell if an object is frozen by calling `Object.isFrozen`). For example, imagine you have an object that you use to store immutable information about your program (such as company, version, build ID, and a method to get copyright information):

```
const appInfo = {
    company: 'White Knight Software, Inc.',
    version: '1.3.5',
    buildId: '0a995448-ead4-4a8b-b050-9c9083279ea2',
    // this function only accesses properties, so it won't be
    // affected by freezing
    copyright() {
        return `© ${new Date().getFullYear()}, ${this.company}`;
    },
};
Object.freeze(appInfo);
Object.isFrozen(appInfo);    // true

appInfo.newProp = 'test';
// TypeError: Can't add property newProp, object is not extensible

delete appInfo.company;
// TypeError: Cannot delete property 'company' of [object Object]

appInfo.company = 'test';
// TypeError: Cannot assign to read-only property 'company' of [object Object]

Object.defineProperty(appInfo, 'company', { enumerable: false });
// TypeError: Cannot redefine property: company
```

Sealing an object prevents the addition of new properties, or the reconfiguration or removal of existing properties. Sealing can be used when you have an instance of a class, as methods that operate on the object's properties will still work (as long as they're not attempting to reconfigure a property). You can seal an object with `Object.seal`, and tell if an object is sealed by calling `Object.isSealed`:

```
class Logger {
    constructor(name) {
        this.name = name;
        this.log = [];
```

```
    }
    add(entry) {
        this.log.push({
            log: entry,
            timestamp: Date.now(),
        });
    }
}

const log = new Logger("Captain's Log");
Object.seal(log);
Object.isSealed(log);   // true

log.name = "Captain's Boring Log";          // OK
log.add("Another boring day at sea....");   // OK

log.newProp = 'test';
// TypeError: Can't add property newProp, object is not extensible

log.name = 'test';        // OK

delete log.name;
// TypeError: Cannot delete property 'name' of [object Object]

Object.defineProperty(log, 'log', { enumerable: false });
// TypeError: Cannot redefine property: log
```

Finally, the weakest protection, making an object nonextensible, only prevents new properties from being added. Properties can be assigned to, deleted, and reconfigured. Reusing our `Logger` class, we can demonstrate `Object.preventExtensions` and `Object.isExtensible`:

```
const log2 = new Logger("First Mate's Log");
Object.preventExtensions(log2);
Object.isExtensible(log2);   // true

log2.name = "First Mate's Boring Log";       // OK
log2.add("Another boring day at sea....");   // OK

log2.newProp = 'test';
// TypeError: Can't add property newProp, object is not extensible

log2.name = 'test';                  // OK
delete log2.name;                    // OK
Object.defineProperty(log2, 'log',
    { enumerable: false });          // OK
```

I find that I don't use `Object.preventExtensions` very often. If I want to prevent extensions to an object, I typically also want to prevent deletions and reconfiguration, so I usually prefer sealing an object.

Table 21-1 summarizes the protection options.

*Table 21-1. Object protection options*

| Action | Normal object | Frozen object | Sealed object | Nonextensible object |
|---|---|---|---|---|
| Add property | Allowed | Prevented | Prevented | Prevented |
| Read property | Allowed | Allowed | Allowed | Allowed |
| Set property value | Allowed | Prevented | Allowed | Allowed |
| Reconfigure property | Allowed | Prevented | Prevented | Allowed |
| Delete property | Allowed | Prevented | Prevented | Allowed |

# Proxies

New in ES6 are *proxies*, which provide additional metaprogramming functionality (metaprogramming is the ability for a program to modify itself).

An object proxy essentially has the ability to intercept and (optionally) modify actions on an object. Let's start with a simple example: modifying property access. We'll start with a regular object that has a couple of properties:

```
const coefficients = {
    a: 1,
    b: 2,
    c: 5,
};
```

Imagine that the properties in this object represent the coefficients in a mathematical equation. We might use it like this:

```
function evaluate(x, c) {
    return c.a + c.b * x + c.c * Math.pow(x, 2);
}
```

So far, so good...we can now store the coefficients of a quadratic equation in an object and evaluate the equation for any value of `x`. What if we pass in an object with missing coefficients, though?

```
const coefficients = {
    a: 1,
    c: 3,
};
evaluate(5, coefficients);      // NaN
```

We could solve the problem by setting `coefficients.b` to `0`, but proxies offer us a better option. Because proxies can intercept actions against an object, we can make sure that undefined properties return a value of `0`. Let's create a proxy for our `coefficients` object:

```
const betterCoefficients = new Proxy(coefficients, {
    get(target, key) {
        return target[key] || 0;
    },
});
```

As I write this, proxies are not supported in Babel. However, they are supported in the current build of Firefox, and these code samples can be tested there.

The first argument to the `Proxy` constructor is the *target*, or object that's being proxied. The second argument is the *handler*, which specifies the actions to be intercepted. In this case, we're only intercepting property access, denoted by the `get` function (this is distinct from a `get` property accessor: this will work for regular properties *and* get accessors). The `get` function takes three arguments (we're only using the first two): the target, the property key (either a string or a symbol), and the receiver (the proxy itself, or something that derives from it).

In this example, we simply check to see if the key is set on the target; if it's not, we return the value `0`. Go ahead and try it:

```
betterCoefficients.a;           // 1
betterCoefficients.b;           // 0
betterCoefficients.c;           // 3
betterCoefficients.d;           // 0
betterCoefficients.anything;    // 0;
```

We've essentially created a proxy for our `coefficients` object that appears to have an infinite number of properties (all set to `0`, except the ones we define)!

We could further modify our proxy to only proxy single lowercase letters:

```
const betterCoefficients = new Proxy(coefficients, {
    get(target, key) {
        if(!/^[a-z]$/.test(key)) return target[key];
        return target[key] || 0;
    },
});
```

Instead of doing our easy check to see if `target[key]` is truthy, we could return `0` if it's anything but a number...I'll leave that as a reader's exercise.

Similarly, we can intercept properties (or accessors) being set with the `set` handler. Let's consider an example where we have dangerous properties on an object. We want to prevent these properties from being set, and the methods from being called, without an extra step. The extra step we'll use is a setter called `allowDangerousOperations`, which you have to set to `true` before accessing dangerous functionality:

```
const cook = {
    name: "Walt",
    redPhosphorus: 100,         // dangerous
    water: 500,                 // safe
};
const protectedCook = new Proxy(cook, {
    set(target, key, value) {
        if(key === 'redPhosphorus') {
            if(target.allowDangerousOperations)
                return target.redPhosphorus = value;
            else
                return console.log("Too dangerous!");
        }
        // all other properties are safe
        target[key] = value;
    },
});

protectedCook.water = 550;          // 550
protectedCook.redPhosphorus = 150;  // Too dangerous!

protectedCook.allowDangerousOperations = true;
protectedCook.redPhosphorus = 150;  // 150
```

This only scratches the surface of what you can do with proxies. To learn more, I recommend starting with Axel Rauschmayer's article "Meta Programming with ECMAScript 6 Proxies" (*http://www.2ality.com/2014/12/es6-proxies.html*) and then reading the MDN documentation (*http://mzl.la/1QZKM7U*).

# Conclusion

In this chapter, we've pulled back the curtain that hides JavaScript's object mechanism and gotten a detailed picture of how object properties work, and how we can reconfigure that behavior. We also learned how to protect objects from modification.

Lastly, we learned about an extremely useful new concept in ES6: proxies. Proxies allow powerful metaprogramming techniques, and I suspect we will be seeing some very interesting uses for proxies as ES6 gains popularity.

CHAPTER 22

# Additional Resources

While my epiphany that JavaScript is an expressive, powerful language came some time ago, the journey of writing this book has driven that lesson home. JavaScript is not a "toy language" to be taken lightly or dismissed as a "beginner's language." You've made it through this book; you know that all too well!

My goal in this book was not to exhaustively explain every feature of the JavaScript language, much less explain every important programming technique. If JavaScript is your primary language, this is just the beginning of your journey. I hope I have given you a solid foundation that you can build on to become an expert.

Much of the material in this chapter is taken from my first book, *Web Development with Node and Express* (O'Reilly).

## Online Documentation

For JavaScript, CSS, and HTML documentation, the Mozilla Developer Network (MDN) (*https://developer.mozilla.org*) is without equal. If I need JavaScript documentation, I either search directly on MDN or append "mdn" to my search query. Otherwise, inevitably, w3schools appears in the search. Whoever is managing SEO for w3schools is a genius, but I recommend avoiding this site; I find the documentation is often severely lacking.

Where MDN is a great HTML reference, if you're new to HTML5 (or even if you're not), you should read Mark Pilgrim's *Dive Into HTML5* (*http://diveintohtml5.info*). WHATWG maintains an excellent "living standard" HTML5 specification (*http://developers.whatwg.org*); it is usually where I turn first for really hard-to-answer HTML questions. Finally, the official specifications for HTML and CSS are located on the W3C website (*http://www.w3.org*); they are dry, difficult-to-read documents, but sometimes it's your only recourse for the very hardest problems.

ES6 adheres to the ECMA-262 ECMAScript 2015 Language Specification (*http://www.ecma-international.org/ecma-262/6.0/*). To track the availability of ES6 features in Node (and various browsers), see the excellent guide maintained by @kangax (*http://kangax.github.io/es5-compat-table/es6*).

Both jQuery (*http://api.jquery.com*) and Bootstrap (*http://getbootstrap.com*) have extremely good online documentation.

The Node documentation (*http://nodejs.org/api*) is very high-quality and comprehensive, and it should be your first choice for authoritative documentation about Node modules (such as `http`, `https`, and `fs`). The npm documentation (*https://npmjs.org/doc*) is comprehensive and useful, particularly the page on the *package.json* file (*https://npmjs.org/doc/json.html*).

## Periodicals

There are three free periodicals you should absolutely subscribe to and read dutifully every week:

- JavaScript Weekly (*http://javascriptweekly.com*)
- Node Weekly (*http://nodeweekly.com*)
- HTML5 Weekly (*http://html5weekly.com*)

These three periodicals will keep you informed of the latest news, services, blogs, and tutorials as they become available.

## Blogs and Tutorials

Blogs are a great way to stay abreast of developments in JavaScript. I've often had those critical "ah ha" moments when reading some of these blogs:

- Axel Rauschmayer's blog (*http://www.2ality.com/*) has great articles on ES6 and related technologies. Dr. Rauschmayer approaches JavaScript from an academic computer science viewpoint, but his articles start out very accessible and easy to read—those with a computer science background will appreciate the additional detail he provides.
- Nolan Lawson's blog (*http://nolanlawson.com/*) has lots of great detailed posts about real-world JavaScript development. His article "We Have a Problem with Promises" (*http://bit.ly/problem-promises*) is required reading.
- David Walsh's blog (*https://davidwalsh.name/*) has fantastic articles about JavaScript development and related technologies. If you struggled with the material in Chapter 14, his article "The Basics of ES6 Generators" (*https://davidwalsh.name/es6-generators*) is a must-read.

- @kangax's blog, Perfection Kills (*http://perfectionkills.com/*), is full of fantastic tutorials, exercises, and quizzes. It's highly recommended for beginners and experts alike.

Now that you've read this book, the available online courses and tutorials should be very easy for you. If you still feel that you're missing some basic pieces, or just want to practice the fundamentals, I recommend the following:

- Lynda.com JavaScript tutorials (*http://bit.ly/lynda_js_training*)
- Treehouse JavaScript track (*https://teamtreehouse.com/learn/javascript*)
- Codecademy's JavaScript course (*https://www.codecademy.com/learn/javascript*)
- Microsoft Virtual Academy's intro course on JavaScript (*http://bit.ly/ms_js_intro*); if you are writing JavaScript on Windows, I recommend this for the material on using Visual Studio for JavaScript development

## Stack Overflow

Chances are good that you've already used Stack Overflow (SO); since its inception in 2008, it has become the dominant online Q&A site for programmers, and it is your best resource to get your JavaScript questions answered (and any other technology covered in this book). Stack Overflow is a community-maintained, reputation-based Q&A site. The reputation model is what's responsible for the quality of the site and its continued success. Users can gain reputation by having their questions or answers "upvoted" or having an accepted answer. You don't have to have any reputation to ask a question, and registration is free. However, there are things you can do to increase the chances of getting your question answered in a useful manner, which we'll discuss in this section.

Reputation is the currency of Stack Overflow, and while there are people out there who genuinely want to help you, it's the chance to gain reputation that's the icing on the cake that motivates good answers. There are a lot of really smart people on SO, and they're all competing to provide the first and/or best correct answer to your question (there's a strong disincentive to provide a quick but bad answer, thankfully). Here are things you can do to increase the chances of getting a good answer for your question:

*Be an informed SO user*
: Take the SO tour (*http://stackoverflow.com/tour*), then read "How do I ask a good question?" (*http://stackoverflow.com/help/how-to-ask*) If you're so inclined, you can go on to read all of the help documentation (*http://stackoverflow.com/help*)—you'll earn a badge if you read it all!

*Don't ask questions that have already been answered*
: Do your due diligence, and try to find out if someone has already asked your question. If you ask a question that has an easily found answer already on SO, your question will quickly be closed as a duplicate, and people will often downvote you for this, negatively affecting your reputation.

*Don't ask people to write your code for you*
: You will quickly find your question downvoted and closed if you simply ask "How do I do *X*?" The SO community expects you to make an effort to solve your own problem before resorting to SO. Describe in your question what you've tried and why it isn't working.

*Ask one question at a time*
: Questions that are asking several things—"How do I do this, then that, then the other things, and what's the best way to do this?"—are difficult to answer, and are discouraged.

*Craft a minimal example of your issue*
: I answer a lot of SO questions, and the ones I almost automatically skip over are those where I see three pages of code (or more!). Just taking your 5,000-line file and pasting into an SO question is not a great way to get your question answered (but people do it all the time). It's a lazy approach that isn't often rewarded. Not only are you less likely to get a useful answer, but the very process of eliminating things that *aren't* causing the problem can lead you to solving the problem yourself (then you don't even need to ask a question on SO). Crafting a minimal example is good for your debugging skills and for your critical thinking ability, and makes you a good SO citizen.

*Learn Markdown*
: Stack Overflow uses Markdown for formatting questions and answers. A well-formatted question has a better chance of being answered, so you should invest the time to learn this useful and increasingly ubiquitous markup language (*http://stackoverflow.com/help/formatting*).

*Accept and upvote answers*
: If someone answers your question satisfactorily, you should upvote and accept it; it boosts the reputation of the answerer, and reputation is what drives SO. If multiple people provide acceptable answers, you should choose the one you think is best and accept that, and upvote anyone else you feel offered a useful answer.

*If you figure out your own problem before someone else does, answer your own question*
: SO is a community resource; if you have a problem, chances are, someone else has it too. If you've figured it out, go ahead and answer your own question for the benefit of others.

If you enjoy helping the community, consider answering questions yourself: it's fun and rewarding, and it can lead to benefits that are more tangible than an arbitrary reputation score. If you have a question for which you've received no useful answers for two days, you can start a *bounty* on the question, using your own reputation. The reputation is withdrawn from your account immediately, and it is nonrefundable. If someone answers the question to your satisfaction, and you accept their answer, they will receive the bounty. The catch is, of course, you have to have reputation to start a bounty: the minimum bounty is 50 reputation points. While you can get reputation from asking quality questions, it's usually quicker to get reputation by providing quality answers.

Answering people's questions also has the benefit of being a great way to learn. I generally feel that I learn more from answering other people's questions than I do from having my questions answered. If you want to really thoroughly learn a technology, learn the basics and then start trying to tackle people's questions on SO. At first you might be consistently beat out by people who are already experts, but before long, you'll find that you *are* one of the experts.

Lastly, you shouldn't hesitate to use your reputation to further your career. A good reputation is absolutely worth putting on a résumé. It's worked for me, and now that I'm in the position of interviewing developers myself, I'm always impressed to see a good SO reputation (I consider a "good" SO reputation anything over 3,000; five-digit reputations are *great*). A good SO reputation tells me that someone is not just competent in their field, but they are clear communicators and generally helpful.

## Contributing to Open Source Projects

A great way to learn is to contribute to open source projects: not only will you face challenges that stretch your abilities, but your code will be peer-reviewed by the community, which will make you a better programmer. It also looks great on a résumé.

If you're a beginner, a good place to start is by contributing to documentation. Many open source projects suffer in the documentation department, and as a beginner, you're in an excellent position: you can learn something, then explain it in a way that's useful to other beginners.

Sometimes the open source community can be intimidating, but if you're persistent and stay open to constructive criticism, you will find that your contributions are welcome. Start by reading Scot Hanselman's excellent blog post "Bringing Kindness Back to Open Source" (*http://bit.ly/hanselman_kindness*). In that post, he recommends the website Up for Grabs (*http://up-for-grabs.net*), which helps connect programmers to open source projects. Search for the tag "JavaScript," and you'll find many open source projects looking for help.

## Conclusion

Congratulations on starting your journey to becoming a JavaScript developer! Some of the material in this book is very challenging, and if you took the time to understand it thoroughly, you will have a strong foundation in this important language. If there were parts you struggled with, don't be discouraged! JavaScript is a complex, powerful language that can't be learned overnight (or even in a year). If you're new to programming, you will probably want to revisit some of the material in this book in the future—you'll find new insights in material you found difficult the first time.

ES6 brings with it a new generation of programmers—and along with them, many wonderful ideas. I encourage you to read all you can, talk to every JavaScript programmer you can, and learn from every source you can find. There is going to be an explosion of depth and creativity in the JavaScript development community—and I sincerely hope that you will be part of it.

## APPENDIX A
# Reserved Words

The following words can't be used as an identifier (the name of a variable, constant, property, or function) in JavaScript:

- `await` (reserved for future use)
- `break`
- `case`
- `class`
- `catch`
- `const`
- `continue`
- `debugger`
- `default`
- `delete`
- `do`
- `else`
- `enum` (reserved for future use)
- `export`
- `extends`
- `false` (literal value)
- `finally`
- `for`

- `function`
- `if`
- `implements` (reserved for future use)
- `import`
- `in`
- `instanceof`
- `interface` (reserved for future use)
- `let`
- `new`
- `null` (literal value)
- `package` (reserved for future use)
- `private` (reserved for future use)
- `protectd` (reserved for future use)
- `public` (reserved for future use)
- `return`
- `super`
- `static` (reserved for future use)
- `switch`
- `this`
- `throw`
- `true` (literal value)
- `try`
- `typeof`
- `var`
- `void`
- `while`
- `with`
- `yield`

The following words were reserved in ECMAScript specifications 1–3. They are no longer reserved words, but I discourage their use, as JavaScript implementations may (incorrectly) consider them reserved words:

- `abstract`
- `boolean`
- `byte`
- `char`
- `double`
- `final`
- `float`
- `goto`
- `int`
- `long`
- `native`
- `short`
- `synchronized`
- `transient`
- `volatile`

## APPENDIX B

# Operator Precedence

Table B-1 is reproduced from the Mozilla Developer Network (*http://mzl.la/1TSIkTt*) for reference. ES7 operators have been omitted.

*Table B-1. Operator precedence from highest (19) to lowest (0)*

| Precedence | Operator type | Associativity | Individual operators |
|---|---|---|---|
| 19 | Grouping | n/a | ( … ) |
| 18 | Member access | left to right | … . … |
| | Computed member access | left to right | … [ … ] |
| | new (with argument list) | n/a | new … ( … ) |
| 17 | Function call | left to right | … ( … ) |
| | new (without argument list) | right to left | new … |
| 16 | Postfix increment | n/a | … ++ |
| | Postfix decrement | n/a | … -- |
| 15 | Logical NOT | right to left | ! … |
| | Bitwise NOT | right to left | ~ … |
| | Unary plus | right to left | + … |
| | Unary negation | right to left | - … |

| Precedence | Operator type | Associativity | Individual operators |
|---|---|---|---|
| | Prefix increment | right to left | `++ …` |
| | Prefix decrement | right to left | `-- …` |
| | `typeof` | right to left | `typeof …` |
| | `void` | right to left | `void …` |
| | `delete` | right to left | `delete …` |
| 14 | Multiplication | left to right | `… * …` |
| | Division | left to right | `… / …` |
| | Remainder | left to right | `… % …` |
| 13 | Addition | left to right | `… + …` |
| | Subtraction | left to right | `… - …` |
| 12 | Bitwise left shift | left to right | `… << …` |
| | Bitwise right shift | left to right | `… >> …` |
| | Bitwise unsigned right shift | left to right | `… >>> …` |
| 11 | Less than | left to right | `… < …` |
| | Less than or equal | left to right | `… <= …` |
| | Greater than | left to right | `… > …` |
| | Greater than or equal | left to right | `… >= …` |
| | `in` | left to right | `… in …` |
| | `instanceof` | left to right | `… instanceof …` |
| 10 | Equality | left to right | `… == …` |
| | Inequality | left to right | `… != …` |
| | Strict equality | left to right | `… === …` |
| | Strict inequality | left to right | `… !== …` |

<table>
<tr><th>Precedence</th><th>Operator type</th><th>Associativity</th><th>Individual operators</th></tr>
<tr><td>9</td><td>Bitwise AND</td><td>left to right</td><td>… & …</td></tr>
<tr><td>8</td><td>Bitwise XOR</td><td>left to right</td><td>… ^ …</td></tr>
<tr><td>7</td><td>Bitwise OR</td><td>left to right</td><td>… | …</td></tr>
<tr><td>6</td><td>Logical AND</td><td>left to right</td><td>… && …</td></tr>
<tr><td>5</td><td>Logical OR</td><td>left to right</td><td>… || …</td></tr>
<tr><td>4</td><td>Conditional</td><td>right to left</td><td>… ? … : …</td></tr>
<tr><td>3</td><td>Assignment</td><td>right to left</td><td>… = …</td></tr>
<tr><td></td><td></td><td></td><td>… += …</td></tr>
<tr><td></td><td></td><td></td><td>… -= …</td></tr>
<tr><td></td><td></td><td></td><td>… *= …</td></tr>
<tr><td></td><td></td><td></td><td>… /= …</td></tr>
<tr><td></td><td></td><td></td><td>… %= …</td></tr>
<tr><td></td><td></td><td></td><td>… <<= …</td></tr>
<tr><td></td><td></td><td></td><td>… >>= …</td></tr>
<tr><td></td><td></td><td></td><td>… >>>= …</td></tr>
<tr><td></td><td></td><td></td><td>… &= …</td></tr>
<tr><td></td><td></td><td></td><td>… ^= …</td></tr>
<tr><td></td><td></td><td></td><td>… |= …</td></tr>
<tr><td>2</td><td><code>yield</code></td><td>right to left</td><td><code>yield</code> …</td></tr>
<tr><td>1</td><td>Spread</td><td>n/a</td><td>... …</td></tr>
<tr><td>0</td><td>Comma/sequence</td><td>left to right</td><td>… , …</td></tr>
</table>

# Index

## Symbols



## A

## B

## C

## D

## E

## F

## G



## H



## I

## J



## K



## L

## O

## P



## Q



## R

## S

## T

## U



## V



## W



## X



## Y

## About the Author

**Ethan Brown** is Director of Engineering at Pop Art, a Portland-based interactive marketing agency, where he is responsible for the architecture and implementation of websites and web services for clients ranging from small businesses to international enterprise companies. He has over 20 years of programming experience, from embedded to the Web, and has embraced the JavaScript stack as the web platform of the future.

## Colophon

The animal on the cover of *Learning JavaScript*, Third Edition, is a baby black, or hook-lipped, rhinoceros (*Diceros bicornis*). The black rhino is one of two African species of rhinos. Weighing up to one and a half tons, it is smaller than its counterpart—the white, or square-lipped, rhinoceros. Black rhinos live in savanna grasslands, open woodlands, and mountain forests in a few small areas of southwestern, south central, and eastern Africa. They prefer to live alone and will aggressively defend their territory.

With an upper lip that tapers to a hooklike point, the black rhino is perfectly suited to pluck leaves, twigs, and buds from trees and bushes. It is able to eat coarser vegetation than other herbivores.

Black rhinos are odd-toed ungulates, meaning they have three toes on each foot. They have thick, gray, hairless hides. Among the most distinctive of the rhino's features is its two horns, which are actually made of thickly matted hair rather than bone. The rhino uses its horns to defend itself against lions, tigers, and hyenas, or to claim a female mate. The courtship ritual is often violent, and the horns can inflict severe wounds.

After mating, the female and male rhinos have no further contact. The gestation period is 14 to 18 months, and the calves nurse for a year, though they are able to eat vegetation almost immediately after birth. The bond between a mother and her calf can last up to four years before the calf leaves its home.

In recent years, rhinos have been hunted to the point of near extinction. Scientists estimate that there may have been as many as a million black rhinos in Africa 100 years ago, a number that has dwindled to 2,400 today. All five remaining species, which include the Indian, Javan, and Sumatran rhinos, are now endangered. Humans are considered their biggest predators.

Many of the animals on O'Reilly covers are endangered; all of them are important to the world. To learn more about how you can help, go to *animals.oreilly.com*.

The cover image is from *Cassell's Natural History*. The cover fonts are URW Typewriter and Guardian Sans. The text font is Adobe Minion Pro; the heading font is Adobe Myriad Condensed; and the code font is Dalton Maag's Ubuntu Mono.